THE JOURNEYMAN

The original idea had been to try and write a girls and boys own adventure story and how a man too old for a mid-life crisis found himself unexpectedly enjoying his own Indian summer.

First though I had a problem. I didn`t know how to write the book that I thought I had in me. I neither knew how to start or where to start. I had a working title and then a second and third working titles These kept changing when someone says to me that title's just like whatever and another one went in the bin I did take some of them back out again and reassign them to chapter headings and in the meantime kept writing. Part of the problem was how much information do people need to understand what's going on and why things are happening so I figured that if I just start with a couple of quick sentences on how, where, when, and why and then fill up any gaps as the story progresses. I figured this might be a way of telling a tale without boring my readers to death before they've got to anything interesting.

I came up with Journeyman, someone skilled, trained, but not yet a master, employed by others to do a job of work, competent and trustworthy and also a pun and I decided to run with it from here on.

When I first started out on this, new for me, outdoor education venture. I had to develop my own self-promotion programme that regularly found me at an event or a prospective employment sort of meeting. Everyone's making small talk. I have a badge pinned onto my top; it tells others my name, but I see no harm in introducing myself. "Hi. My name's Rob, Robert Platt. I am by trade a woodworker and by profession an expedition leader." Generally, I don't get much further than that. People unsurprisingly want to talk about themselves not listen to me.

Nevertheless, that's my starting point for how I describe myself, but I've probably done a hundred other jobs that don't fall into either of those categories, however all those jobs and small pieces of experience have been a bonus and have stood me in good stead, when I have been in another country minding a group of students and teachers.

Then having got myself established with work being offered rather than my having to pursue it, another change of direction.

A car crash, not in some isolated area on a dodgy road surface in a vehicle that would have been scrapped ten years earlier in the UK; but a couple of miles from my home on Merseyside.

So, I am now, an aspiring writer, as I've said, with about as much of a clue as I have had with every new job I started in my past.

Let's go back a couple of years.

I'd been working as an instructor on a Duke of Edinburgh award job. I did quite a lot of these and they provided me with a much-needed source of income and also an opportunity to meet other instructors and finding out what was or might be happening workwise.

This morning I'd left home at 6am and, after a couple of hours of driving, I am travelling along the A49 going south from Shrewsbury to the village of Marshbrook a journey remaining now of around sixteen or so miles.

A short time later I pass the traffic lights at the junction for Church Stretton. I am listening to Paul Simon on the CD player   and I know that I have only a couple of miles to the turn into the village. It is on an S bend and easy to miss if you're going too quickly.

 A train passing over the level crossing at the road junction makes the decision for me and I have had to stop to let it through. A few years back I went over the bridge to Skye playing Runrig having carefully timed my journey to cross at the exact right moment on the CD.

 We are meeting in the car park behind the Station Inn. I and three other instructors are working on a bronze award programme, planned to run over Saturday and Sunday that, if all goes well, will get the trainees up to speed and able to go for assessment in a couple of months' time. It is a good place to meet. There is ample space for parking, for instructors to meet and enough space for a coach carrying the students from the school, to drop off safely, and turn around and it has with a campsite behind.

 More importantly it serves good coffee and cake. I can see the others sitting in the small walled area outside the café, taking the early morning sunshine with their drinks.

I have done this weekend on many occasions. The first time was around five years earlier when I`d been working part time as an outdoor instructor in order to gain the knowledge and to pay for qualifications. Like any other job you learn the trade by doing the work on the ground and putting in the hours to get the experience and become known to prospective employers and working with fellow instructors to develop relationships, that will open future doors. I believe it`s now called networking.

It doesn`t matter how many qualifications you`ve got if you can't talk the talk and walk the walk you are no use to any employer. This job is about walking whilst talking in more ways than one. If you can`t put a pack on your back and instruct whilst your students are doing the same, you`re in the wrong job. Success is never instant, and I have one acquaintance, who is an international mountain guide, he started on his career, by washing dishes in an outdoor centre, just to get his foot in the door.

Previously, whilst again doing a Duke of Edinburgh award training programme, I met another freelance instructor named Steve Smith. We found that, as is quite usual, several friends and acquaintances in common. We hadn`t worked together before, and talking to each other, found a lot of common ground. We promised to keep in touch. We never did, and though we never worked together again, it was Steve who told me about a company, he was freelancing for, that they were looking for instructors for UK work, and expeditions abroad. Although, at the time, I wasn`t interested in working overseas I was certainly keen on the idea of getting into an organisation with plenty of work available.

Then another fortuitous meeting on a different D of E job, followed by a weekend spent training a school about to spend a month in Kenya, and suddenly, I find myself looking at going abroad and I`ve been catapulted and fast tracked onto a training and assessment programme with that same company I`d started freelancing with not long before.

We are about to go away for further training and peer assessment in Tunisia; as I am required to have a proven capability at being able to handle situations in developing world and able to keep my cool, basically, when I`m being stretched and stressed and pushed for any length of time. The object of this trip is to see if I can pass muster.

I am looking forward to the challenge and my love affair with Africa is about to begin; and like some schoolboy on his first date, I am both excited and in fear of messing it all up.

Tunisia

It is Sunday morning. I have travelled down on the overnight coach from Liverpool, I am standing outside the company offices in the London outskirts waiting to meet the other members of the team. We are about to get chucked in at the deep end in Tunisia.

I had got the London tube, from near the bus station, and for the first and only time a seat; a couple of stops and I'm only a short walk from our headquarters. I make a point of being on time for appointments and at all times I try to be early. For my efforts I have just received a text message to tell me that the 10am meeting will now be at 2pm as the flight has changed to a later one.

I was way too early now, some five hours, but as irritating as it was the timetable of coaches from home wouldn't have made any difference. I had got the only one that would get me here, so, I spent my time walking along the road in front of the building along to the shops and back again. After an hour or so another likely looking candidate arrived his name was Julien, an ex-military policeman, known as Julien Le Bastard, not his real name but his way of dealing with issues, and he would be the man I ended up sharing rooms with for the next seven days.

We found a Lebanese café that had just opened and retreated into it to sound each other out, pick each other's brains and to sample the coffee.

 A little later, on a walkabout, we met another one of the guys. who turned up wearing a lot of clothes and some winter mountaineering boots. Like all of us he had been given a kit list and possible itinerary for Morocco but not the information that we actually were going to Tunisia. Unfortunately, he`d packed for 4000 metre peaks and not for 4000-foot peaks. Rather than write another kit list the organisers had sent a standard North Africa stroke Atlas mountain stroke Morocco kit list trusting that the information that Tunisia was the actual destination would also be made clear to the team. Nobody thought to put both itinerary and information in the same email and Gerry had spent the last four days in a snowhole near Aviemore and literally came off the mountain and got the overnight train down from Aberdeen. Pissed off would be a fine and accurate description of his mood when we told him where we were going.

Eventually the rest of the team arrived. Seven males and one female to be assessed by two male senior expedition leaders. Nine males and one female made for an unusual looking group; and the implications of this odd look may well have added to some future problems. Something we were all totally unaware of, at that time.

This trip had two parts. One was to look at the possibilities of trekking in Tunisia, whilst the second part was designed to simulate what would future job situations might entail for us. There would be peer assessment and the two staff instructors would also be assessing our abilities. What we were to do was play the part of the students, we would be taking on expedition, whilst two of us would be leaders. This would rotate through the week until such time as we had all gone through at least a day of planning and organising, not dissimilar in theory to an actual expedition, but on a reduced scale. On the real thing we would be responsible for making certain that everything that would be happening on an expedition ran safely, if not necessarily smoothly, as that was for the students to discover as part of their experiential learning curve.

The main difference was that normally a lot of the planning and the recces have already been done for us. All we had was an out and return ticket and a brief and a location to go and see if there were possible trekking opportunities in there. We did not have an itinerary as such but two of the management team had been out previous, and we did have a rough idea which direction we should be going in and an even rougher idea as to what we might be doing.

Just like any other expedition we split up the kit, cookers, tents, first aid kits and safety equipment so that we were carrying the kit as part of our personal luggage, just as well, as Air France that week had adopted a change of group kit policy. Previously it would consider group kit as part of a collective weight, but all had now changed; however, it was easier to separate it and carry it as we were going to have to do this at some stage anyway.

So, kit check sorted, passports checked, everything run through emergency procedures agreed, lost person programme plan talked through we walked to the rail station and caught the tube to Heathrow and booked in for our flight to Tunis via Charles De Gaulle airport, where you can buy coffee for a price similar to the hire of a small car.

We arrived in Tunis shortly after midnight, changed some money at the bureau de change and then spent the next twenty minutes or so haggling with taxi drivers to get a reasonable fare into the city centre. None of us spoke Arabic and though our French was fine taxi drivers seemed reluctant to do a deal with Lucy. It made for an interesting confrontation. The only advantage we did have was that it's difficult to bully ten people into some sort of submission when most of them are cranky from being on the go for the best part of twenty hours or so. We finally did a deal and got ourselves into three taxis and headed for The Hotel Metropole. We'd found this on the internet, in a somewhat frantic search, as affordable to replace the original choice of The Grand Hotel de France, which had been picked by the management team, due to its close proximity to the railway station; but no one had bothered to reserve any rooms for us and when we let them know we had arrived they knew nothing about us and so sorry we are full., was what we got.

We signed in, handed over our passports and headed for bed and a late good night's sleep, which was what we all desperately needed.

The following morning, a later than expected start, was initially a disappointment, but in retrospect was fortuitous. Our plan was to buy tickets to get to Bou Salem, the town, where we hoping to start a potential trek from, and spending our second night in Tunisia there. Outside the hotel was busy with people, trams rattled along the road, and the first thing we noticed how many people held hands. This wasn't restricted to a male female thing as more often than not it would be two males hanging on to each other. This seemed to be nothing other than a friendship rather than a relationship.

The whole team, all ten of us, trooped off to the train station to buy tickets. Until we had got tickets and train times there was no value in making plans.

 None of us were holding hands. As yet we had not had enough time to remember each other's name let alone become friends.

The morning was dry and bright and the walk to the station across the market was pleasant. This was February and we had left the UK to its cold and damp. Tunis was well awake and the sounds and noises typical of a big city during a working day.

We spotted a man who looked like a ticket collector or inspector or a man whose job title might have ended in "or"

"Bonjour monsieur. Parlez vous francais"

"No but I speak great Arabic."

"Nous voulez vendre billets pour le train."

"Je ne comprends pas. Try English"

"Nous"

Forget it guys speak to me in English

We want to buy some tickets to get to Bou Salem

You`re in the wrong station it's over there.

The man pointed towards another booking office and we trooped over feeling extremely stupid. We were mastering the art of trooping a good sign team was starting to bond on more levels perhaps than just stupidity We had been given information as the man spoke to us in English and patently we had ignored it. A lesson learnt.

There was only one more train that day to Bou Salem and we did not have enough time to pack, check out and return to the station before it left. Plan B is normally to get plan A to work but there was plenty to keep us occupied, in doing surveys around Tunis, and checking hotels, cafes, supermarkets and transport for future expeditions would keep us all busy for the remainder of the day.

 The two staff members left us to our own devices; and in four pairs we wandered around Tunis trying to pick up information and maps, visited the souk and some roadside cafes, before finding a café for an evening meal.

As I`m sure you are all aware finding somewhere to eat in a major city anywhere in the world is extremely easy. Finding somewhere cheap makes it a little more difficult but not in Tunis. If you really want to make life difficult you bring Peter with you who's a vegan. The Muslims we had met thus far didn`t understand why anyone wants to eat food without meat in it. Even when Peter ordered a plain salad in a restaurant it came with egg and fish. Chips with chips was to become Peter`s, 'meal of choice' and we eventually found a restaurant cum café that we will be able to find our way back from in the dark, and there, we eat well. The plates are plenty full, and the place is buzzing with locals which is always a good sign, in my opinion, of its quality. The following morning packed, breakfasted and making our way to the station, two guys have got the shits.

At this point let me explain how odd we looked. We are a group of ten as I`ve said nine males one female. We are carrying 80 litre backpacks, some with bits of camping equipment strapped on the outsides. Also, we have about 40 litre sacks strapped onto our fronts. We are walking through the streets of Tunis heading for the station in what appears to be some sort of handicapped conga line. Unlike yesterday when we were mostly ignored this morning we attracted a lot of attention and looks of amusement.

At the station three of us went off to buy tickets to Bou Salem, whilst the rest stood in a group minding the huge pile of luggage. The station was getting fuller by the minute, and when they did finally get the tickets, after standing at a window only to be moved to a different one and then another one we returned to the dance again and congered like the handicapped eel along with numerous others heading with us for what appeared to be the same gate and presumably the same train. The tickets showed to the man on the gate and we headed for the platform.

We had got aboard the right train more by luck than any sound judgement; It was the only one and as no one apart from the original railway man spoke any English and we spoke only English and French we got aboard with our fingers crossed. Julian's voice shouting through to us from the carriage behind confirmed how, I don't know, that we were on the right train. Eight had got into one carriage with myself and Peter standing in the vestibule of the next one, jammed like sardines, with I assume a whole lot of Tunisians. No one was going to fall over at this time there was no room and the jolt of the train starting just gave everyone a bit of a rib squeeze.

The journey will, if there are no delays, take around three hours and shortly after we started a few passengers went to stand up in the carriage aisle, breathing became easier and I felt relieved that we were finally on our way. After a couple of stops on route and around half an hour into our journey, I couldn't help but notice a young and pretty Tunisian lady standing near me.

Bonjour Ca va she says

Ca va je parle francais un peu.

We can speak in English I have a little English.

She spoke English better than I spoke French. She probably spoke English better than I did and we managed a small amount of conversation using a bit of both. She told me that we had turned up during what was a long bank holiday and that getting about was not going to be easy because of this. We made even smaller talk for a short while. She told me she was practising her English as long as I didn't mind. I didn't mind, she was adding information to my knowledge bank, but I was pleased that some of the passengers had moved or left the train altogether and more space allowed us to talk at a distance that would not have compromised her from any religious point of view.

At a later stop, a number of soldiers have boarded the train and are standing near us, in the corridor. They found Peter and me amusing and whatever they were saying was amusing some of the other passengers.

"They are ignorant pigs" my new friend says. "Do not worry about what I`m saying they don't understand they speak only Tunisian Arabic and have no French or English at all. They are ignorant peasants going on leave from their unit for the holiday". She spoke to them a couple of times and during one exchange she looked to be worried about what was said to her. She did not tell me what was said but wished me luck and advised me to be careful. Before she left she told me that our stop was the station after the next.

Peter was not having the best of times with the other squaddies. He is a big lad and it wasn`t getting violent so sod it, worry about it if it does. At our station a few were getting off and the corridor got quite cramped with people jostling. My main pack was on the floor by my feet where it had been for the last three hours, and my other pack was on top of it. From the far side of the corridor, I could see the others outside having got out of their carriage fairly easily. The squaddies motioned me to pass my small bag over and they`d pass it out. I shouldered my other bag and got off the train.

Where`s my small bag guys? I asked the team. "No bags come off the train Rob."

"Bastards" I turned around and I could see the soldiers just inside looking out at me. I was going back for my bag and I did. They rushed away from the doors and got into the main compartment with the rest of the passengers. They didn`t seem to have my bag on them. I kicked open the toilet door next to the exit door and that`s where they`d hidden the bag. I picked it up and got off the train, just as it was leaving. I`d done the unexpected and got away with it. Stupid and impetuous it may have been, I was lucky they hadn't stayed by the exit ready to kick my teeth in if I got back on the train but all my personal stuff including my phone and camera was in that bag and I didn't care at that moment, even if they were the Tunisian army.

All our other kit was accounted for, and after the train had left, this motley crew, then crossed the railway lines, and once again congered out of the station. heading into the town, to look for a hotel or a hostel for the night.

Neither Rough Guide nor Lonely Planet had been able to advise us, but as we had been pointed in this direction by our management team, we assumed they would have checked the accommodation situation out. So, we figured it was only going to be a simple "Hello where is a hotel?"

Finding someone who spoke English didn`t happen; and finding someone who spoke French didn`t happen either. But we found a small walled garden like a miniature village green and sat down in there, to work out a plan.

We decided that the easiest thing to do was find a policeman or the police station or post office as there didn't seem to be anything like a tourist information office about. Three were sent to look for assistance, whilst the rest of us remained in this little garden. It didn`t take long for us to become noticed and quite soon we were being watched by a few the locals. Quite soon after that word had spread around, numbers increased, and we were being observed by quite a lot of the locals. Word was going around and shortly after, as we obviously had become a bit of a novelty, we seemed to be outnumbered by about five to one. Camping in this little walled area suggested as a bit of a joke had rapidly lost its funny side and all of its appeal.

The guys arrived back with a policeman in tow who fortunately spoke reasonable English. He told the crowd to disperse which they did, but not too far away, that they couldn`t see what was going on. He got on his radio and two more officers arrived. I'm not certain whom they were protecting, but the taking of sides was not a question that in the end needed answering. We were told that there was no hotel, no hostel and nowhere for us to sleep in Bou Salem. What he would do for us, was that he would organise some transport to take us to another hotel in the next town, where we could stay the night, and tomorrow we could return here and by that time he would have some information and advice available for us that would hopefully get us sorted out with regard to seeing about trekking. There was nothing we could do but take his offer and move on.

He told us to follow him. One policeman, nine males, one female, twenty bags, two policemen and too many locals to count headed off in a line behind our friendly policeman to a taxi park, where he negotiated for two people carriers to take us to the hotel with a return deal; so, they would also pick us up the following morning and bring us back here. "You pay only half today" he said "and the other half tomorrow. It means they will be there. They will ask for it all today, but they may not turn up if you pay it all in one go."

We traded information with the policeman. He explained about the lack of accommodation and couldn't understand why anyone would assume it was easy to find here and in return we gave him the name of our contact, and the name of the hotel where we had arranged to meet him. We asked if he would be good enough to contact our prospective trekking agent, and let him know what was happening, and that we hope to be with him as arranged tomorrow. We had struck lucky his English was better than we could have hoped for and his willingness to help had taken the problem solving out of our hands. Our very helpful policeman waved us goodbye and assured us that all would be fine and sorted as per the request.

 We booked into our hotel and settled in for the night. Eating there saved us any further potential confrontations and given our performance this far it was almost certainly the best option we could have hoped for. The hotel was clean and friendly, dinner was excellent and reasonably priced and breakfast was included in the stay. The following morning, we had eaten early, continental, croissant and coffee. There was cereal for those that had wanted it. Thankfully we had all had a quiet night's sleep, now showered and packed, and filled with food we were ready for when the taxis came to pick us up to take us back to Bou Salem. The taxis appeared exactly on time; someone somewhere was making things happen. That'll do for us thank you.

We were met back at the taxi rank by the same policeman as yesterday.

He walked us from one taxi rank to a different one explaining that taxi companies operated from allocated areas and as we were now going in a different direction we were required to go with a different company. Again, the morning sun was comfortably warm for sitting around in but walking only a short way across the town carrying all our kit left us damp and sweaty. Gerry who was carrying all his winter mountaineering gear for the high Atlas in Morocco was getting red faced and irritated. He felt that it was so badly organised that he swore he'd never work for this company, and as far as I know he never has. We were like a mardi gras parade; people didn't applaud us as we passed but again we attracted a significant amount of attention. Although the walk was maybe only five minutes or so, we ended up with a bit of a following by the time we had reached the other taxi park.

Once again negotiations took place and it was interesting watching the wheeling and dealing that went on. We needed two taxis it took about six people to do the deals. One policeman and three taxi guys with Lucy and Paul our team accountant. Eventually after lots of shrugged shoulders looking up to the heavens and walking away in apparent disgust before returning back to the bartering again the deal finally got done. Like in a lot of other places, haggling is an art form here and important in making people feel that a fair deal has been done.

We took time to look around the area as it had a small open-air market selling just about everything, it seemed the only thing new was the food everything else appeared to be the sort of thing that western society would have sent to the charity shop. Footwear seemed to be in abundance as did well worn clothes. One of the guys bought a second-hand watch that looked like a poor Rolex copy and some of the crew laughed at him. It kept perfect time and he was still using it a week later, so one expects that it might go on forever. We grabbed some snacking food and bottled water from the market whilst the wheeler dealers had negotiated our taxi fares to the Royal Rihana hotel.

This is a journey of around 50 kilometres according to our policeman and will take at least an hour. Now that everyone was satisfied with the price; we boarded the two minibuses and headed off. Our nice young, smart, freshly shaven, helpful policeman saluted us as we left, and we waved him goodbye. He looked like he was going for an interview He let us know that he had arranged for a representative from the tourist office to come to see us and we could then discuss with him trekking in the area and he would advise us on how we could go about developing it. Things were looking up.

Normally these minibuses, or louages, as they are called here, carry ten persons, but when each of us is carrying around a hundred and twenty litres of baggage we need two vehicles and, even then, it can be cramped.

But this morning I am in relative comfort it is now my day to lead and so have been given the front seat. This is really a smart move by the rest of the team as its normally called the death seat for obvious reasons and more so today for when I try to put the seat belt on my driver is insulted by the action that suggests his driving is going to be anything less than impeccable. He starts shouting at me and although I don't understand the words I do get the drift of what he means. I think. I decide anyway not to bother as there is nothing to plug the seat belt into and as I do so the driver takes off and once again we are on the move.

I am not sorry to be leaving. Although we didn't have any trouble as such the possibility of things going awry were closer than they should have been and being sent to a place without accommodation was distinctly poor planning. We were fortunate in finding a helpful policeman and in retrospect lucky that it was not a couple of years later, at the start to the Arab Spring, when things in the area were not so friendly towards some non-Tunisians.

 At the risk of unintentionally maligning the whole of the British army our management team of two ex-army officers had been true to form.

There are three possible routes to our destination and our drivers are taking the most northerly one. We will be travelling towards the North West. This route appears to be shorter than the others but probably, according to our maps, no quicker. The central one I don't know about, but the southerly starting route would have taken us via Jendouba, which had been an alternative beginning to our expedition and where we had planned to finish.

We pass through the North African countryside, mostly reclaimed scrub desert with irrigated parcels of land between showing signs of a healthy-looking abundance of green crops our speed too quick to be totally certain of what each of them were but certainly a variety of food plants and plenty of people working the fields.

We speed along straight lengths of tarmacked road and then carefully negotiate a hairpin bend before again we are speeding to the next hairpin, the road bending around a huge piece of immovable rock or a deep ravine easier to redirect the road than to remove one or bridge the other. Our journey continues like that for most of the way. We are climbing up a steep road when the driver turns sharply, into a gap, between some concrete walls and we arrive at the hotel where we are due to meet our contacts.

The vehicles stop at the front of the hotel and we all get out. Its higher here but the weather is still warm, and we look for somewhere to shade.

Paul and the guys doing the accounts today pay the drivers. They are expecting tips, but our budget won't extend to this. They move their vehicles from in front of the hotel and park up a few yards down the drive towards the exit.

I take Anthony and John with me to the reception desk and explain who we are and that were awaiting our contact who we expect to arrive shortly. We cannot afford to stay here the budget is not going to last past one night and we are expected to be in Tunisia for a further five days.

Our reception manager tells us that we can wait on the balcony which is on the first floor where we will find seats and shade. We are welcome to order drinks and he passes me a priced menu. He tells me that the view from the balcony is very good, especially today as the sky is clear. When I ask him about our contact he says, "I will let you know if he calls." The conversation comes to an end with a shrug of the shoulders. I am presented with a language difficulty that says I`m not saying anything else.

I let the others know and we all wander up the staircase to the first floor and out onto the balcony, which is not like a Romeo and Juliet one but more in keeping with a five aside football pitch.

We hear another vehicle coming up the driveway, a stubby 4x4 with tinted windows stops by the minibuses. Two men get out from the back seats. They are wearing bulky bomber jackets, cargo trousers, highly polished boots and what appear to be puttees. They have a short conversation with the two minibus drivers who then leave as the two get back into the 4x4 and continue up the drive to where the driver reverse parks the vehicle, near to the steps.

The two big boys get out and go inside. We assume that they will come to visit us but don`t. We`re nosy and quite interested in finding out what`s going on. We haven`t got it totally sorted yet as this is something else to fit into the equation but and not without good reasoning think the two guys below are police or military; it`s too warm for those jackets so they are certainly carrying weapons of some sort. The driver has not wound down any windows or opened their door. A minute or so later we see them walk down the steps and get into the rear of the vehicle. The engine starts but the vehicle stays put. The air con is on.

Our hotel reception manager appears at the door. 'Someone will be here soon to speak to us about trekking.' His perfect English soon lost in a lack of understanding and shrugged shoulders when we ask him who will be arriving. Will it be our original contact, but we are talking to his back as he has departed for the safety of his desk.

We sit and wait.

The sun is cracking the flags; we are all sitting around on the first-floor terrace. And as the sun is getting warmer, we keep drinking expensive soft drinks from the bar below. There is a washroom on the ground floor we are advised not to drink the water. Ok for washing but not drinking.

"Not going to plan this is it" asks Martin to no one in particular but to all in general. "We`re out of place and look wrong" Julien, the redcap, says. There`s nine men and one lady and apart from Rob we`re all in late twenties early thirties short hair fit and healthy almost like what proper out door instructors might look like. We`re carrying huge packs and we turn up unannounced in a town in a foreign country; is there any reason we should be surprised that we have attracted attention. To us we are here to look at trekking in the local area but with Rob, who could be the old colonel, we also look like a wet squad and I think they`re justified in being suspicious of us. If I was still in the military I would want to know what you were all up to."

What`s a wet squad?

"An assassination team" replies Julien and there it lay for a while each of us with our own thoughts. There didn`t seem anything else we could add to the statement at this time. We would have to wait to see where it was going next.

The men from the 4x4 are wandering around, now and again, presumably stretching their legs. They are appearing as nonchalantly as two big gun toting guys can be whilst the driver still hasn`t left the vehicle since they arrived.

The views across from the hotel terrace are quite spectacular. That's a good reason for coming but that's not why we`re here this morning. We know we can`t afford to stay here and the management is either unlikely or unwilling to do us a serious discount that would allow us to do so. A number of guests arrive and leave, and their transport makes us realise that this is a serious money hotel; why we thought we were going to go trekking from here is becoming difficult to believe. I`m thinking of starting smoking again as the waiting is starting to get boring and just as I`m about to bum a cigarette from Laurence, the only smoker on the team, again we hear the sound of tyres crunching on the gravel drive. John looking down into the parking area from the balcony calls across. "Looks like our man has arrived" he says, "A blacked out Mercedes and the big boys below have left their vehicle and suddenly jumped to attention".

The car stops in front of the hotel. The passenger door is away from us and we are unable to see whom they are talking to its left-hand drive of course and once again we can`t see the driver; tinted windows will hide more than sunshine. The conversation is short one of the guys' opens the door and a man wearing a dark suit gets out. As he is coming into the hotel his car parks up next to the 4x4 and the other two men return to their vehicle.

Seconds later and he comes through the door, like he owns the place, the hotel reception manager trailing a couple of feet behind him Bonjour Ca Va. He says and starts to shake hands with everyone on the team most of whom now are resigned to patiently waiting for whatever they think destiny holds for them and are currently trying to make the best of the sun and get themselves a tan. "Je m`appelle Mohammed" he said working his way around the balcony. He moved like a cat he looked everywhere and at everyone he was getting a measure of what he was dealing with. Most have taken to sun loungers and lazily some of them shift their bodies when he greets them but close their eyes, soon after the handshake, appearing to lose interest in the proceedings.

I rise from my chair as he comes to me. We are around the same age and politeness requires that I stand up to greet him. He is smartly dressed, good suit well-tailored, clean white shirt and a black knitted tie. He is as smart as I am scruffy. He too has given me the once over as he has with the others. Whatever he is he isn't stupid. His shoes are black and smart too. Our boots are designed for walking. He surely has noticed but what he has made of it I am not yet privy to. His conversation is way too quick for me to understand My French is not that good I said. My English is not that good either He replies. As I am leader of the team today it has befallen to me to speak to our tourism official.

I call Lucy over and introduce her as our translator. I didn`t tell Mohammed, that Lucy teaches modern languages to A level, and is fluent in French, German, Italian and Spanish with a smattering of others as this would have started to look even more suspicious. But now having explained why there might be the single female with the team, I leave it at that. Our two senior instructors joined us for the discussion and after some preliminary explanations what we were trying to do with regard to trekking and linking up an educational programme with the historical site at the Roman ruins of Bulla Regis at Jendouba, the other town which is not far away from Bou Salem. If we can do more than just trekking with these expeditions than just a long walk it provides a better reason for going and it does enhance the experience for the participants.

We explained that there was no particular reason for starting at Bou Salem rather than Jendouba the options had been left at our discretion and we had only been able to find one hotel in Jendouba that we could afford so we thought it a good idea to leave it until the end always expecting to find accommodation in or near Bou Salem the rest of the time we would be camping.

The door behind us opened and two waiters appeared one carrying a well laden tray and the other pushing a trolley. "I ordered some soft drinks and a snack our man explained "Do help yourselves". The sunbathers sprang into action like they'd been let loose from a skeet trap confirming my suspicions that not one of them wasn't listening to what was going on.

What were your other plans?

Well we hoped that there might be some good trekking to the North West of Jendouba we were told that there was some wild boar up there, so the area might lend itself to being good expedition country wild boar permitting, and as no one was doing it at the moment our company thought that being the first there might be to our advantage assuming of course that we could get it all organised. Hence our visit today. "You know about wild boar?" "I know they can be dangerous." I replied, "We will take advice from your people". He took a glass of fresh orange and continued.

"I tried to get in touch with your company this morning but kept getting an answerphone. I left a message, but no one has got back to me." Mohammed said in perfect English. He did not see it as a mistake this was his party and he could play it any way he wanted to. Mohammed was the most unlikely tourist official I had ever met in my life.

They're probably needing to get director level approval to phone back said Alan who had been filling in the details of what where and how the business end was being considered. You've probably been logged into our system but as we don't currently work in Tunisia it's likely that the office staff don't know what's going on and they've passed it upstairs. Lucy was still translating as Alan had been speaking but our man knew what had been said without the need for Lucy to repeat it.

Trekking is not possible at this time. I have informed your contact here that it will not be possible to organise any expeditions this season, and consequently you will not meet him today. If your company will get in touch with me on the telephone number I left with them, we will try and put together some possible routes for them. You are talking about trekking less than ten kilometres from the border with Algeria. Therefore, the trekking will be organised by the police they will provide the mules and assistants and the guards as required. You are proposing to trek in an area where insurgents cross the border from Algeria and where there is possible criminal and probable terrorist activity occurring. We cannot therefore allow you to go wandering around up there without our assistance and protection and should there be any change for the worse we will cancel and there will have to be a change of location.

This was supposed to be Enid Blyton "The Famous Ten Go Camping" and it was turning into a Jean Luc Goddard.

I suddenly realised I was loving every moment of this and getting into it in a big way along with the rest of the team who were no longer pretending to be asleep but listening intently.

As you aren`t staying here we have found a reasonable hotel for you on the coast in Tabarka. We are in the middle of a national holiday and hotel accommodation is difficult to get at reasonable cost I will however accompany you on your journey and negotiate on your behalf a fair price for your stay.

The louages will return shortly and we will be on our way soon after. I expect to take around one hour to the hotel assuming no delays. Do you have any questions?" "Not at this time" I replied, "but if one occurs may we ask." "Certainly" We looked at each other decided there wasn`t anything we could say. This was a 'non-negotiable' and rocking the boat was not on our agenda. We had, potentially, through no fault of our own, been dropped in the mire and extricating ourselves in a damage limitation exercise was what we needed to do.

"Thank you for your help"

"You're very welcome. I suggest that there is time for a wash and tidy up before we leave there is a bathroom just inside, at the bottom of the stairs, as I`m sure you are aware. I will have some extra towels put in there,"

The conversation was at an end.

He nodded to us about faced and he was gone. Like a professional dancer he moved swiftly and smoothly towards the door to the staircase which opened as he did so by the hotel reception man who had been clearly keeping an eye on proceedings.

"Ok guys. Just in case you missed any of that. Listen up. we will be on the move soon. Off up to the coast to a town called Tabarka I`ll look it up in Lonely Planet and in the meantime, we need to get ready for an hour's taxi ride there will be extra towels in the washroom. And we can use the toilets for a freshen up if we think we need it. Its free may as well take it."

As leader it was still my responsibility to organise the day.

"If he`s from the department of tourism I`m a Dutchman" said Julien. "Blacked out windows, minders jumping to attention too much muscle for tourism, definitely military or police, I reckon though I would suspect some kind of anti- terrorist unit. I doubt we`ll ever know the full story. Reminded me of the old days. Like being back in the army again."

I went to the bathroom for a wash and brush up and left everyone to it. Julien may not have been exactly spot on but there was certainly more to the tourism work in Tunisia than there seemed to be in the UK.

The louages, that we had arrived in, returned about twenty minutes later and quite obviously they had not gone back to Bou Salem but stayed close by, having had instructions from someone in authority.

We loaded up the kit and climbed aboard again same places as before; this time I made no effort to clip the seat belt into a non-existent keeper.

We descended slowly out of the hotel driveway and tucked in behind two police cars who were leading the way from the hotel. The 4x4, with the muscle in, was immediately behind us and the Mercedes followed behind the 4x4. We had ourselves a convoy which drove gently along the tarmacked road. Our driver seemed twitchy as if it was all too slow for him and he obviously wanted to get going. We continued at this somewhat sedate pace for reasons unknown it may have irritated our drivers but at least with a shortage of seat belts the journey was considerably less hazardous.

Around thirty minutes after we started the two police cars pulled over on the opposite side of the road the louages pulled up on the right facing our direction of travel and 4x4 and Mercedes pulled up behind the police cars on the left.

"What's going on now?" came a voice from the back of the bus

Don't know said Julien but I'm not going to worry unless something big and noisy on a tripod, comes out. The louage drivers had got out and were across the road with the others chatting through the open windows that we still hadn't seen into. We sat and waited. Maybe it was a test, maybe there was nothing to be concerned about, but we were on a learning curve and we didn't know what the subject was. Five minutes or so we waited it had felt like half an hour but five was all it was when two police cars arrived from the opposite direction pulled up reversed in to a gap and turned around to face back from where they came. Our first two police cars started up, turned around and presumably returned to where they had come from and then we realised that all that was happening was a probable change of jurisdiction. Perhaps, the Tunisian police had, like the louage drivers, directions and boundaries within which they worked. It provided a reason for the slow start to the journey and our drivers returned, and the convoy was back on the move again, in what appeared to be a desperate bid to make up lost time.

My driver having put the only seat belt in the vehicle on proceeded to give us an upper body workout as we tried to stop smashing into each other as we were thrown around inside the minibus as he careered, down steep and narrow roads, for the remainder of the journey. He seemed happy turning it into the most dangerous part of the whole day and I was pleased and relieved to arrive in Tabarka, in one piece.

There was no difficulty, in finding a hotel. The Tabarka police knew exactly where we were going and drove us straight there. We paid our louage drivers as we had been instructed to do, by Mohammed, and followed him with our kit into the hotel. There was conversation in what we assume was Tunisian Arabic which I believe is different from other Arabic dialects not that I can understand any of them but if you are travelling to another country I think it`s always a good idea to do some research first.

Mohammed was true to his word; bed and breakfast was well within our budget and we went through the process of signing in and showing our passports. I would put money on that Mohammed got a copy of everything.

"Enjoy your stay here it's a very nice resort there is a castle on the hill overlooking the bay" he said "and you can get bus tickets to get to Bizerte which is halfway back to Tunis and then after a night in Bizerte you can travel back to Tunis on Friday. Friday is our holy day and travel can be difficult on Friday and Saturday but the journey from Bizerte to Tunis is easy as buses are more often, and the road is easier too." Our itinerary was being rewritten and in truth we had little option other than take Mohammed's advice he shook our hands and we never saw him or any of them again though I suspect that we were watched by others if only to make certain they hadn't made a mistake about us.

Some lunch and maybe a visit to this castle which Lonely Planet tells us is "Genoese, overlooks a beautiful sandy bay and is now linked by a causeway and is in a most picturesque town in northern Tunisia just 27 kilometres from the Algerian border". Considering how far we seem to have come today and how long we've been on the road we haven't managed to get that far away from our original objective.

Apart from the distance to the border I can confirm that everything else is true, and we spent an easy pleasant afternoon researching the local area taking Mohammed's advice buying bus tickets in advance and making copious notes for any future exploratory forays.

We found a cheap pizza place with space for all ten with seating outside on trestle tables and bench seats some of the team ordered a beer while the rest settled for the national drink of coffee.

Our senior assessor decided to call a review of the days`
proceedings to see what we all thought and though most
seemed happy one or two felt we`d been backed into a
corner and moved very much against our will to suit the
Tunisians.

"As leader today; I some observations to make. This
morning we were in Bou Salem looking to go trekking
around Jendouba which is about 50k from the border with
Algeria and south west of Bou Salem. We have spent the
day talking and travelling about 80k in the opposite
direction as we cannot go trekking in that area and now we
are according to our Lonely planet guide only about 27k
from the border. We are a lot closer to the border than we
were this morning, but the authorities are happier with the
situation or they wouldn't have moved us here. Any
reasons for this on my part would be a guessing game or
pure conjecture and I figure we should go with the flow as
someone else is in charge of whatever programme we have
found ourselves in. I don't know if we can do anything
else or can we?

I`ll answer that said Julien. We don`t know what`s going
on here they could be in the middle of some sort of clean
up in the hills the guys who were watching us might just
have been there for our protection as well. Look what
happened yesterday when we arrived at Bou Salem. We
attracted a big enough crowd of people to do us all some
serious damage had they chosen to do so and if our
friendly neighbourhood policeman hadn`t arrived and
called up some reinforcements maybe things would have
worked out differently.

When in Rome do as the Romans do or in this case what
they tell you to do. We are in someone else`s country and

we should always bear that in mind. There is no advantage to be had, alienating either the government or the people when we`re trying to do business here. The people we have dealt with have treated us well and taken care of us we should be grateful and thankful; and when we get back home we should consider nailing someone`s scrotum to their desk for dropping us in the shit."

That`s why he was Julien Le Bastard and we knew he meant it. "Anyway that`s my opinion for what it`s worth."

 Anyone else? I asked No one had anything to add. "Here endeth the review and discussion were my final words" and I handed over the leadership reins to Martin who would hopefully get us to the bus station on time and on the right bus to Bizerte.

The journey to Bizerte is given as 3 hours. The bus like all buses in countries without subsidised public transport goes when it`s full. Today it filled up quickly and then was filled a bit more, not excessively but like the train, it served to stop passengers from rattling around on the bends. We have seats and there is no obvious need to rush. Except for the guys who`ve got the shits and maybe would prefer to stay here today near a toilet. They seem to need to rush in and out of everywhere. We do not have an hotel, but Bizerte is a substantial size and accommodation should be easily sourced, we reckoned somewhat naively, given our performance to date, and after a bumpy journey of a good three hours we arrive at the terminus in Bizerte. The four with the clenched buttocks and funny walk head for the nearest toilet while we wait, minding the bags. The toilet a stand-up job over a hole in the floor apparently left a little to be desired and though I didn`t visit I had no reason to suppose otherwise as public toilets anywhere in the world can leave even the least fastidious in search of tissue and hand gel.

Bizerte is heaving with people; its Independence Day and a public holiday and the whole of Tunisia, as expected, appears to be trying to get a bed in Bizerte. A lot of military and service personnel are walking around their uniforms making them fairly obvious and they are keeping themselves with their comrades. As long as the paras and the marines don't spot each other or those squaddies on the train aren't here all should remain calm fingers crossed.

Hard negotiations with a hotel manager gets us three rooms between ten of us. He has demanded that he is paid in full in advance. If we agree we can stay if not we can't. Another non-negotiable but its within budget and we get a receipt. It's written in Arabic and could just as easily be a laundry list.

 There`s enough beds, but Lucy will have to share a room with three males which we think is against their religion, but we have acquired some curtaining from the manager and he seems satisfied with the covering around her bed not to give us any further grief. Needless to say, Lucy doesn`t mind. It's a lot safer than sleeping in a room on your own and even with door wedges and rape alarms it's still better with three men even if they do snore and smell a bit musty after spending three hours in an oven of a bus journey.

Julien, Peter and I have a three-bed room en-suite. We have a toilet a shower and a washbasin all three can be used at the same time without moving your feet they are separated from my bed by a curtain less substantial than Lucy has and as a result my bed has a damp feel to it even though it`s not had any use all day.

The group with dodgy stomachs don`t wish to go walkabout so we split into two groups of three and take different directions from the hotel. I go off with Lucy and Martin in search of the bus station which our lonely planet tells is fairly close, while the others go in search of the Ksibah also known as Fort Sedi Henni, where there is apparently an oceanographic museum that might be worth a visit though the guide book blurb doesn't sound too promising. It's not too far from the Kasbah and so well within walking distance for them. We spent the day working on accumulating as much information as possible about Bizerte. Should trekking in Tunisia become viable, even if initial thoughts weren't promising, it would have been criminal as professionals, given the chance that we had, if we had wasted the opportunity. Our gathered info and the format the company ran concluded that at that time Bizerte was for travelling through rather than staying in. The day therefore had not been wasted and with some satisfaction we got cleaned up ready to eat.

Later after an evening meal, cheap and cheerful, of fresh fish and rice, and thick black coffee we make our way back to the hotel. The streets are noisy with people celebrating Independence Day and even with the windows shut finding sleep was difficult and even worse for Peter who spent most of the time awake, in a bed with some form of infestation that had bitten him throughout the night. The following morning, he looked like he had some sort of highly infectious disease, his whole body was covered with spots and lumps and although my bed had been damp, I`d faired a lot better than he had.

Luckily for Peter, he being a vegan, and I for unknown reasons don't have the shits this morning but the other eight do and it's a brave man that farts today.

We will be happy when we get back to Tunis and the Hotel Metropole, having learnt now, we believe, how to book in advance.

Our management duo have set us the speak a foreign language test again. Although, with Lucy we have no problems with numerous languages, she has been taken out of our list of available assistance. So, we must manage to get ourselves sorted, without resorting to her expertise. Though she will monitor any conversations as an insurance policy.

 French and English and mobile phones and patience write it all out before you start and hope no one asks questions you don't understand. By some miracle we have managed to book an extra night as we were only expecting to be there Saturday; but they have managed to find space for us and though the journey from Bizerte to Tunis is short it can`t be over quick enough for some who on arrival head for their rooms and will not be seen for any length of time, until shortly before we leave for the airport and home.

Saturday our last full day, and those who were up to it, took a trip to Carthage, for some Roman historical culture, as it`s only a short train ride from Tunis. Later, on our return to the city centre, we got ripped off at a perfume-sellers, had an argument at an alfresco café over coffee prices, nearly came to grief with some very intense and demanding carpet dealers, and to top it all, were met by a hail of stones and significant pieces of brick by some less than friendly youths, when we took a wrong turn in the souk. Worse was to come even later in the afternoon when the two accounts people told us that we had run out of money part way through the weekend. "you mean we're going to have to pay for this?" "fraid so". We ended up clubbing together to pay for our Saturday meal and taxis to the airport. A fairly normal sort of happening for nine men and a lady on a weekend away, in a foreign country. I suppose.

We sat in the airport lounge and reviewed the week and what we had achieved and although we hadn`t really established if trekking was possible we had established that if it was going to take place it was not going to be a case of sending a school out here and everything would fall into place for them; We had survived the trials and tribulations the dodgy stomachs and the stress and we had come out at the end of the week still talking to each other. Always a good sign.

At Charles de Gaulle Airport we traded email addresses with each other and had a chat individually with our assessors. At Heathrow we would mostly be off in different directions, so Paris was our final opportunity all together. I reversed my journey from a week before and found myself waiting again.

I was ten minutes too late for the bus from Euston and it being a Sunday I would have eleven hours and fifty minutes before the next one. Eventually you can fall asleep on the floor at the bus station; but if the last week in Tunisia had taught me only one thing it was ways to strap my bags to myself when I needed to make with the zeds.

On the strength of my performance, the company offered me an 'expedition leader' role for a month in Namibia. My learning curve was in the ascendancy and I was wishing my life away to go to a place I had dreamed about going to, ever since I had seen a film about the Namib desert many years before.

I told my wife where I was off to, and she managed to get me a copy of that same film, 'The Beautiful People' made by a South African film director named Jamie Uys, which had originally seeded my desire to visit there. My passion for adventure was being nurtured and unwisely given my age I was wishing my life away and urging the onset of summer, not only was I going to a place I'd longed to go to, but I was being paid to go there as well.

Namibia

Walking with children and other wild animals

It takes a fair-sized team of people to put one of these expeditions together. In addition to what we had attempted, on our feasibility study to Tunisia, there would be further checks on transport, hostels, campsites, medical and emergency situations, costs to all of these, shopping for food and also frequently an in country search to find a charitable project to take a part in during the time away.

A lot of these projects are group efforts and may take place over a couple of years and involve more than one school and numerous visits. A lot of teams will do some teaching and education projects. Quite often some sort of building work will take place. Some students will get involved in a physical way believing they have not much else to offer. Stop selling yourself short is part of what this is about. A building project at a school or orphanage would add mutual value to the experience and leaving a project with some clear changes completed will provide an indelible mark of satisfaction a job well done glad we came feeling.

Often the most benefit might not be visible on departure. The cross-culture fertilisation between students from different backgrounds, a look into other people's lives, works in both directions and frequently in retrospect has a greater lasting impression than the newly painted clean toilet block. Those toilets will need painting again before you forget about the games you played, the English you taught, and the songs you sang with those plastic shoed worn-out clothed kids in an some isolated village, in the desert or the rainforest or out on the African plain. Those memories will stay with you forever and if they don't you did it wrong.

Getting in to a country once you've got the visa and the flight sorted out is relatively easy, getting around and out again, as we were well aware, can be a lot more difficult. Normally there is someone that can be easily accessed if problems occur that can't be resolved without difficulty and these local agents can provide a lot of help and advice. They would if it's felt necessary, meet us when we arrive at the airport, in country.

In the UK, my colleagues will have met with the school, on many occasions, usually over an eighteen-month period, during which they will have discussed, where they wish to go, what they would like to do when they get there, and how this can all be accommodated in roughly on average a month-long programme, that with travelling added, will make 31/32-day expedition.

When a plan has been agreed, they will have drawn up an approximate cost for this and then it's up to the students to work out how they are going to finance it. The person who has the job of liaising with the school, our school programme manager, will give them advice on how they can collect and make money. They will offer ideas such as organised coffee and cake sales, bag filling at the local supermarket, car washing and also sponsored runs and abseils that we will help to organise and provide the technical expertise for and hopefully at the same time get the students working together and bonding as a group.

At an agreed time, a training weekend will be organised where they will have to do a couple of days walking and camping, cooking and cleaning of equipment. This will give an opportunity for the instructors and assessors along with the schoolteachers to check on their fitness and attitude to teamwork and leadership. The instructors who are all experienced expedition leaders will provide them with information and advice which they can take away and work on together.

At some point I will go to the school to give a short talk on how I fit into the programme. I will tell them of my experiences how I've run previous expeditions and how I see the month away, working out. Plus, what I expect from them and what they can expect from me. We normally finish with a question and answer session which, when finished, should give everyone assurance that all will be all right. I try to make the evening as useful and entertaining as possible with information that I give to the parents and minders of the students.

Frequently students don`t turn up to meet me and even more frequently neither do the parents; which bothers me now and again. I think if I am going to trust my child with someone, I'd want to know who he or she was and feel confident in them.

I've done it a lot of times now and I'm comfortable with the way I go about it, but that first time was a different happening altogether.

My plan was to give a talk about what they didn't know.

Therefore, with the information that they already had.

That most of the admin has already been handled by the planners at headquarters, that is they who have put numbers and costs together, done deals for flights and worked out exactly how the time away could be used effectively by liaising with the school and putting together a cost-effective programme that would satisfy all.

That all of this has taken place long before the expedition leader gets involved. Team numbers and teacher, minder ratios need to be confirmed in order that the local education authority is happy that they comply with their criteria.

As I've said this all normally takes about eighteen months from start to finish. After the original idea, numbers are confirmed, costs are estimated, and plans are made, tweaked, changed, adjusted and played with until it looks like it might work if it goes alright. Then a final costing is arrived at and team balance is assessed with a view to finding a suitable leader. It's not acceptable to have an all-girls school and two male teachers and a male expedition leader in place for a month away in the rainforest say. This is when a female leader and maybe if a female teacher wasn't available perhaps a female assistant leader as well.

And obviously the same thing applies the other way around.

So it`s normally nearer the going away time when the prospective leader will meet the team at the school and say hello to the parents and try and convince them that they should trust their offspring, the gentle little fragile loves of their lives, to this stuttering idiot who when he did it for the first time was nearly ready to be sick with panic and grief, trying to assure everyone present, he can take twenty-four students and two teachers and solve any problem that might occur and bring them all back safe and sound which is exactly how I found myself trying to convince a group of unsmiling less than friendly parents one Wednesday evening in a school just outside Cambridge and trying to get my breathing into some semblance of normality.

Warren Buffet reckons that public speaking is one of the most important things that a successful person should learn. If he had said this a lot earlier, in my life, I might have practised beforehand. Talking to one`s peers in a meeting I was well used to; but this was a more demanding crowd who had to believe in me, before we left, or they were going to need sleeping pills for a month if they were going to get any rest at all.

On my drive down, I had stopped and rewritten my speech, a little further down I stopped again and tweaked it a bit. Then I got to the school and sat in the carpark and rewrote it again. I took out the jokey bits, made certain I wasn't getting into areas I didn`t know anything about, and put my trumpet back into its case. There wasn`t a lot left after that, and I was expected to talk about my experiences for around fifteen minutes. I don`t think armed militia, diarrhoea, stone throwing teenagers, dodgy and aggressive carpet sellers was what they wanted to hear from me. Nor about taking drunken climbers around Spain or halting meetings in the toilets after midnight when we caught two different D of E groups trying to do something that was not prescribed as a part of the award.

I am sitting at the top table facing my audience. Our school rep has run through so much stuff most of what I had allowed myself to say she has now covered my most of my talk and I am even more out of waffle than I had ten minutes earlier.

Then she gave me the sort of introduction one might give to the winner of the best Oscar.

I did a quick resume of running groups inside the UK and training DofE up to gold standard, teaching bush craft and team building for several years. This didn't take very long it was woefully short of substance and it held little in the way of style. "Does anyone have any questions?" It was the only way I could think of stringing it out, and it would have to be done anyway. My thought desperate as it was that maybe a question and answer slot now would fill out the allotted time, make all think it had been worthwhile coming, and then everyone would go home certain in the knowledge that I was the right man for the job.

 I had the usual questions about making contact. "If it`s an emergency, via our office, they have access to me via my satellite phone which I sign in to daily."

 Why can`t they take their phones?

"Because no news is good news, if there is a problem the office will contact you directly. You should therefore make sure your emergency numbers and contact information are up to date when we leave".

Once on a mountain road in South America on a late evening drive on the way to their hostel when a lot of the team had gone to sleep two coaches had to carefully slowly squeeze around a long bend due to a wagon having broken down in exactly the wrong place. One student sent a message home that whilst out driving late at night they had nearly been off a cliff edge certain that it was only a matter of time before they were all killed. By the time our people on 24 hour watch had got back to the leader in South America just about every parent had been on the phone worried about their child. No phones.

What about clean water for drinking?

"In their kit list, we ask that they carry at least two water bottles of at least one litre size each, which they can fill as required. Having two bottles allows for one for drinking whilst the other is being purified."

Where can we buy a waterproof sac from?

"You can't they will all let water in. Some are better than others, but the easiest way is a decent sized plastic bag inside the sac, big enough for the top to rolled down because if it's open all you will have put in there will be a big bucket. In Namibia we are however unlikely to see any rain. It is extremely dry. And there is no need for a dry bag inside. Carrying a few plastic shopping bags is a good idea to put the washing in and also for any cameras especially ones with zoom lens or other moving parts as sand is good at infiltrating just about everything."

We battered a few minor questions around about food safety, water purification and what might happen in a medical emergency and a couple more times why can`t they have mobile phones? "

As I've said No news is good news. This expedition is for people to work together, learn to lead groups, develop as individuals and understand what sharing and taking responsibility is."

Anyone else have any questions?"

"What experience do you have of taking twenty-six people away for a month to Africa?" A man's voice from the back row.

Until that moment it had been going quite well. This question was the only question that not only I couldn`t answer but no one else could answer it as far as we knew either.

Twenty-eight if I and the driver are included is a huge group and getting it to work on paper had been a logistical nightmare. No one else had ever had that many and having met the teachers who were as street-wise and as naive as any I have ever met I realised that I was in at the deep end.

"Numbers are not that much of an issue. One problem person in a team of six could spoil it for all and create issues difficult to solve but if everyone has the right attitude and having met the team this afternoon I believe they do. So, the size of the group will work in our favour there will always be someone to talk to and there is the added bonus of safety in numbers.

It went quiet for a moment

When the man from the back started again." Can you guarantee then that there won`t be any problems and everyone will be ok on their return"?

"No"

It`s gone quiet now and I have everyone's attention.

The only way to guarantee, without a doubt, that nothing will happen to someone on an expedition is to not allow them to go. No one wants to hear that as an option. I'm not about to say it but;

Fire with fire time? or bull muck time or trumpet blowing maybe.

"It's the same as you can`t guarantee that nothing can happen to anyone when they leave here and go home. You won`t walk along the white line in the middle of the road in the dark and neither would I. Because we can risk assess and we run, what we call a dynamic risk assessment, where we are constantly evaluating and adjusting for any changes in circumstances. That`s my job and I`m good at it which is why I`m here" A couple of people clapped a couple of times and the school rep jumped up and closed the meeting with "There`s tea and biscuits outside in the corridor for those who would like some and I`d like to thank Rob for coming down this evening and giving us an interesting talk. There was then a reasonable round of applause after which most of the parents started to head for the teapots and plates of biscuits. Some spoke on the way out shook my hand and wished us a good expedition. The voice from the back came over. He was a big man late fifties big hands that looked like they`d done a lot work, he oozed physical power, but his handshake was no more than firm; there was nothing he needed to prove.

"I`m sure you`ll take care of them" he said. "I worked in Africa a lot. Left a few friends out there. I hope it goes well. Thank you for the talk. Bon voyage." He didn`t speak to anyone else on the way out nor did he stop for tea and biscuits I saw him put his arm around a young girl and the two walked down the corridor he opened the door and she linked his arm as they left. My belief that there is no stronger bond than fathers and daughters had once again been confirmed.

Namibia

My wife bought me a Timex "Expedition" watch, to use whilst away, after I had told her about the guy buying a watch in the market at Bou Salem. This was instead of wearing one she had bought me as a wedding anniversary present, which had a lot more personal value.

Just over three months later and we are going to Namibia.

The flight was direct from London to Windhoek the capital of Namibia and we arrived on time at Heathrow, sort of.

I had stayed at a small b and b, near the school two days before we travelled to the airport hoping rather than trusting that everything would be all right. It was a quick and easy journey for me then to arrive the day before departure at the school with plenty of time on "our check it all over day".

I always have contingency plans then nothing will go wrong. Things only ever go awry when there is nothing to fall back on and even less likely when the contingency plan is better than the original.

I check passports, telephone numbers of parents, personal kit, make copies of passports in case anyone loses theirs, make certain that any medication they need is enough for the time away and take my responsibility in loco parentis.

We will then spend the rest of the day together. We will run through our itinerary try to foresee where and when there might be a problem look at food menus and any allergy requirements, medication etc. This time we will be sleeping at the school.

Seeing all the students together gives me a chance to meet them, see how they shape up as a group, and an opportunity to assess their needs with the teachers present. It's a day for bonding sorting out final details discussing the expedition and what the students hope that they're going to achieve, what they're looking forward to and also what they might be apprehensive about, so that minds can be put at ease. The expedition is designed to stretch them and to take them outside their comfort zone. It is not my job to beast them around southern Africa for a month. With 24 students getting the balance right isn't going to be as simple as it is in theory if you say it quickly. It's also an opportunity for me to get to know the teachers better.

Originally, I had two lady teachers, but now I have one male and one female, things are already looking better. The female is Alex and the male is Gary, they are both in their late twenties, according to my information sheet and we sit down together, to agree some ground rules regarding discipline, health and safety, etc. I have met neither as Alex was not at the parents meeting I did a short while back and Gary was not even in the starting frame then and has only joined to replace the other lady teacher.

A lot will depend on the teaching staff with a group this size, and talking to them, I'm becoming a lot more relaxed about our time away. I've been fortunate getting Gary he has backpacked during most school summer holidays in various destinations around the world. I am looking forward to the prospect of working with them. Selfishly, I'm not sorry to see that the teacher who was not going now was the one without any relevant experience. Her time abroad hadn't amounted to much more than Ibiza clubbing and holiday camps by the seaside. Not the sort of expertise I need in an assistant for a month away.

Whilst we are going through the paperwork all three mobile phones go off. I have got an e mail, as have the teachers to say that our flight time has altered and will be an hour later than originally planned.

"Should we delay our coach?" Gary asks. "We're only a couple of hours down the road to Heathrow."

"No let's leave it as it is we can just as easily sit in the airport as sit here in the school and it will give us some time if we are delayed." I replied. "I much prefer to be in an airport an hour early rather than a minute late."

They agree that an hour is not going to make any significant difference to our waiting time and it will give the students a better chance to get lost in the airport and a panic to set in, before we leave. I've been there it's not as funny as we were making it out to be. We have sorted everything by late afternoon and its chill out time for everyone. Alex and Gary disappear to the staff room to organise some more coffee and to sort out their 'who's in charge?' between them.

I've found out via the student grapevine that Gary and Alex are maybe becoming an itcm. Seems it's since Gary became involved in the expedition and though only brewing for a short time, it's probably why the school found it so easy to recruit a replacement for the original teacher, that's according to the whispers I am told. Nothing like a good dose of gossip to create a belief whether it's the truth or not

We all slept in the school hall, had cereal for breakfast, packed our sleeping bags, went through a 'let's check it all again' check, and because we hadn't had any replies to our emails from the headmistress at the school in Namibia we spent the rest of the morning planning how we were going to run our project which was to be at an isolated village school in the south of the country.

The students had a lot of ideas and differing opinions on how they could be achieved, and I realised then that democracy was going to be a cause of procrastination. They had also had a discussion as how they were going to allocate jobs and positions. Some would be for the whole of the expedition such as accounts and transport, food and cooking whilst being in charge was to be individually and on a day by day rota. They hadn't finalised the exact way they were going to achieve this and came to me looking for some advice.

As we had an exact split of twelve boys and twelve girls an alternating male female leader was proposed and excepted. Apart from the "who's going first" issue being resolved, this had an added benefit of integrating them more as the whoever the leader might be had as their assistant the next day`s leader. It might avoid the boys on one side and the girls on the other as often happens and all we had to do was keep them out of each-other`s tents. Every silver lining has a cloud.

When the coach was heard pulling into the school car park, we were all ready to board. The caretaker having heard the coach arrived at the same time, checked nothing wanted or needed had been left and locked up behind us.

Quite a few parents were there, to see them off. There were some tears as there always are and some of them apparently were already home sick, having only been away at the school for one night. The bags are packed away underneath, and we wave goodbye to anyone watching as the coach heads out of town for the M11 then onto the A1M.

A call comes through to the driver from the coach company. There's been a crash on the motorway and we are far enough from it not to know what's happening but past the junction that would get us off before it, and quite soon we come to a halt with all the other vehicles. An ambulance and fire engine a couple of police cars have blue lighted down the hard shoulder and nothing else has moved. We wait about 30 minutes and the traffic starts to creep forward again. Rubberneckers slow the progress down, but we are well ahead of schedule and arrive at Heathrow with a little time in hand before we need to check in. The desk is checking in passengers for South Africa, so I leave the team to check in when called and go off to pick up expedition funds, which will be waiting for me at the American Express counter.

When I get back there is panic going on. It appears that there was no postponement to our flight and the check in desk have been waiting for us to arrive. They have got us all on board, even though I haven't checked in yet the desk is aware that I am here. The students have managed to put my bag through, (I don't know how) but we are split up and dotted all over the aircraft.

"No one's dead. We're all on. Stop fretting. Ok?" It was quite a positive don't start worrying now it's only day one statement. Our leader today is Jacob, as he had taken responsibility for organising transport from the school it seemed only fair that he should be first. I also promised him that he could lead in Namibia as we would still be there when the rest of the team had taken their day at it. "Yo Rob", and high fives me. Well sort of his is more a low five for him, he's about a foot taller than me and I need glasses to see his hand if it's that far in the air.

The students are happy, the two teachers are well irritated, as they've been separated, and it won't be for the last time on this trip. I've reminded them all about deep vein thrombosis and that walking about when possible will get the blood flowing and at the same time provide a chance for some chat. It's a long journey some of the girls are on the pill and some have a higher BMI than desirable and though it's unlikely to happen it does no harm to have a prevention rather than cure programme, which is my first rule of solving possible medical issues.

The flight is just over 12 hours. We are fed often, and I take every opportunity to put food inside me even if it is on an aeroplane. Spending long periods in remote areas, trekking, has taught me to eat whenever I can. I have an aisle seat, next to man, with a noisy laugh, who has managed to watch comedy films throughout the flight and consequently sleep is fitful, but when we arrive at Eros airport in Windhoek the sun is shining and though it's still early morning it's comfortably warm outside as we descend steps to the tarmac in what is by international standards a very small airport.

Clearing customs was no great ordeal but there was no rush and it was 6.30 before we were through immigration and I went off in search of our driver and the in-country agent.

One of life's pathetic little pleasures for me is leaving a cold airport in the UK and arriving to sunshine and warmth. I like to text home at that stage adding a few extra degrees on for good measure and await the reply. "It's raining again" I commiserate and sympathise, but they can't see you smiling in a text message as long as you don't do emoji's.

At the meeting I had had with team prior to talking to their parents at the school we had discussed the options for the first few days. Where would we buy food? where would we stay when we arrived? how much money did we have available to spend? etc. I'd let them know that we would be given a budget for the time away which would be for everything including food accommodation and essentially everything that we were required to pay for. Our transport around Namibia was mostly sorted beforehand, from our office, by hiring an overland trucking company for the all but the last couple of days of the expedition and it was the first of these trucks that had been arranged to pick us up at the airport on our arrival.

Now where's my driver? I bet he's been given the wrong time as we were. Yep bang on exactly one hour late but right on time for his information our guys turn up to meet and greet. It was just in time. They were getting close to either kicking off or crying "I want to go home".

"Welcome to Namibia" we receive the customary greeting from our agent and driver. I introduce our leader today and as is proper, our agent tells the leader what is happening and checking where we should go. He is aware that I am listening, and he will later check with me that all is ok.

The team had booked camping at a well know backpackers hostel named "The Cardboard Box" and our agent and the driver both know where it is. It is a good choice as it provides a reasonably quiet time with easy access to the main shopping centre and the banks to change our currency.

Our transport is a converted Mitsubishi truck. It was parked in the road outside the terminal building and our driver, a good description would be, Eddie Murphy moonlighting, set the rules when he had the team aboard. "No walking around when we're moving wear your seatbelts all the time don't throw rubbish on the floor sweep the truck when it's dusty and sandy. This will be often. This is your transport for a few days but it's my truck when you leave, and I expect not to have to clean it on the inside." I think they got the message.

 It was delivered with a big smile and they took to him immediately. Amazingly his name was Eddie but spelt differently or he made it up to suit the persona he had created. I never found out and it didn't matter what the truth was. All my drivers in Africa have had English names their African name often difficult to pronounce or remember accurately.

The truck is what's classed as an overland truck, supplied by Nomad tours, based in South Africa. This one is a functional box with seats and seat belts windows to see out of and a huge roof rack that will store most of our packs and kit whilst we're travelling. It's not as sophisticated as the international space station nor so well appointed, but there's more leg room and a better view than you get from the back seats of an aeroplane and it was a pleasure to climb aboard and start the journey to Windhoek itself, and our lodgings for the next couple of days.

It was customary to allow the leader of the day and their assistant to sit up front with the driver as communication was easily catered for by a sliding window between the cockpit and the rear of the truck, just like a huge black cab. The route from the airport to the city is on tarmac roads and as it's early morning with a drive of less than an hour to the 'Cardboard Box' we head straight for there, to get ourselves established and pitch our tents before we go changing money and shopping for food.

Namibia is a huge country, the size of Germany and the UK put together, but with a population of less than two million. It has concentrations of inhabitants, obviously in the main near to the towns, and extremely sparse everywhere else. It also closes on a weekend. Sunday opening is unknown and Saturday morning doesn't happen everywhere.

You must shop for everything you need when you can during the week, too much is a lot better here, than not enough and as long as it isn't quickly perishable it will be ok. We have plenty to cook on but no refrigerator. The cooking and planning teams need to get their acts together as soon as we get to our camping ground. They have a couple of days to sort themselves out for the week ahead, but it would be good to eat today as well; and for that they need to plan some meals and go to the bank before they can buy the food.

They need to change money either to the Namibian dollar or the South African Rand. The two are interchangeable in terms of value but the Rand is the one that easily changes back outside the country and the only one with coins that go into slot machines for drinks etc.

The formalities completed at the cardboard box, team members going to the bank and to do the shopping have eaten breakfast first, at the café at the campsite.

They have an idea what they're going to buy and how they're going to change the money and having been dropped off by Eddie and his truck we are now, six in number, sitting waiting for a cashier to change most of our US dollars into the more easily spendable currency.

The US dollar is certainly the most readily acceptable currency in the world but if you're in a little shop in a tiny village in Namibia you ain't going to get what you need without the local currency and if by some miracle you do, it will justifiably be at a premium.

We had entered the bank via a security lock system, possibly based on the airlock in any tv space drama. We had trouble getting through. Unlike the television only one person was allowed through at a time and one customer was expected to leave before another would be allowed in.

One out, one in, which made for good security and attempted robbery difficult and therefore less likely.

Eventually, on showing all our passports and explaining what we were about, we managed to get us all into the bank and we sat patiently whilst the head cashier carefully counted and checked our notes. The rate we got was slightly better than expected and gave us a little extra for our budget. It came half in South African Rand and half in Namibian Dollars. The money was split evenly around the five team members. After I have picked it up I do not hold any of their money. It's up to them to manage it and as insurance only covers robbery of money up to two thousand pounds, they need to split funds carefully and safely between themselves.

It's probably were most problems occur on any expedition keeping track of the funds when students unintentionally mix in their money with group money, accountants change often on a weekly basis and when the right hand doesn't know what the left hand's doing, disaster can occur.

I have access to emergency funds which they are not aware of; however, I will offer advice when I think they need it, which if I do, I expect them to take it.

Five was not a big enough team to handle the amount of shopping that we are doing and now with eight trolleys full of food they are faced with the dilemma of how we're going to get it to the truck which is parked about a quarter of a mile away. They haven't got a sim card yet for their phone which if they had, they could phone the driver with, if they had managed to remember to get his number, which they haven't. I suggest they ask if they may borrow the trolleys to transport the food to the truck and three staff to assist with the pushing of the trolleys which they could then bring back.

"We only need two. There's six of us and eight trolleys." Louise is telling me.

"I don't carry anything or push anything" I said, "I always have my hands free just in case. I'm sure the management will be happy to loan you staff who will be only too keen to give you a hand. You've just spent a lot of money."

I was not wrong and after a couple of minutes conversation with the supermarket manager Louise and Martin return with three young men in tow and a big smile that said she'd done what she set out to do. A lesson learnt. Ask if you need something.

Like a camel train crossing the desert they made their way to where the truck was parked I followed at the back from where I can see what's going on. It seems to be a forte of mine and once again we have attracted some strange looks but no problems. The trolley contents were boxed and stowed quickly into the back of the truck, and the last I saw of our helpers was them running back from whence they came racing each other with the empty trolleys.

"I gave them fifty dollars to share" our accountant informs us as we start back to the campsite "Seems fair" one of the others agrees. "

"I hope that was Namibian and not American I said and added "Lesson number two. Fifty dollars is around a good day's wages here. Possibly even more than a day's work. Adjust your measurements to Africa. It's not Cambridge. Even in Cambridge half a day's pay each is a good tip for less than ten minutes work." I think I've got them sulking as we arrive back at the campsite.

"Mistakes will be made. The problem is not learning from them. It was a cheap lesson by UK standards. Learn from it and do SUMO."

"What's sumo?" "Shut up move on." I told them "Look at it on the bright side you've made three guys extremely happy and no one's hurt. Now smile. Today is the start of a big adventure and the first day of the rest of your life; more mistakes will be made believe me. If they are only as small as that one, and you learn from it then we will have a successful expedition."

We have been to the bank done the shopping and some of the others are still waiting to get their breakfast. Welcome to Africa.

Most travellers arrive with food looking to cook in the communal kitchen, and the attached café does the occasional meal, but mostly coke and coffee when needed. Suddenly finding they have to cater for twenty plus mostly hungry teenagers requires them to go, where they don't do so often, and so the meals got cooked one at a time instead of en masse.

If nothing else, it's got the team focussed on sorting out the provisions and properly planning menus and who will do what and when. They need to organise how they're going to prepare the food, cook the food, wash the dishes and give everyone a fair share of the work, rather than leaving it all to some as I've seen on other expeditions. They come up with a plan, which doesn't sound great, because it's too complicated and requires a computer or a ream of paper to manage it. Some aren't happy, and this is day one in country.

"Give it a try and if it doesn't work you can adjust it as it's going along. That way you will arrive at something that works satisfactorily for all of you." They reluctantly agree with a view to having another meeting that night if they feel a different plan is warranted.

They're tired and a tad fractious but they have work to do, rest and play comes after the chores are done.

They have alternative ideas.

There is a swimming pool and the idea that it's holiday time rather than an expedition that is in early stages of planning and will benefit from some serious thought and they to a person all reckon that chilling out around the pool will do them no harm.

It's got a lot warmer, I suggest that factor fifty and not too long without clothing is what they should be thinking. "Yeah yeah ok Rob" I have visible skin the colour of mahogany and they all want to get to my colour. That's twenty years of working outside and it doesn't go lower than my neck or higher than my biceps. My bodies white; sunburn is not good for you. Thirty minutes at the most to start with and even that's too long here sometimes.

They're still on the yeah yeah Rob and I keep my fingers crossed that someone won't prove me right. Stay hydrated you need to be going to the toilet regularly for a wee and it should be light, not the colour of dark marmalade. Ok? I'm resigned to the fact that this is their expedition and all I want to do at this stage is gently coax. There isn't a universal answer to problems as there isn't a perfect way for an expedition to progress. It's a development programme their decisions at this time.

Alex and Gary, both wearing long shorts and t shirts, join them at the poolside and I go in search of my driver who has been out again to sort out some travel arrangements for his next job in a weeks' time.

He and I need to do some planning even if the students are busy on their skin cancer; I still have work to be done.

Eddie is from Zimbabwe. He has a wife and four young boys on a small plot of land that is just enough to support them as long as he works away sends money home and doesn't eat there. He admits that it's an arrangement that suits him. He sleeps in his truck, drinks beer, when he isn't working and has friends dotted around south west Africa where he can spend time and share beers and a good time when he's passing through.

He's drinking coffee and chatting up a lady from The Netherlands by his truck which he has managed to squeeze into the campsite and off the road which will make keeping all the kit safe, a lot easier. The truck has an awning on its side below which are drop down stainless-steel doors that form a work surface the whole length of the side of the truck. Hidden behind these hatches below the floor of the seating are the gas bottles, the hobs, pots, pans and sundry cooking utensils for on the road and remote campsite cooking.

Like transporting livestock its crammed as tight as it can be so that kit doesn't fly around loose and get trashed, but there are empty spaces available in separated compartments that will provide us with some much-needed storage space.

The kettle is boiling, and I make myself a coffee. The pretty young lady realises that he and I need to talk, she excuses herself, and though I'm possibly queering his pitch I don't care I need to check journey times, alternatives, what ifs and numerous other possible problems to get them sorted before they happen. Some leaders like to let the teams continuously make mistakes working on the premise that they will eventually get it right. I don't mind them making mistakes if I know how to get us out of it. Whilst the team are cooking themselves in the Namibian sun Eddie and I go through the next seven-day programme. Although we are here for a month he will leave us when we get to our project. The team will then spend ten days or so in a school, on their project after which another truck and driver will come and pick us up. The next driver will be with us for the remainder of our road trip; leaving us at Swakopmund, for our r and r and, from where we will be returning to Windhoek by train.

We will need more propane gas, on the way, there's a lot of cooking to be done and Eddie knows where to get that and where we might pick up supplies en-route. The distances between towns are mostly measured in hours and nipping down to the shops for a bottle of milk and a loaf doesn't happen, as we were to find out.

Eddie and I run through the logistics and times for travel over the next seven days and with a list of things they must do before we leave here.

The coffee is long finished, the day has got even hotter. Eddie shuts up the kitchen and we make our way back around the building to check on the students. Most of them have had the sense and taken advice and are now sitting inside around the bar undercover. A few of them are still working on their skin cancer programme so I call a meeting which means they need to join the rest of us in the bar area and tell me how they're getting on with the planning.

The rest has done them good. Once again, they've not been idle and have changed the rota system for cooking and washing to one more easily managed, sorted out who is going to run the accounts how they will rotate the leader into the other tasks, and how everyone should get at least a go at things they want to have a go at.

That will do for me. They have started to take ownership of the expedition. The more you put in, as with many other things in life, the more you will get out. Hopefully they will be able to look back on it at the end with pride and say, "I did that". Well I hope they will.

 Now who's doing the evening meal as its now mid-afternoon? Some haven't had anything since their late breakfast and its best to cancel the idea of lunch. We have a vegetarian with us and for some reason we will be all going veggie for the month rather than adjusting her meal they have decided to cater to her needs in preference to the rest of the team.

They have Trangia stoves to cook on, as well as the hobs on the side of the truck. They have bought a couple of large pots to cook for twenty-eight people, as we are required to feed our driver too, but they are too wide to fit on the hobs of the truck, so they will be used by putting three or four Trangia burners together to provide enough heat to cook this large pan of pasta on. They will use one of Eddie's pans for the sauce tonight as it fits easily as it should on the hob. From tomorrow they will take advantage of the propane cookers and use Eddie's bigger pans as well as they fit on his stoves to cook the pasta

This evening's meal will be pasta and vegetables with a tomato sauce. Sounds good enough to eat until you come to eat it. The sauce is nearer cold than hot the squash does everything, but squash and el dente is how the pasta should be, but somewhere between raw and uncooked is a more accurate description. The meal has sand in it. In the end it took me nearly a month to get them to cook food somewhere near edible, but I don't think I ever got a team cooked meal without grit of some sort.

"Listen guys meal wasn't cooked properly, and a lot of food got thrown away. There's people starving in this world and you've just wasted enough to feed quite a few people a decent meal. Don't waste food and if you can't eat it see if someone else wants it or if you can't find someone don't make it obvious that it's been binned as you are likely to attract unwelcome visitors both two legged and four." They're looking at me like I'm from another world. "and you're more likely to eat it if its cooked properly."

Later that evening we had a meeting to review the expedition thus far. Twenty-four plus teachers plus me if needed, with something to say can take a long time and this was no exception here and some two hours later we had confirmed exactly what we'd established in the first ten minutes via a show of hands. However, democracy was seen to have been satisfied, and for some that was more important than any decisions that might have been made. The two teachers had spent most of the meeting whispering to each other and had avoided getting involved in any decision making, which was as they were supposed to do. It was not their expedition and like me they were there to mind the team not run the programme.

The following day we had a journey of over three hundred kilometres to make to Sesriem, but before that we had to go to the rail station in Windhoek to buy our tickets for our travel back from Swakopmund at the end of the month.

 I advised them to get an early night so that we might be bright eyed and bushy tailed, ready to go as early as possible without missing breakfast and reducing travel time in the hottest part of the day. They disappeared into the bar area to drink coke and coffee and I sat in my tent writing my report and reading through the paperwork and advice I got from our office which detailed any possible problems and potential pitfalls.

I had pitched my tent so that I could keep an eye on as much as possible from the doorway and a lot of them were still talking in the bar when I fell asleep.

The teachers joined Eddie and me at the side of the truck at about 7.00am for toast and coffee. They were in good spirits and looking forward to getting on the road and by 7.30 we had breakfasted packed our tents filled and treated our water bottles and were ready to rock and roll. Some of the team may have been properly awake but other than a trip to the toilet none had ventured out into the real world.

Last night they had decided to do a deal for breakfast with the cardboard box which because of the favourable exchange rate was well within their budget so cooking this morning was deemed an unnecessary chore.

 At 9.30 the whole team had packed their tents loaded all the group food onto the truck loaded the bags onto the roof filled their water bottles sorted everything, but some had not yet eaten their breakfast. This, after yesterday's breakfast disaster, should have been lesson number two but they hadn't learned anything from that, and they weren't going to learn anything from this one either as they were happily playing pool in the bar area whilst they were waiting.

Too long after 10.30am I had finally got everyone on board. They had gone through a check that nothing had been left and Eddie is carefully easing the truck out of the narrow gateway and our journey via the station to get train tickets has begun. Four hours from waking up to leaving needed some radical improvement.

We had picked up sim cards for the group's mobile phones that we supply on loan (no personal phones known to be in existence here) checked that they were charged and working ok and phoned ahead to tonight's camp to let them know our ETA.

We stopped for lunch around 1pm having spotted a small group of trees at the side of the road, with a parking stop and some seating. This would provide some shelter and give the girls a chance to go to the toilet with a little more privacy than normal on roads that pass mostly through scrub desert. There was jam or cheese sandwiches for lunch. Either or but not both and only two slices of bread each. Water or black coffee or black tea as they couldn't locate either the boxes of powdered or long-life milk assuming them to be jammed up under the kit inside the truck. The day was not as warm as yesterday yet there was still no cloud and stopping and stretching our legs was much needed relief from sitting on the bus.

If you spend eighteen months saving to go to another country, you would think that taking in the view and looking through the windows might be high on the list of opportunities not to be missed. Scrub desert is not the greatest viewing spectacle in the world but its surely better than spending the whole of the time en route reading books which is what most of all were doing and this included the two sitting up front with Eddie.

Some six hours after we left cardboard box, we arrive at Sesriem park campsite. We have been allocated an enclosed circular area to camp in. It has a boundary defined by a dwarf stone wall and is one of the original sites when the area was first opened. We have a tree for shade and three forty-gallon oil drums, with their tops removed, in which, we should put our rubbish. There are two recycle bins one for glass the other for metal with the third bin for everything else. The truck fits neatly inside this area as well, so no problems over cooking this evening.

Its Friday we have been in Namibia for two days and though things aren't quite as clockwork yet, they are starting to slot together. We still have more to do I will give them time. The meal is a repeat of last night pasta vegetable and tomato sauce. We have different cooks today. Tonight, it is hot. It's still not cooked very well and again it has been garnished with sand, not as much as last night but that may be more to do with surroundings rather an improved level of hygiene. By last night's standard its significantly better but it's not going to win any cookery competitions.

We can't find any of the milk and some of the food seems to be lost. We have found one of our large tubs of drinking chocolate and as its now dark it's a good idea to have our chocolate drink and go to bed. Tomorrow we definitely must be up early in the morning if we're going to do what we've planned.

The park gates open at 5.00 am and we have a nominal 45-kilometre drive to dune 45, where, if we get ourselves sorted, we can witness the sun rise from the top.

They have all done well they are up and ready to go at a little before 5am and very soon we are at the front of a queue that is now building behind us. Eddie has the engine running trying to get some heat into the truck. The morning is cold, and our breath hangs in the air even inside the vehicle. Coffee would be welcome and hot food but that will come later after our morning hike.

We are checked through the gates, vehicle, documentation, number of personnel and entrance tickets. We have saved time having organised our entrance tickets before our arrival. The company had done one of numerous deals with the park authorities given that these were school children here for a month on a self-financed expedition the park authorities had been generous with their discount and the extent of their hospitality.

We rattle along the road once we're through the gate but soon we're overtaken by a couple of Landcruisers and Hilux's the African workhorses. The vehicles that overtook us have passed dune 45 and presumably gone on to Sossusvlei and we are alone as we turn off the road into a parking area on our left. It is no warmer when we stop. What heat has been in the truck is lost as the doors are opened and we stand around in our cloud of foggy air. I point to the top and the ridge they should walk up and advise them;

"Don't rush up" I tell them "take it slowly it's a lot further than it looks, and the sand is hard work." Then there off like it's the Epsom Derby and my advice is lost on the morning wind. My hands have been in my pockets and they have not got any warmer my fingers are cold and the batteries in my camera, though almost new, are not working. I stick my hands back in my pockets and wander behind the teachers who it appears are more than happy to amble gently upwards.

 They can help each other by holding hands, what a good idea, they would call it teamwork I suppose. If there was a power struggle, which there might never have been, was definitely non-existent now. Alex was in charge and although she didn't seem to be pushy I got the feeling that if push came to shove Gary would be right behind her no matter what. When she was in control she was sweetness and light, but she did have a look about her when she had a mind to.

We picked up the first straggler after maybe 100 metres or so, she was puffing and blowing for England and now reduced to sitting on the edge of the sand dune wheezing. "Why are we going to the top of a hill to come back down it?" asked Lizzie "You're not by the sound of it" said Alex and kept on walking. Gary got caught off guard and didn't know what to do. There was a moment's hesitation before he shot off behind Alex, who was now striding out for the summit, still a good distance off.

The sunlight was creeping over the horizon. It didn't make a sound, but it was there alright and trying to burn my eyes out. At least now it would get a bit warmer. There's a price to pay for everything.

Lizzie was unfit and that was all it was. Her medical records had specified nothing to cause us any concern, but her BMI looked like it needed work on. She was starting to breathe better and so I suggested that she should wait around for a bit longer then decide for herself if she wanted to continue up or wait here for some of the others before she went back down to the truck where Eddie was. She reckoned she was not going any higher under any circumstances and would wait for someone else to walk back down with her. I didn't really want to leave her on her own but further on I could see a small group in a similar position. Alex and Gary were still heading for the top with Alex a few metres in front and not taking any prisoners by the look of it. Although the others were not going so quickly I couldn`t see any more walking wounded or casualties.

Cambridge is not famous for mountains or even hills and these guys had no idea when it came to pacing oneself and going upwards and the learning curve here was too steep in more ways than one. There were four in the next group two boys two girls looking like another cosy gathering as the two boys were the ones in trouble and the girls had stopped to help them. They too weren't going any further and so I suggested that when they were up to it perhaps they could wander slowly back down and pick up Lizzie on the way. I got the feeling they weren't in any rush to do this from the looks that greeted the suggestion and as there still weren't any more bodies visible on the route I turned around to check Lizzie was ok and not freezing anymore.

My camera still wasn't working but would be soon, as the Sun was well over the horizon and making me wish I'd not left my sunglasses in my bag on the truck. My breath wasn't hanging in the air anymore, always a good sign, and a gentle walk down would suit me fine. Carrying a sat phone, an epirb and a medical kit at any time is a nuisance. On sand that goes three paces up two paces down it's a ball-acher.

Lizzie has suffered in the cold and as she`s my only known problem I suggest we head back. She is more than happy to walk down with me, and when we arrive Eddie has the kettle on the go with the bad news that we definitely don't have any milk, as he's been right through the truck whilst we've been on the dune and the 20 litres of long life and the powdered milk are both missing. Lizzie reckons they put everything in the storage area or the truck after the shopping trip because she was one of the shoppers and also had wanted to be the main cook on the expedition, which is what had been promised her when she signed up for it. She was due to go to college on a cookery course when she returned to the UK having finished at the school this last term.

"We'll have a discussion after breakfast let's wait for the others to come down." There was little point in us spending our time talking about it to do it all again later. Lizzie had a black coffee with us and then retreated to inside the truck.

Most of the students had got to the top. When my camera had finally come alive I had taken a picture from the bottom up the side of the dune showing a huge lump of sand with tiny matchstick figures slowly making their way down its ridge. Alex and Gary were the last two down. There were no injuries most of them were tired out. Many of them were neither wanting breakfast nor another walk this morning. As we had brought food for breakfast I over ruled them and insisted that the ones who wanted to eat should do so and then they could review the options for rest of the day and decide then.

Lizzie cooked a huge pot of porridge with sugar and drinking chocolate to substitute for the no milk. She may have looked glum on the dune, but she was a shining light after, when in charge of the cooker and on the cooking. The porridge wasn`t great as meals go but we were hungry, and we ate a good breakfast.

 Figuring now, they would all feel a lot better and fit again I approached the idea of walking down at Sossusvlei, which is further down the road and more so than dune 45, the most photographed scenery in the park, with its stark distorted blackened Acacia trees.

 They weren't interested so I gave them all the good news about the milk and that we needed to go through our list and check we haven't lost anything else.

They couldn't do this here as they had a lot of the foodstuffs in the tents and everyone was certain that they didn't have the milk. There was no porridge left to be got rid of so dish scraping and washing was going to be left till we got back to the campsite.

Christine, one of the successful summiteers, leading from the front having organised the packing, area checked for anything left, everything that was supposed to be in the truck in, and not liable to be flying around loose, kit on roof secure? All done?

Good

Time to go. I had made the leader of the day responsible for going through this process even though I went through it myself it made them take responsibility for every aspect of the trip. It's their expedition they need to take as much ownership of it as possible. Well as much as I give them.

We've been up for hours and it's only mid-morning. My stomach is crying out for more food, but I settle for a coffee as Eddie has the kettle boiling soon after we get back to the campsite. I also have powdered milk in my tent having bought a tub for my own use. The team have emptied the tents of all the food, pots, pans and cleaning materials they have bought and it's not looking good. The volume of food and provisions would suggest that at least two shopping trolleys worth of goods are missing. The accounts team have the original receipts from the supermarket and although it takes a while the process of elimination leaves us with around two days' worth of food available for what was to be five days of self-sufficiency.

We were due to go tomorrow morning to the Namib Naukluft national park to begin an acclimatisation phase of walking and trekking to prepare them for their main trek later in the month. We knew that the park would not be able to supply anything in the volumes that we required. Plan B time.

"Who is leading tomorrow?" I ask.

Reluctant Simon who didn't want to lead at all, due to a huge lack of self-confidence and belief puts his hand up. "Me sir" the voice almost a tremor worried as to what is coming next.

"We will have a change of plan I will keep you posted" He was unhappy. "Don't worry" I said, "We'll sort it" The relief was immeasurable, and he instantly stopped slumping inside his body.

"We will be here as planned for the rest of the day as per schedule we will go to the canyon this afternoon again as planned and then tomorrow we will go in search of food. I will ask Eddie to speak to the guys at the Cardboard Box, just to make certain that the food isn't there. However, we will still need to source supplies or change plans. It's too long a journey to drive back to Windhoek and then back to the next park in one day. Eddie and I will work out what can be done and then we will have a meeting. D'accord?"

I really wasn't interested in going any further with it until.

"Can't we just go and buy more from the town we came through on the way here?"

"What day is tomorrow?"

"Sunday"

"And what opens on a Sunday?"

They were quiet again now they had just realised that they had managed to make a discovery of some importance at the only time of the week when we couldn't do anything about it.

"Leave it with us for now. Make a complete list of what we need. Accounts team, work out how we are doing budget wise and what we have left over and above the original projected spend at the end of our stay in the Naukluft Park in four days' time". Christine as today's leader should join us along with Simon and bring a mobile phone."

I got the mobile phone and telephone number book from Christine and asked Eddie to phone the Cardboard Box to see if they had discovered any of our missing food, and whilst he went off in search of a signal we opened our road map and looked at the options we had. I didn't believe that Eddie was about to bring us any good news so plan B needed to be implemented.

Alex and Gary had stayed with the rest of the team and were helping sort out a list of missing foodstuffs or more accurately she was telling people what to do and what she needed from them. Maybe it wasn't any worse than what I was doing but I couldn't help believing that she was overstepping the mark. I'd given the phone to Eddie as he spoke the local dialect even though he was from Zimbabwe, he had no problem finding a common language with everyone we had met so far. But I could tell from his face when he returned without any need for conversation that there was none of our missing provisions still there for us. Eddie gave the news to Christine and Simon and asked me if we had any plans.

I was waiting for his return, hoping that he would have an idea, having travelled quite extensively around here, where if there was anywhere, we might be able to source our missing food. According to Eddie this wasn't something that had happened before, and groups had always either been catered for by him in which case the food was all locked away inside the truck until needed or groups of solo travellers brought their own provisions and cooked for themselves on either the truck cookers or their own personal stoves. But mostly Eddie cooked for them and bought everything for each trip as required keeping only small amounts of rice and tinned meat and veg to tide him over between jobs. Time to look properly at the map maybe and though it didn't look very full of information and it didn't tell us anything we didn't already know. There was nothing for miles according to the map, but we knew that there was, it was just unlikely to be of sufficient significance to replace our losses.

We had only two options we either went north to Solitaire or back around the route we had come in on to a town named Maltahohe. Our trip had sent us back in the direction we had come in on and then turning east so splitting between our choices. That way gave us only a small village named Bullsport and with reading what Lonely Planet said and what Eddie knew from other drivers both Bullsport and Solitaire as nice as it was would be unable to refill the larder. So, we plumped for Maltahohe keeping our fingers crossed that as the town was significantly larger we thought it was possible that somewhere might be open and if it weren't we had the option to remain in the area and buy our needs on the Monday. Plan B as it stood was not only are better option but the only one workable.

We returned to the team and called them all together. I asked the accountants how the money situation was.

"Teachers have told us sir that we have extra funds available for emergencies and that we don't need to worry over the money."

"I am holding extra money. It isn't your money. It's money that I am responsible for and is to be used only if a disaster requires me to spend it. The money is given to me by the company that has organised your expedition. If it was your money it would have been available for you to spend with the rest of your budget. It isn't. It's there for me to use should I think we need to. You are holding sufficient funds to complete this expedition without using any of this extra. And given that we haven't even got to the end of week one it's hardly an emergency when given the very favourable exchange rate you got and the current usage. You are going to have to take responsibility for this problem. Work out what you need. Work out your budget. Work out what is still available and come to me with a plan and where should you need to do so you can save money. Then we will discuss it further." They all looked at me. No one spoke some had their mouths open and all of them realised that at the end of the day it was actually me that was in charge.

"It is early for lunch, but we got up early you should start getting it ready asap and then we can eat, snooze, if you wish to and later this afternoon we shall go down to Sesriem canyon and having seen the sunrise this morning you can watch the sunset tonight."

I turned and went back to the truck to top up my cold coffee with some hot water from Eddie's permanently boiling kettle. "That'll make you popular" said Eddie as he passed me the coffee from our store under the counter. The teachers followed. "We were told that you always carry funds to top up if necessary" Alex was being sweet.

"Who told you that?" I asked "it's not common knowledge even within our company. And it's not for every trip."

"One of the leaders at the expedition meeting she says they use it all the time and at the very least for a party at the end if there's not enough money left over."

"She's out of order on every level." I could feel myself getting just a little irritated with her.

"Well she should know her brother is a director, and should you be drinking the coffee all the time if we're trying to save funds?"

"It's my coffee" I said "We four have been drinking coffee I bought along with sugar and powdered milk when we did the shopping in Windhoek. And I have the receipt to prove it. That's why Eddie keeps it out of the way under the counter with his spare food. Anything else?"

I think she realised she'd irritated me and she flounced. I think that's what she did. One second, she was there, and in an instant, she was gone. It took Gary off guard and once again he was three steps behind her as she hotfooted it to her tent. I permitted myself a smug sort of smile and made a mental note to remind me to let the office team know who was giving out confidential info. Only a couple of days into the expedition, four days since I'd been at the school and I find myself at loggerheads with just about everyone but my driver. Seems about right I wonder why it took this long?

The accounts team arrive sooner than I expected. It appears that most of them have done `A` level maths this last year with Gary to do accountancy at university as he teaches sixth form maths. They were up to speed fairly quickly on what was required of them. I'd already found out on my original visit to the school some months back that Alex taught English to A level, so they had had a lot of contact with these students again this year. Hence, they had already an established bond, having taken them for their `AS` level as well last year.

We took our map and moved away to one side to allow the chefs and food preparers access to the kitchen. Paul who considered himself as the senior accounts man had been nominated himself to speak.

"If we're careful and if we can get what we need at the same price as we bought the other stuff we will have a short fall but as you said if we can keep buying what we need at the prices we paid originally we should be ok until the end of the expedition."

"Are you all happy with that as a fair estimate of where you are?"

They nodded their agreement.

"Then we shall continue as we are. Do not starve us. It will only spoil it for everyone. We will look again after our four days in the Naukluft Park and review what has happened and where we're up to then. Same again after each phase. We were always going to do that anyway, but you realise how keeping a check on how the money gets spent is important. If you guys are going to be studying accountancy, you may well learn enough for a 2-2 whilst were away. They did laugh which is what they were supposed to do. "If you hadn't spent money at the Cardboard Box on meals you may have still been quids in.

Another lesson learnt. Spend it when you know its buckshee. If you're careful enough there is normally enough for a farewell meal at the end of an expedition there is always extra money squeezed in to the budget the trick is to spend wisely without depriving people. Ok? Let the others know please"

"Thank you, sir,"

My name is Rob I would prefer to be called Rob.

"Ok Rob" replied Paul and off they went back to the group who apart from the chefs preparing lunch were waiting spread about the site in and around their tents but very obviously keeping one eye on proceedings.

Lunch was once again two slices of bread with either jam or cheese slice and in my case an extra cup of coffee to keep my blood sugar levels up or awake at night whichever need came first. The teachers didn't bother with coffee and spent lunchtime together and slightly apart from the group. Eddie and I stayed with the team mostly because that's what I'm here for but at the same time I didn't want to lose them over a small issue that wasn't of anyone here's making. Eddie is getting on so well with them I leave him to tell stories of his life on the road and his farm and family in Zimbabwe and entertain them. He has led an extraordinary eventful life or has developed the stories with each telling. They are quiet, and they listen intently and when he finishes to go back to his truck a number follow him gently pushing and shoving, each other, to get close and fire questions at him. He is, as I suggested to everyone, going to siesta and almost because he's doing so they decide. "it's a sound idea Rob". And disappear into their tents.

It was an early start we have breakfasted, lunched and our plan is to see the sunset after a walk in the canyon which is only a short drive from here; and even taking a walk in there it shouldn't be more than a couple of hours activity before the evening meal, which I'm looking forward to. It's pasta, vegetables with a tomato sauce, sounds delicious. I can't wait.

After half an hour in my tent I am regretting having the second coffee. Sleep is alluding me, so I settle for working my way through the group accounts, trying to foresee any avoidable problems, and keep mulling over in my head where the equivalent of two shopping trolleys full of food could have disappeared to and how.

The walk in Sesriem Canyon was a lot better than had been described. The snooze had been beneficial from a physical point of view and a successful way of filling in a quiet afternoon. It had recharged slightly depleted batteries and stimulated some enthusiasm in the students to go on another excursion.

They had done their reading on the canyon and being clever kids having found an interesting subject they probably should have spent more time in there. But it is going dark now, and I need to get them out to see the sunset, but more importantly, so I know where they all are as darkness here is like having a black bag pulled over your head. It will be easier to keep a watch on them on the top rather than trying to locate them in the dark in the canyon. Sadly, the sunset was a disappointment and as exciting as watching paint dry. They felt when we reviewed the day that evening the day had almost lost its sparkle and sun set was a poor end to a day that saw sunrise from the top of dune 45 and a walk down Sesriem Canyon.

They thought that the evening meal needed something to improve it. I wanted to suggest cooking it, but, in my mind, I got the feeling that that might be taken as a sarcastic remark and was probably going to lower my standing in the popularity stakes even further and Lizzie, who has taken over responsibility for all the cooking, is proving to be extremely sensitive to criticism. She will not survive in a commercial kitchen, as she is, and needs to toughen up. It isn't wholly her fault as she has different help at each meal. The problem is she isn't taking control and directing but trying to do it all herself whilst the others are left hanging around watching. I'll let it run a bit and see if it improves. If it doesn't I will need to speak to her otherwise we will all die of malnutrition. Losing a bit of weight might not do some of this group any harm, however, they will need digestible calories to complete the treks successfully.

Sunday morning and most of the team have got themselves out of their tents toileted and are awaiting their porridge breakfast. I keep suggesting that cooking the porridge with some salt would dramatically improve its taste. They reckon salt is bad for you and prefer to put chocolate powder or vast quantities of brown sugar on it. They believe that because its brown it's healthier than white and six spoons of sugar is better for you than a pinch of salt. It wouldn't be so bad if the six spoons were spread between twenty-six, but it appears to be about six spoons each. We need to buy bigger bags of sugar.

Most of the others on the surrounding campsites have gone into the park though its light and the sun has risen the morning has, once again, a chill about it and the hot porridge and hotter coffee are as good as any comfort food around and a lot of the team unusually, have taken hot drinks this morning, as well and my powdered milk has all but disappeared.

After breakfast we need to hustle. It's after eight and the dishes, pans and cutlery need cleaning, tents need to be taken down and they and the kit need to be stowed in and on the truck. We can't afford to waste any time nor trust to good luck about picking up our extra supplies. We are ready to leave in an hour, which is surprisingly good considering what they needed to do, and we have a drive of around 160 kilometres and if all goes well we should make it there for around noon.

Our reluctant leader is happy to sit in the back with his mates, rather than taking a front seat in the cab. His assistant a young lady, named Caroline is quite indignant when I send her into the rear as well. Feisty is a fine word.

I have taken the front seat to talk through our options with Eddie, should we not get our supplies, and having a solo schoolgirl sitting between two men is not what I would consider as a good idea. 30 minutes driving and we come to a fork in the road left to Naukluft is the way we should be going to Naukluft National Park, but we need to turn right and take the C19 road to Maltahohe another 130 kilometres down the road. The road is clear and as long as we keep going as we are our eta will be as we predicted.

Eddie would have driven straight through I suspect had some of the team not started asking about a toilet break and given that we had not seen another vehicle in the last hour Eddie stopped the truck in the road almost immediately.

I suggested everyone should get out and stretch their legs even if they didn't need a leak. "Where do we go to the toilet?' "Just go off to the side of the road as long as you're not near a stream or water hole you'll be fine. Be careful if you're squatting ladies that there are no thorns or long plants below you. Girls up the road boys behind the bus" I pointed in the direction they should go and off they trooped. I shouted at the boys. "Gentlemen you have nothing no one has seen before and if you go any further you will be back at the campsite."

Alex had gone with the girls and I hoped she would take care of them. I had gone through a toilet procedure a couple of times with the team prior to today and until today they all seemed comfortable with what they should be doing. Drink water and urinate pale urine and you will stay healthy. Avoid drinking because you don't want to go for a wee or avoid going for a wee because you don't want to be seen and you may get cystitis. I have treated cystitis and urine infections more times than everything except blisters and diarrhoea. I checked with Alex, discreetly, to see if they'd all gone to the toilet. Not all but that may have been because they didn't need to. I asked her to make a mental note just to make certain they all stayed healthy.

It was a little after twelve when we arrived at Maltahohe. It's closed or appears to be. We are looking for someone to ask about a food shop when we spot the Maltahohe hotel. "May be a good place to start" I said. "Hotels with restaurants need to get what they don't grow or shoot from somewhere" I called Simon in the back of the truck to remind him that as he is leader today he should be the one asking at the hotel on behalf of the team.

 "Caroline you should go with him"

She is up for it and is out and ready to go Simon half hanging back searching for inspiration or courage or whatever he thought was missing. I climbed down from the front and joined them on the walk to find reception.

The day has warmed considerably. I had noticed a lot of the students had nodded off on the drive. They were still reading books rather than looking at the view. It takes all sorts I suppose.

We have found reception and enter through a doorway into a cool comfortable area, a lady has heard us arrive and comes to meet us as we enter. She is apparently the owner and with the niceties over with we get down to what we need. We explain who we are, what we need and our reasons for having this problem. She is quite happy for the rest of the team to come in buy soft drinks use the bathroom and Caroline goes back to the truck to let them know.

There are a few guests sitting quietly reading in the lounge and Simon is sent to the front door to make certain they all understand to be quiet and respectful. We are being treated as guests and should at least behave responsibly. The lady owner has taken our rough ideas list and has gone behind a small counter and is making a call when the students file through the door and make their way to the bar area. I ask Gary to keep an eye on them. It won't be the first time someone's had a quick beer whilst I'm not looking.

Once I found some sixteen-year olds watching a rugby match and drinking beers in a pub when they were on a Duke of Edinburgh award assessment. The teacher who was in the pub with them stupidly couldn't understand and wouldn't accept why I failed them there and then. For some unknown reason the school has never used me again.

Alex has joined us in the reception area and timed it nicely as our host rounds the counter to talk to us. "About a five-minute drive away there is a small supermarket. The lady who owns it has said she will be there in around thirty minutes or so and she seems to have most of what you need available and if not possibly something that could be substituted. She would like you to be there waiting rather than opening up and waiting for you as she's not open today. She likes to have her Sundays off. I can vouch for her prices in that they aren't as cheap as what you might pay at Shoprite in Windhoek but even though she has a captive market here she keeps her prices reasonable."

This lady doesn't have a sticky out dress, a tiara nor even a star topped glittery wand, but our new-found fairy godmother has produced some super magic here that may well have saved the day.

 "So, we need to leave in around 15 minutes?" I ask

"Yes" she says, handing the shopping list to me. "I will draw your driver a simple map it's not difficult to get there and there's plenty of space for even that truck of yours.".

"Thank you in a minute I'll let him know what we're doing. We are extremely grateful for your help and hospitality."

"You're welcome. Fortunately for you, we are quiet today and we can accommodate the children." Simon went to organise the full shopping list and some pickers and carriers and money from the accounts team. I called after him "Get one of them to come with us and they can pay the bill. Saves going through it all later with them. Ok?"

He gave me a thumbs up and I could see him at the bar drinking coke from a bottle one of the others had passed to him whilst he organised them, for our shopping trip.

I went out to see Eddie who as usual had parked the truck and put the kettle on. Coffee was ready to drink. I explained what was happening. The coffee drunk and kit put away I left him turning the truck around to face back out onto the road. The kids were coming out with lists map and money and big smiles. The thought that their supplies were going to be replenished soon along with lemonade in a cool bar had lifted their spirits as we walked to the truck.

"Take the map to Eddie, Simon, and climb up front with him you're still leader today" Simon`s smile stayed were it was, and I was pleased that he'd been ready to take back responsibility, as today's leader, now that we had a plan to implement.

Although the shop is not huge by supermarket standards it is big for the area it serves and certainly well stocked. Though we clean out some of the shelves we have replaced our losses as much as we have needed to do and if we're not stupid we will have enough to see us through our time at Naukluft and a bit beyond.

I have restocked my coffee, sugar and powdered milk. What I have bought will last until the end of the expedition, assuming that no one steals them.

After Naukluft we will be going to our project site, which is a school near Keetmanshoop, a journey of some 420k but here there are numerous large supermarkets and fresh food is easily obtained, so I am told.

We will be saying farewell to Eddie the day after we arrive, so I suggest to the team that they make a comprehensive shopping list, for here, as we will not have the benefit of his truck but may be obliged to hire taxis. This will make excursions into town more expensive. Though I have not been previously to the school one of my colleagues, who has set the project up, has written me some handy notes to make certain that surprises are avoided. Times and distances, were as per standard operating procedure, of course wholly inaccurate.

Our purchases have been mutually beneficial, but nevertheless we are extremely grateful to our friendly shopkeeper for opening today for us and we wish her well and hope that her Sunday off has not been too disrupted.

If they were to be honest they'd admit that they didn't really care how disrupted her Sunday had been they'd got their supplies and we could now continue on our way back up the road to the Naukluft National Park still on our daily schedule, albeit later by a couple of hours.

We picked the rest of the team up from the hotel. They thanked the owner for her assistance probably in the same obsequious sort of way and settled into the truck for the couple of hours it would take Eddie to drive to the park. I made a mental note to suggest that sounding sincere will go a long way with most people and maybe there's a fine line between the two but that they were on the wrong side of it.

The Rangers at Naukluft were pleased to see us as they knew we were coming but didn't know what they should do should we not arrive. We were due to arrive early in the morning, it not being that far from Sesriem and I explained that we'd tried to phone them but couldn't get a signal. Although I have a satellite phone for emergencies, I didn't think arriving later than expected constituted an emergency.

We booked in at the office, and whilst there, we were provided with both maps and written information about the two walks we were planning to do here.

They had allocated us a camping area close to the car park. There we could park the truck, which would be handy for cooking but also it was close to the toilet and washrooms so long walks during dark would be unnecessary.

They did a person count as my colleague had booked our time here with the park authority and we had a permit for three adults one driver and 24 children. I believe it was making sure we didn't sneak any more in, but it's just routine so they told me. You can't fault someone for doing their job even if you think what they're doing is trivial.

The team are putting up tents and getting the cooking on the go, its late afternoon after we have done all the admin stuff with the ranger's office and although it's not dark yet it will be soon enough. Eddie is trying to teach Lizzie and the rest of them how to cook and I keep my fingers crossed that he may have some influence over the end result, as the teacher's and my efforts have fallen on deaf ears.

At the same time on the camp is another school group from Newcastle same company as me so I wander over to introduce myself to their leader and see what she and the school have been up to. The other leader is Tracy and although we have not worked together before, we know each other to nod to from courses and groups that we have run in the UK. This is their last night here and they are off up north tomorrow morning and going to Etosha via Windhoek and then into Zambia.

They are just over halfway through their time away and the couple of days that they did here was their trekking phase. Her group were not wanting to do much walking but were keen to complete a good project and then see some wildlife in Etosha National Park before going into Zambia and flying to Joburg and then home.

Tracy gave me a heads up on the two walks we'd be doing here at Naukluft but other than those our itineraries were so different we were unable to swap any useful info.

I was getting a call to tell me the meal was ready. I wished her bon voyage as they were leaving very early tomorrow, grabbed my bowl and fork and joined the queue at the chuck wagon. Pasta, squash and a tomato sauce no wonder my trousers are starting to fall down. Eddie has managed to get them to cook the pasta longer it's not quite as gritty this time but cooking it doesn't hold their attention like a television programme, so they are quick to tire of watching it and finish it early so still maintaining that new meaning to al dente. I'm getting fed up with unimaginative catering for our vegetarian. They need to sort out a better menu with something akin to protein in it before we succumb to malnutrition.

We are at the park to experience some "wild" country walking. This is an opportunity for me to assess their capabilities and plan accordingly; for them to assess themselves and to rationalise their kit and how they're going to carry food and equipment on their five-day excursion in Fish River canyon later this month.

We are here for two days trekking as we leave on Wednesday to go to our project and I think the students will miss Eddie. Most are sitting with him as he again tells stories and answers questions about his travels around Africa. They are probably learning more about customs, different cultures geography and life from him than in a whole term at school. The teachers like myself have had the sense to stay out of it and let him do what he obviously enjoys. Once again there is a mutual benefit but more importantly we are achieving what it says on the back of the can and broadening their knowledge and horizons and if Eddie is the tutor and it's working I have no intention of not going with the flow.

When Eddie suggested it was time to shut down they all made a mad dash to get to the washrooms first and whilst they did so we put the kettle on for those that wanted hot chocolate before bedtime. They got to bed at a reasonable hour. The teachers had spent most of the evening with the team but apart from whispering to each other now and again they had had little to say. They joined us for hot chocolate before going to their tents and when I was certain that everyone was sorted I grabbed my towel and headed for the shower, clean, brushed teeth, cicada noise in the trees, fall asleep, happy days.

Chapter 4

It's Monday morning, the dawn is up and running. Tracy and her team have packed up and I say goodbye again and wish them a safe journey as they leave for Windhoek.

They are hoping to get all the way to Etosha in one push but it's an eight-hour drive plus stops, and they need to shop in Windhoek for supplies en route.

That's someone else's job, mine is to get this lot around the route they have chosen to do today.

We have a choice of two routes. One is 10k called the Olive trail and the other is 17k the Waterkloof trail. The team have opted to do the Olive trail first and the Waterkloof tomorrow, figuring that 10k today will give them a warm up for 17k tomorrow.

Breakfast is the best meal of the day even though they still won't put salt in the porridge and they shudder when I put a tiny bit on mine. "If you leave it to stand after you've mixed it for a short time the salty taste disappears. It's not as good as cooking it in but I don't need eight spoons of sugar to make it bearable. We will have to disagree, and they won't let me make the porridge in case I sneak it in there.

We are breakfasted, toileted and water bottles are filled.

Water is frequently in such short supply and especially when you are out on the road that we have bought around two hundred litres of water in large bottles to make certain that we never run out. Storing this has not been easy but we have managed to squeeze it into every available space on the truck, and although we will use Namibian water which we have been assured doesn't need treating. We always do treat the water but will maintain these extra bottles as an emergency supply.

We share the loads out. We should keep the hard stuff away from the soft stuff to avoid damage. I am carrying some safety equipment, karabiners, slings and what we call a confidence rope, which is a short rock-climbing rope, and I have two of these. A first aid kit a satellite phone and an EPIRB which translates into Emergency Position Indicator Radio Beacon.

If they're good enough to find Tony Bullimore in the South Pacific Ocean they should be able to locate us in Naukluft Park. But they're for emergencies and we won't require their use though I must have them with me. The rangers are aware of our proposed route today, so they would be our first resort if there was to be a problem.

"Who's got the lunch"? I am met with blank stares all round. "Come on guys we're out all day we need lunch. Who is leader today? I know its Caroline because she was Simon's assistant yesterday. We are running a programme that tomorrows leader is todays assistant. Caroline has forgotten that she is in charge today and although she was good as Simon's assistant, leadership has taken on an unforeseen dread and mental blockage. Yesterday's confident young lady is todays bag of nerves. Caroline can't talk and puts her hand up. We need lunch" I continued "who's on cooking duty today?" Half a dozen hands go up. "Ok let's do enough sandwiches for us all before we leave. It's going to be a lot easier here than out on the trail later. Share them out before we leave then we know everyone's got lunch and the safe transportation thereof is the responsibility of the eater. So, says my Philadelphia lawyer friend". I thought I'd made a joke, but no one found it funny I think they thought I was being serious.

Eddie and I had another coffee whilst we were waiting. He had grabbed an old rucksack from his truck and he offered to take some of the kit from me. I gave him one of the ropes and some slings. Gary offered to take the EPIRB and as that was within our standard operating procedure, to split sat phone and EPIRB within the group I was quite happy to let him lug the beast around.

They didn't have enough wrapping to separate the sandwiches into individual lots so Kevin, todays assistant leader, had emptied his rucksack of everything and they had carefully put all the sandwiches back into the bread wrappers and he had volunteered to take responsibility for their safe carrying.

Half hour later than planned but we are ready to roll. We know from where we're starting, and the route is marked with footprints strategically painted on rocks and conveniently pointing in the direction of travel.

We have been told that the path is constantly used, and so the route should not be too difficult to follow. I have put Lizzie up front with Caroline, as she is the one who didn't want to go up dune 45 so it allows her to set the pace. The trek is over terrain similar to a Duke of Edinburgh silver walk, so 10k should take no more than about five hours, an hour for lunch makes six, plus a bit of site seeing, say eight in total, back by 5pm in a worst-case scenario, which will give us a daylight window with an hour and a half to spare. Eddie has taken the front with Lizzie and Caroline and as they lead off I can see a huge cascade of fair wavy hair, I have seen before, and I realise that Caroline is the girl whose father asked the awkward questions at the school meeting some months back.

I think I can trust Eddie to keep a steady pace. After Gary and Alex's performance on Dune 45 I figured that maybe they would be trying to push them too hard. I like to bring up the rear because I can see what's going on in front of me and can always shout the leaders to slow down if I feel they need to. After an hour, walking the sun was getting warmer and I suggested a short rest, a drink and a sun cream top up. Everyone seemed ok and I was pleased that they all seemed to be enjoying the day. We continued for another hour or so, during which time we had passed over some rocky parts, got off route and took a short time to relocate ourselves. Satisfied that now, we were back on the intended path again and although there weren't any more footprints to follow the path was well trodden and when we came to a burnt-out tree, which we had been told was on our route, we knew we were definitely on the right line.

A little further on, according to the rangers, was a good place to stop for lunch, as there would be some shelter out of the sun. The burnt-out tree had been a weaver bird's nesting complex that had gone on fire. The rangers thought this was a result of sunlight hitting something shiny that had then caused the dry leaves and twigs that the nests were made from to burst into flame. Sad as it was it nevertheless provided a good landmark. The path started to descend down into a canyon and as advised we took the opportunity to take our lunch where there was some shelter available.

Though this wasn't perfect as we were sheltering under trees, and space was limited due to the size of our group. However, as we weren't sure there would be anything any better further on we settled on a quick lunch here and then with a view to taking a rest later when the sun would be lower, and we could use the canyon wall for shade.

The sandwiches and biscuits had survived the journey in Kevin's sack and he was given an embarrassing moment when he was applauded for his efforts. His embarrassment was short lived when he was reloaded with kit from other people's bags and his protestations were ignored.

It took a bit to get them started again. A certain reluctance due to food sunshine and a bit of tiredness had brought on a level of lethargy that was irksome more than worrying and our quick lunch had turned into an hour. I was disappointed that they struggled to get going. They were disappointed in having to get going. Fortunately, our route was now downwards rather than upwards so progress, though not quick, was easier to begin and a reasonable pace was easy enough to maintain.

The canyon took on the look of the dry riverbed that it was and as it got deeper so the walls got closer and the temperature cooled enough to make our journey even more pleasant. We continued as we had been with Eddie up front and myself at the rear minding the stragglers.

His brief was if anything should crop up that was out of the ordinary he should stop and wait for me to assess any potential problem. Either it had slipped his mind, or he didn't consider it a problem but suddenly I'm being shouted from the front and I quickly headed up there to find Eddie and two of the team across a part of the walk known as "the chain walk".

The two teachers are telling the ones who had arrived to sit down away from the edge in case they fell down the drop. Richard and Caroline are on the other side of what is a fault in the canyon floor. It drops maybe twenty feet into what is now a shallow pool of water in a hollow. If you can imagine a wall with a substantial chain on it at chest height above a narrow path that easily accommodates size fourteen feet you may wonder what the panic is about.

I certainly didn't see a problem, but the teachers' opinion was that under no circumstances could the rest of the team cross without safety ropes being rigged and my taking responsibility for getting each one of them singularly and safely over. The school rules won't allow for us to take any chances like this.

Personally, I thought the rigging was just a bit overboard from a health and safety issue. If anyone needed a hand getting over walking across with them would have sufficed and Eddie and I could have managed the whole thing without any difficulty but now, Alex and Gary had slipped danger into the equation and more than a few of the team were feeling that safety ropes were needed which killed off any discussions as far as those two were concerned.

The difficulty was not getting any one of the team over but in retrieving the limited amount of personal equipment that we had to ensure that we complied with the teacher's demands or school rules whichever was the truth. In the end I made the crossing twenty-two times and it took nearly two hours to complete the exercise. Most of the kids hadn't been worried one or two were glad of the extra confidence of the sling and rope support but it was Alex who didn't have the bottle to get herself over and I had to coax and coach her all the way across. She hung onto the chain white knuckled and when she let go to move her hands along they shook like a leaf in the wind. I felt sorry for her she was further out of her depth than she would admit. There was a loud cheer from the group when the final one was over, and I had retrieved the safety equipment I grabbed a quick drink of water thanked Eddie for his work and then we got quickly on our way.

As we had taken over two hours to complete the crossing other walkers, on the same route, passed us by taking the other more difficult side of the canyon, probably wondering what the hell was going on, on our side. Darkness was starting to creep in, progress was slower than I would have hoped, though the distance to the four by four track was not too far, the travel was hindered by numerous trees that had lost their grip on the meagre soil and fallen across the river bed, turning the route into a hurdle course.

We were slowing down. The side walls of the canyon were blocking out what little light was left, the trees were exacerbating the problem and only three others beside myself were carrying head torches. Why would you need them? We were going on a four-hour walk but thus far we had been out the best part of nine hours with distance still to do. I was pleased that some had brought their head torches; it wasn't on the kit list today for obvious reasons, but we were managing, and it was good to see them work together as a team. I was looking at it on the bright side when Kevin whispered to me that he had overheard the teachers saying that they were going to set the EPIRB off as they figured they needed rescuing before they were attacked by wild animals. Here we go I thought. I caught up with the two of them and interrupted their conversation.

"Give me the EPIRB" I said.

"Are you going to set it off" Alex asked?

"Not under these circumstances" I said, "it's for emergencies and this is not an emergency we're walking in the dark that's all".

"We could be attacked" said Alex.

"If you set it off. The signal will go to satellites up there I pointed to the sky with my torch. Then it will go to UK. They will look at the identity and who it's registered to. They will phone our ops desk who will then phone me on the sat phone and I will have to explain to them that I'm following standard operating procedure have split the safety equipment as per norm, but the teachers have panicked fearing entering the food chain lower down than usual and there is no emergency. They will then tell me that the EPIRB is now no longer able to function as it was originally intended and I need to keep my fingers crossed that we don't actually have an emergency as we will probably not get another EPIRB on this expedition as there are no spares in country."

I took the box from them and pointed them in the direction of travel. When it comes down to the bottom line I am in charge and told once again they should be very aware of that now.

A couple of minutes later I was getting called to the front the trees had gone and the countryside had opened up; there was no moon yet, but it was a tad less dark and we had arrived at what looked like a possible ford in the river bed had there been water in it.

I went up the right-hand side of the bank and did a short walk. This was our four by four track, not travelled often maybe but there was sign of traffic in the surface and what looked like the remains of tyre track just about visible with my failing battery. "It's heading in the right direction," I said "so, we'll take this route". The last hour or so had seen off most of the good side of all our batteries and I wouldn't risk an accident in the canyon. We made good progress the surface was typical of off road but with the torches off night vision was enough to get us along the route if we didn't try going too quickly. The night vision didn't last forever though as a land rover with its headlights on came bouncing along the track towards us.

The cavalry in the form of park rangers had come to find us as we are too long overdue, they had made the decision to work backwards along our route. Though I hadn't doubted it, it confirmed we were on the right track with about twenty minutes walking still to do.

Happy days indeed as we walked behind the Landrover not unlike the pied piper but no music with this one. They, having found us, were unwilling to leave us trekking back on our own, presumably to avoid the necessity of having to venture out again should we again be presumed to be lost. Even given that we were on the right track and heading in the right direction their belief was that we didn't know where we were and therefore needed shepherding back to camp.

 I gave up trying to assure them of our ability to get back to camp safely and did a SUMO. Sometimes it's the best way forward and arguing with the rangers was not going to make me any friends. Even though, the Landrover lights were wrecking everyone's night vision, the fact that the rangers were with us made them feel that all was not lost; and group confidence now restored, made for quicker progress back to camp.

No one was injured and what little niggles I had heard as we trekked through the dried-out river bed seemed long forgotten and it was a happy team that entered the park gates and headed to toilets and washing, prior to cooking and the evening chores.

I thanked the rangers the team having as normal disappeared from view.

The rangers asked what our plans were for tomorrow. I think they knew as well as I did that the chances of them doing eighteen kilometres tomorrow using today's performance as a guide was on a par with the snowballs chance in hell.

I suggested that we'd have a group discussion about it and give them an answer tomorrow morning, as it was not my decision to make at this time. Nevertheless, it had been a reasonable excursion not as successful perhaps as we might have hoped for but were back and smiling well most were. I knew the teachers were pissed off with me and I was almost certainly in line for crossed finger repetitive injury strain, but I figured a tick in the "good day" box was in order.

The main advantage to cooking the evening meal on the side of the truck in a car park was there was less sand than usual. Sadly, the urgency to get it served caused by the late finish further enhanced their reputation as the worst expedition cooks I had ever experienced.

It is the following morning some of the group are awake and functioning like normal human beings whilst some are doing what teenagers are good at and making with the Zeds still. You did, when You were their age someone will tell me, but I don't remember doing it on expedition in Namibia.

Coffee and porridge have obliterated the memory of last night's culinary delight. Eddie is around the back of toilet block like a secretive miscreant having his morning cigarette. He smokes two per day one first thing and one before he sleeps.

Kevin, our leader today, wishes to discuss today's excursion. Actually, he doesn't want to discuss it, he wants to tell me that they had meetings last evening, in small groups, and have decided that yesterday was sufficient for acclimatisation purposes and today they would prefer to go out for two hours, have lunch and reverse the same path back to camp.

"It's your expedition" I said "And it`s your responsibility to take ownership of it. Though I would have preferred you to have completed an 18 k walk today yesterday`s performance left me with the worry that we may well need rescuing properly this time. Let's see if we can plan the day, put times figures and ideas together and come back with a plan that you all agree to and then let's see if we can stick to it and accomplish what we're setting out to do."

Kevin left me, a big smile on his face, to join the others that were about and give them his good news. I figured we might learn more about their capabilities and expectations with a walk they'd planned to see if they were taking the team as a whole into consideration. I knew quite a few hated walking and rough ground yesterday had added a couple more into the "don't like this" group.

I gave Eddie the news and he too decided to join us for the short walk today. He was good company and he entertained the troops. He would be leaving us shortly and I knew the team were going to miss him. They had come to me asking about giving him a tip and I had suggested that if they all put in only a small amount because there were so many of them it would by Namibian standards quite substantial.

The rangers were pleased with the news of today's trip in the national park and shortly after ten am we set off with a plan to take an hour for lunch at 12.30 returning at around 3.30 thinking that the return journey would be quicker as the route was already seen and stops for viewing should be less. Kevin was proving well organised as the leader and lead from the front he did.

Eddie walked with him and told him and those in listening distance about any interesting finds en-route.

Kevin and the others up front hoped to see some animal life but the only animals they would be likely to see here would be dead ones. There was nothing predatory that would stay around long enough to tackle a group this size. The chances of meeting a superior eating machine was not like in many other parks and there was no elephant or wild boar or big cat that had the sort of right of way mentality that was generally reserved for small tanks or gun toting armoured vehicles. Sensible animals had vacated the area well in advance of any group that could be heard from miles away.

Well before lunch, we came across a small clean rock pool, about the size of a squash court and not too deep. I spotted what I thought might be Kudu prints in a sandy area near the edge, but these were instantly obliterated when the team surged forward to view the water. A brief discussion and it was decided that a stop on the way back would be available for those who wished to sample. I told them that I would risk assess on our return and we continued on our way, the conversation now almost exclusively about the thought of sitting around the pool. Some of this group should have gone to Butlins not spent a lot of money on a paddling trip to Africa.

Eddie provided a running commentary on Namibian wildlife. He seemed to know lots about which animal had done any stool we came across and although he may have made it all up there was no one able to argue with him as to what had done what and when.

Richard had carried the sandwiches for lunch today and again had done a fine job in keeping them safe. We had cheese or jam very enjoyable when you know that breakfast tomorrow will be the next thing edible. Importantly they were a happy team, Alex and Gary, the Velcro twins, kept themselves quiet and out of conversation. There was nothing for them to be involved with.

This walk is on the same level as a Sunday afternoon ramble with the family in the local municipal park and even the lunch break today was shortened, the team happier to spend any extra time available near to the pool, we had found on the way in. They proved if nothing else they could get a move on if they either needed to or wanted to and well within what might have been an expected time we arrived back at what had become their main objective for the day.

I had a look around and walked in it was half-way up my thigh at its deepest easy to swim in and safe enough as long as it didn't get too boisterous. "You're not all going in at the same time, no bombing, no underwater, no wrestling or ducking. Clear? Good." They had reluctantly agreed. "Anything to add?" I asked Alex and Gary. They shook their heads.

"Any messing about and I'll shut it down and no going for a wee in the water. Enjoy yourselves." Eddie took up a position on the far side of the pool and together we kept an eye on proceedings. Eventually everyone was wet and quite happily sitting around drying off. "Put sun screen back on when you've dried off I said you're likely have left it in the water for the Kudu to drink when they come back later." They looked at me like I'd said something rude. "If you were an animal thirsty and looking for a water supply you could do worse than this". There were Kudu footprints in the sand areas when we were here earlier on. You have walked over them enough times now, so they've disappeared."

"Are they likely to come back soon?

"Not unless they're particularly stupid or desperate for a drink. It's unlikely but lion might see some of you as a food source, kudu will see you as the enemy and avoid any confrontation with a group this size." Maybe it was the mention of animal life that awakened the teachers to what was being talked about and shortly after they suggested that it would be a good idea to make moves back to our camp site, as we would be leaving early tomorrow morning.

The whole group dawdled back. It was still light and what else is there to do but enjoy the moment whilst you can; and they had enjoyed themselves the pressure of yesterday forgotten and eventually after what could only loosely be described as a leisurely amble we arrived at the reception area to see two happy smiling ranger faces. They had probably been waiting, ready to spring into action and were not disappointed in not having to do so.

The prospect of an evening meal, not dissimilar to all the others we had been eating, did nothing to stimulate my thought that it might be a great way to finish the day. Coffee and one of Eddie's cigarettes was having more appeal and even though I don't smoke anymore and wouldn't in front of the students if I did, sneaking off behind the sheds for a fag was looking like an attractive and welcome option.

I stuck with the meal though and immediately regretted it. They had the food, the pots, pans, cutlery and Eddie's cookers and they could still manage to turn it all into something close to a disaster. I was going to miss Eddie in more ways than one. Lizzie was "plagued by people who wanted to help and were as much use as a chocolate fireguard". Her words not mine. Tonight's looked like it had been in a road traffic accident and I was worried because after tomorrow we would be ten days without anything to cook on but Trangias or what the Southern Africans call a braai, which are barbeques generally made from oil drums cut lengthways in half. The only good thing to be said about it was that my digestive system working so hard to deal with the "food?" was burning more calories than I was consuming and although I was not getting slim some of the spare flesh was disappearing. Again, every cloud has a silver lining, but every silver lining has a cloud and I wondered where and when that was really going to surface.

Chapter 5

We started early, paid our respects to the rangers; who appeared to be relieved rather than glad to see us off, and settled in for our journey to our project site, a school close to a town called Keetmanshoop some 400 kilometres away further South in Namibia.

As the school was not quite in Keetmanshoop the team had decided that it would be a good idea to shop before en route and therefore we would make a detour via Mariental.

It was as broad as it was long in terms of distances and times so having consulted with Eddie the plan was on.

They'd compiled shopping lists, as expected, and worked on somehow getting off the project site to top up the supplies as the job progressed. I was starting to get sore fingers from having them crossed for so long, but we weren't dying of hunger yet, but malnutrition was a potential problem. I needed to see something other than pasta and a tomato-based sauce on my plate. I'm not a big meat eater but some form of protein was desperately required. I figured dropping into the supermarket was the answer and so when we arrived at Mariental I left the teachers with Eddie at the truck and again joined the team on their shopping trip.

I was not alone in my need. Significant packs of biscuits, chocolate and tinned meats were being added to the normal shopping list and I asked if they had had a change in the menu. Apparently, some of them had been buying tinned meats with their own funds on the previous shop excursions and eating them in the privacy of their tents as they too had been fed up of the same meal every single night. Perhaps I should have been more devious or at the very least shopped for supplies other than coffee a bit earlier.

Biscuits with the sandwiches at lunch and a couple of mugs of coffee and we are back on our journey.

We must find a turnoff on this long, dusty, gravel road.

 One of our expedition organisers from headquarters came out here around six months back and made all the arrangements with the headmistress, at the school, and wrote a set of directions for us to find it.

We had amended them with our detour to Mariental, but as planned we are on the main B1 road as per instructions.

All around, as we travel the view is scrub desert, low hills are visible in varying distances from the road but there is little sign of either activity or life. Turnoffs, though not well marked or signposted are so far apart that in theory, it's difficult to miss them. Mariental to Keetmanshoop is around 240k and should take around two and half to three hours. We need to slow down after a couple of hours. We are looking for a roadside sign the size of a shoebox that will tell us that we are close. We spot the sign laying on the ground either the wind has blown it over or time has worn it away as there no obvious indication of it having been hit by a passing vehicle. Vandalism is not an issue here.

 Then quite quickly we are at our turn and Eddie swings the truck off the dusty gravel road onto a dustier dirt track. We pass some corrugated iron clad huts, washing lines and old tyres for fences. Scrawny goats tied up or in small paddocks dog barking now and then at our intrusion into the peace. Small children rush out of the huts to wave, but we are gone by the time they realise what is happening and see only, if they can through the dust cloud, the back-seat students waving from the rear windows.

We don't have a distance to our destination but a time of around 20 minutes from the main road and unless there is a turnoff where we need to make a choice we will slowly make our way along this track looking out for a windmill, which will mark our site. We pass a pointed top hill and almost immediately spot our landmark, which had been obscured by that same hill a "t" junction is here and a small group of similarly built shacks with corrugated iron cladding and standing tyres half buried in the ground, has created a small village with a huge school and a massive church.

The village itself appears deserted and totally empty of people, presumably at work somewhere, for the day, but the school is heaving with small children, who have spotted the truck and are running around in a most excited manner. A metal gate has been opened for us and Eddie slowly and carefully drives in. Running one of the children over as we arrive will not endear us to anyone.

They are dodging around the truck and the teachers at the same time, who are shouting and waving what appear to be canes at them to move them out of way. I suggest to Eddie that stopping might be the safest thing to do and he pulls up which starts a mad rush towards the truck doors.

"Open the doors carefully" I tell them. The schoolteachers are swinging their canes like a scene from Gladiator and eventually some sort of order is restored.

Our students file out to greeted by shouting screaming giggling Namibian children none of whom seem to be any taller than half the height of most of our team. The Velcro twins have sensibly left their exit until the end and they introduce themselves to one lady who is not carrying a cane and appears to be in command if that is the right word.

She is the school secretary and tells us that the head teacher was hoping to be here to meet us, thinking that we would arrive this morning. He had made other arrangements and appointments for this afternoon and is unlikely to be back before tomorrow morning. She continued "He sends his apologies and hopes that you are all well and that he will hopefully see you when he is back tomorrow morning."

I queried the "he" as we were expecting a headmistress. The previous head teacher had retired just a week or so back and the new head teacher was one of the senior administrators at the department of education and they were lucky to get him so quickly. Having taken over the job at short notice he was still trying to complete work started at his previous post hence not meeting us in person. The secretary seemed to have rehearsed the statement almost like a small speech. It hadn't taken me long to discover that Namibians enjoyed speeches and formal statements such as this. The school secretary is Mrs Mutwa and after the headmaster it is she who has the power. But only when the headmaster gives it to her. Although we have introduced ourselves with first names only she asks that we call her Mrs Mutwa to maintain her position of authority.

This is what the headmaster had said was not for discussion, it was a statement and that was as far as it needed to go. We discovered later that it was also just as likely to be changed if it suited him to do so.

We were to camp inside the school grounds, near to a spare classroom, that had been allocated to us, to use for whatever purpose we needed the space for.

 Some of the school's young students were trying to help Eddie unload the truck and he spent quite a bit of time shouting at the kids in language only he and they understood.

It seemed to work. I don't know, nor do I want to know, what he threatened them with, but order had been swiftly restored and whilst one of our school team was charged with minding the door to the classroom those helping, shipped bags, food equipment and everything else into the room. The remaining team members were entertaining some of the other children to games and a bond between our students and the Namibians was fast developing. This is what about half the team had come for and they were wasting no time in getting started.

 The secretary invited us for coffee; took us into her office and gave us some dark strong coffee. No milk no sugar and unknown vintage perhaps not the best coffee I had ever had but nevertheless an act of kindness that would be churlish to complain about.

 I did make a mental note though to provide some powdered milk and a small bag of sugar for her use. The secretary passed us a padlock and three keys.

"They are all the keys" she said. "We would like the lock and three keys back when you leave".

We promised their safe return. The headmaster would discuss the programme with us when and if he came in tomorrow. I didn't query the possibility of 'if'. Thinking I wouldn't get an answer. A couple of times whilst we were talking to the secretary the lighting had flickered, and then went off altogether.

"The water supply is the same." She told us. "The windmill is attached to the water tank. It pumps the water when it's available and if the wind blows. It's stored in the tank and we use it from there. We use it for drinking and cooking, showers are once a week, it's not for wasting."

I had made certain my mobile was charged up via the inverter in Eddie's truck, but a signal here had been more elusive than their electricity supply. Although the village was isolated, I had noticed on our way in that a solar powered, telephone kiosk, probably card operated, had been installed outside the school. I asked her about it.

She told me that she had never heard of anyone ever getting it working in the two years it had been there. The conversation was finished her attention had shifted to the paperwork on her desk. I didn't think she was being rude but uncertain now what to say to us or what information she should give out. She was sorry she had work to complete before she could leave.

We thanked her for her kindness and hospitality and wandered over to see how the rest were getting on. The padlock and three keys were for the door to the classroom. This had a hasp and staple and was only lockable by padlock and the advice was that we should keep it thus when not inside or we would be likely to lose whatever there was of value in there. It wasn't that the village was full of thieves as such, but everyone was poor and an opportunity to improve their situation may well be too tempting.

Nigel, todays assistant leader has taken responsibility for guarding the door.

"Nisus was the guardian of the gate" I said as I passed him going into the classroom to see what goodies we had. He questioned what I had meant "my old Latin exam I said Nisus and Euryalus, written by Virgil. That's Virgil the poet not the one from Thunderbirds" It came out as arrogant it was supposed to be funny. I hadn't meant it to sound anything but amusing. Sometimes even highflyers from Cambridge haven't done Latin at school and when he looked at me not understanding anything I was saying, I could do nothing but apologise and hoped that I hadn't said anything that might have offended him.

I explained how I'd somehow got myself into the clever boy's class at school where I had wasted two forty-minute lessons every week, studying Latin that I had at that time no interest in. However, recently I had started reading a lot more history again and remembered stuff from my school days and took an interest that I should have shown when I was there. I don't know if he understood what I was saying so having apologised I shut up before it got dark.

The classroom was substantial. Empty of desks fortunately, but we had been supplied with enough seating for around thirty. This was mostly stackable plastic chairs and some wooden benches along with a couple of trestle tables that would fold and be put out of way should we need to do so. We had square pin sockets which was a bonus whether any electricity was going to be available and come through them, whilst we were here, was always going to be a guessing game.

Outside the team have pitched their tents in a circle. They have left enough room to walk around and have used the confidence ropes to make another circle around the camp as a stop line for the Namibian children to stay outside of. Eddie has again told them what is expected of them and currently the plan seems to be working. We all know it won't last forever as the natural inquisitiveness of youngsters will have them coming just a bit closer every time.

They are using Eddie's truck to cook at for the final time and some of the team are getting quite emotional about his departure. They have bought him a cake from the supermarket and, it has, surprisingly, survived the bumpy journey here.

The cake will probably be the best thing he's eaten with us and I suspect Eddie will be only too glad to leave to get something to eat that's been cooked properly all the way through. Tonight's has been garnished with sand and it's difficult to tell if one is eating uncooked pasta pieces or grit blown in from the playground. At least eating will only get better from here for him or should do. Becky calls me over to one side. "We've had a collection for Eddie and wondered if you wanted to put anything in?"

That's good of you" I said "I was asked if it was a good idea and as long as you've not got carried away? So how does it look? I asked. We've got about £150 she said.

"That's like at least three weeks wages here. I recommended a couple of pounds each tops I'm not saying he's not been good. But you could spoil it for other teams and other drivers. They will all talk to each other. I could see it was a waste of time continuing with the conversation."

"We can't return it now" was the reply. I put two ten rand notes in which was just over a pound and got a look of disgust.

They made a presentation of the cake and of the collection and we shared in the cake. Becky, I think grudgingly, served me just a spoonful, which was enough to take away the memory of the meal so that was a bonus. There was coffee and some fruit juice that they had also bought for the going away party and I left them sitting with Eddie for one last time before he left.

He would be leaving early tomorrow to return to Windhoek to pick up his next group the following day. I asked him to call into the cardboard box, to confirm our reservation for the end of the month and this he said he would do. We had been unable to make proper contact with them due to the phone signal and or language and although we had sent a text message, we had not had a reply as yet.

We have breakfasted, I have drunk my last morning coffee with Eddie. We have indulged in some small talk about life and work and prospects. The morning has been relaxed, he has plenty of time to complete his journey back to Windhoek and feels in no rush to part from our students. But move he must and slightly later than originally planned, he is ready to leave.

Many of the team had brought cameras with them (pity mobile phones are banned they're often better cameras) and I have some pictures in my collection of Eddie and I standing by his truck, as he is about to climb aboard. We are shaking hands in one and he is hugging me in another. It's been a good few days and I am grateful for his input and his assistance. It will be a cousin of his who will be our next driver and he will be picking us up and driving us around for the remainder of our time here. I wish him a safe journey and he climbs in starts it up and waves goodbye to the assembled here.

The teachers from both schools and all the Namibian children have come out to do the same and it is quite a spectacular send off. Some of our team are crying. They have lost a friend and they disappear into tents to grieve in private.

Another vehicle appears out of Eddie's dust storm and turns right at the junction. As it gets nearer we see it's a Toyota pickup. "This is the headmaster" the secretary says and hurries away into her office.

One of the teachers opens the gates again whilst what remains of the group of children, in urgent haste, scurry back to their classrooms.

The Toyota speeds into the schoolyard, completes a half circle and pulls up facing the admin building. A tall slim man built like a telegraph pole awkwardly climbs out of the truck and without looking in our direction heads straight into his office. I suggest that we should wait for an invitation to join them.

The two teachers and I head back to the classroom where we can avoid the harsh morning sun and the Toyota's dust still hanging in the air. Some of the team are getting organised and sorting out the Trangias and food in readiness in an early preparation for lunch. The Velcro twins have each started reading and I am working through some paperwork when there is a knock on the door and the secretary walks in. "The headmaster would be grateful if you would join him for some tea". It was another of those statements; it was not a request or for discussion but essentially a command. The two teachers and I followed behind our messenger. I called Nigel to follow us. "As the one in charge today he should be privy to what is happening."

The headmaster has not budgeted for Nigel coming with us and Mrs Mutwa is sent for another seat. Not only was there no seat but there wasn't a cup either and she goes without. The tea is ok as a result of our contribution of sugar and milk.

Headmaster apologises for not meeting us yesterday, but he has been organising a cultural festival in a village some 60 k away which had been his responsibility in his last job and as the local mayor and mayoress and some government officials would be there he was responsible for its success and consequently it was demanding much of his time.

We are discussing what it might be feasible to achieve in the time we are here with the budget we have available. It is about what work might benefit as many people as possible. Ideally, we would like to continue an ongoing project or finish a project that would improve the school and at the same time provide interest and satisfaction for the team of students. It is after all the students who have put together the finances for the project and it is they who have been the driving force behind this expedition to do something of value.

We have a budget at our disposal but within minutes of the start of the discussion what the headmaster envisages as a worthwhile project and what we can afford in terms of time and finance are two totally different possibilities.

Rewiring the school, providing a 2-metre-high fence around its perimeter or a new toilet block are out of both our financial capabilities our time scale and technical expertise.

The headmaster is looking at major civil engineering plans and we are just about capable of painting a couple of doors. We need to compromise somewhere, and the headmaster has already lost interest when he sees that our budget won't satisfy any of his new pet projects.

Eventually we settle on redecorating and smartening up the classrooms. They can move the children around so that there is always one room available for us to be working on. We will also build a storage shed in the goat field which will also provide shelter for the goats if needed and we will rotate our students so that they can interact with the Namibian children and teach them English and Maths. We have high flyers as I've said before, these will get their "A" level results during our time away and most of them are expecting to stay with a Cambridge education.

The simple maths says 24 students for ten days is 240 working days. As the UK working year is around 225 days long we would need a lot of work and a biggish budget to keep the whole thing running for the ten days we are to be here. Ideally on projects like this we would leave something useful and lasting. Kilroy was 'ere painted on a wall would be on a par with some of the end results I have been unfortunate to have been a witness to.

A decent latrine or long drop, or a water pipe and tap in a trench requires only a small budget and a lot of time and digging and gives something more useful to the communities after the teams have left.

Our students teaching and interacting with the Namibian children is far more beneficial for all than a nicely gloss painted door with a broken pane of glass in. We now have a plan it's not perfect but as compromises go it should satisfy most.

The headmaster says that we should make a list of our food and material requirements and he will take us into Keetmanshoop later this morning where we can buy materials and any supplies that we may need.

 He does not stay at or even near the school, but has a farm, where he and his family live some distance back along the B1 road to Windhoek.

The discussion is over; we are to quickly make our lists if we haven't already done so and he will take us as soon as we can be ready as journey time is at least an hour each way. During our stay we will see little of the headmaster for reasons only he is aware of.

 I suggest to Nigel that a team meeting well before lunch will be a good idea and he goes off to organise it. We should keep everyone up to speed and we need food and building material lists. Mrs Mutwa follows me to the office door. She points towards the end classroom to show me that behind that school building is the home of the school maintenance man. He has a key to one of the unused classrooms where all paints and materials and any tools the school own are stored.

"Tell him I said he should give you the key to the padlock. I expect to have that one returned too when you leave." Possibly because the headmaster was in earshot; I felt she was talking to me as if I was one of her children and abrupt and officious sounding as she was, I decided to ignore it.

She was being both helpful and informative, and everything it seems comes at a price. I'm not certain how long I wished to keep paying that price but as we were on only day two of ten, and here less than twenty-four hours, I thought it early days for speaking to a lady less than half my age to inform her that my patience had run out with my money.

Also, as I'm not aware of the current building materials the school holds and haven't had time to do any sort of schedule my list will take a while and I have no time to discuss attitudes now.

I took over the meeting more than I would think proper, but we needed speed and I was not looking for consensus or promoting democracy but lists to take to Keetmanshoop. Mrs Mutwa appeared at the door. The headmaster says we must leave soon. However, he will be going into town tomorrow to do some more work and he could make a diversion and pick people up if by then you will have more time to complete your needs. We were about halfway through what we thought we might need but that would be enough to keep us fed and working until past the weekend even; so, we were ready

"We will go into town with the headmaster today" said Alex to do the shopping you can stay here and organise the teams and the work." I got the feeling that she could give the headmaster a lesson in positive communication but decided that nothing would be achieved by questioning her decision. It suited me for the others to go and leave me to get on and I would be unable to do my survey and planning off site. Paul the accounts person and two of the other boys had volunteered to pick up the shopping and I had no reason to object. I asked Alex and Gary if they would speak to the headmaster before they left and get permission to take a teaching group into one of the classrooms with the Namibian children to have a nosy as to what goes on.

 Now we need to go and find the school maintenance man and get a look to see what we have already available."

"I don't know anything about DIY" Nigel tells me. Don't worry I said before I became an outdoor instructor, I used to own a building company and believe it or not a school maintenance company. I'm a woodworker by trade and we joiners know everything and can do everything. I was half joking but he wasn't impressed, assuming that I was lying about my CV or at the very least embellishing it. But that didn't matter to me either. Pudding eating time will come later if necessary. We walked around the outside of the school until we reached a gate, in another fence, which was more a boundary marker than a line of defence. We could hear a dog barking from somewhere close and saw it tied up to a metal frame that must originally have been a child's swing but now a dog's tether. In the property next door, a thin Rhodesian Ridgeback cross maybe, with the distinctive wrong way coat along its spine was standing and barking at us as we made our way to the other shack. It did not run and pull on its lead but stood stock-still and watched us as we approached. As we got closer to the shack, the door opened, a wrinkled. broken nailed. old hand came out holding a string with a padlock key tied on one end. As Nigel took the string the hand disappeared back inside, and the door closed. No words no sight of the key donor, it saved us the issue of niceties in the hot sun and didn't surprise me at all. We turned and left, and the dog stopped barking.

The room was dark and dusty, in truth there appeared to be more dust in here than useable materials, but we did find timbers and nails a hammer with a loose head that I could easily fix with a wedge and a bucket of water, that might be a cup of water, a few tins of paint some still useable with the addition of some white spirit to thin them out. In the corner we found a pile of corrugated iron sheets with which we could build the goat shelter come storage shed.

There was enough timber and materials for us to make a start tomorrow morning. Nigel organised our first couple of volunteers, to sort out what we had into some sense of order. We started with "do we know what this is" and to clear the junk out of the way and into a "we don't need this" corner.

I started to do some sketches, a schedule for seven days and a material list. A good number of small panes of glass were discovered that fitted the metal window frames. I put putty on my list and we also came across two fully glazed ones as well which I thought would provide some light in our goat/store room as there would never be any electrical light in there.

We needed a door for the store, which could probably be made from some pallets that we had found under a pile of tyres.

Things hadn't looked too promising when we first got in here but the possibility of stretching our budget further than we thought possible was looking quite good. Tool situation wasn't that good though I had found a couple of old chisels that had been used primarily for opening paint tins but fortunately also found a hand driven grinding wheel which would put some sort of edge on them. If the temper was still in them they might work long enough to get done what was needed.

We weren't building luxury flats with expensive exotic hardwoods. I could make these work. But I did need a decent saw. Even after seventeen seasons on the rugby field, I still had more teeth than the old one we found. It went on my list as definitely required.

We had a shout for lunch and along with the everyone else headed for our room Sandwiches were dust and sand free coffee was hot maybe things were looking up. After lunch we had to get the teams organised. Nigel called a meeting as we were all in the room.

It didn't take too long before it was losing itself in minutiae; I needed to stop it before it got into petty bickering.

"Ok guys hold it there or we'll still be here at dark. Three teams of eight. Teaching team. Maintenance team and cooking and housekeeping team. We have nine days so that's three days on each phase of the project. If you want to change between them all. Understood?" "Nice one Rob. that'll do." Nigel said immediately. I think he was getting fed up with the nit picking as well.

"We can adjust as needed as we're going along." He continued "Excellent; any more for anymore? Meeting adjourned" he finished. I think the headmaster had even influenced his leader management style. It did the trick and they started to sort themselves into friends and pals' groups.

I said to Nigel "You will end up with something other than three lots of eight. Lizzie will want to stay on the cooking and there may well be revolution later on. But that will be someone else's problem if it happens.

It was early afternoon and quite quickly they had formed themselves into three teams it wasn't a perfect split, but it was near enough to be workable. As I thought, Lizzie wanted to run the cooking and had enlisted Maddy with whom she shared a tent and Allison wanted to stay on the teaching as she was hoping to do children's nursing. As no one else was objecting to any of this I could see no problems with it.

We left the classroom to Lizzie and Maddy and their team to organise the evening meal and create a kitchen and food area.

Today's work group came with me and I left Nigel to get them to clean the windows inside and outside so that we might have enough light in there to see what we're doing, whilst I took the budding teachers and child minders to introduce them to the first of the classes that the headmaster had said we could go to.

The day was turning out well; shortly after 3pm the bell rang, and school was finished for the day. Playtime took on a whole new meaning with all the big people to play with or little people depending on which group you were part of.

Most of the children stayed and slept in a dormitory at the end of the admin block next to the school kitchen. The school was known as a feeder school. Two or three infant junior schools would finish their education at a given senior school when they were old enough. The children would get educated and housed and provided with meals during their weekly stay. A lot would stay for a week as for some it would be a two hour walk home on Friday afternoon. And the long return on Monday morning for an 8 am start. Nine years of age and a two hour walk to school in the dark often on your own. We'd be locked up in the UK if we allowed that to happen.

I had shown Lizzie how to use a big pot on Trangia burners when they wouldn't fit on Eddie`s truck and did so again for Maddy's benefit.

 Typically, a Trangia has its own saucepan, which holds a couple of litres which is fine for a small group; but trying to feed 24 is nigh on impossible. They had already bought other large pans for cooking, some of which they had used on truck. All they had to do now, was do it with three or four Trangia burners and keep them lit. The main problem is that you can't see them properly and they will run out of meths at different times. There is an advantage to that in keeping a constant heat source while one is being refilled.

 I have to explain that on expedition wild animals dragging you off to feast on you is nothing to worry about. Cooking accidents with Trangias are a lot easier to have and can spoil your time away so easily.

 They need to learn how to use the braai, but you can't do that inside you need to go outside, and you need fuel to burn. All of which was tomorrow's jobs. We have struggled to eat again, unsurprisingly we are eating pasta vegetables and yet another tomato-based sauce. I think the squash is starting to rot as its soft, so I think it's more likely to have gone off than successfully cooked. I saw it before it went in the fry pan and it looked like it could have been on the antiques road show. After the meal we have our nightly meeting. Tonight, there is a lot to discuss, even before Lizzie who, as keen as she was this morning to continue has had enough and quit as the cook.

The team has been less than sympathetic to her problem and although they thanked her at the meeting for all her hard work they were secretly more than happy to see someone else take over. Maddy didn't want the job either, so it was decided that as it was rotating on a daily basis everyone could have a go at trying to poison us all. They thought it was funny when Nigel said it. Worryingly, I think it was possibly nearer the truth than I would have wanted it to be.

 The meeting had gone on a long time with talking through plans and ideas. As usual twenty-four people felt a need to have their say. It is dark, we are all tired, hot chocolate and bed seems the way to go. I can't believe that they have already forgotten about Eddie, but no one has mentioned him.

Lizzie and Maddy have come to see me after the meeting to say sorry for giving up on the cooking, but it isn't working for them and it wasn't making any friends either and consequently they were losing what little confidence they had. I try to assure them that it doesn't matter, and they should not beat themselves up. "It's another case of SUMO" I said. Take it as an experience; learn from it; and Shut Up Move On. You have done nothing to be ashamed of or worried about so forget it. And I'll say it again stop beating yourselves up." They were smiling when they left, and I hoped that that was the end of it.

Porridge is not as good as Lizzie and co had got to, but it was edible. just. Salt is still on their list of dangerous substances and no promises from me will satisfy them that it will improve the taste immeasurably. I think I might make a small pan full at some point and let them try it. Possibly soon, before Namibia runs out of sugar. The teachers have compiled the lists and are taking the accountant, Paul, and two of the cooking crew with them. They will all stick together when shopping and although it may take longer it will mean that they don't have to take any more than three on the back of headmaster's vehicle and they maintain their security by remaining in a group of at least four.

Shortly after school starts headmaster arrives does a quick visit into his office and with a brief case in hand comes back to his pickup, ready to go. The shoppers are standing waiting. I have given Alex my list and try to impress upon her that with any of these items missing the job will stagger along. "My father does lots of woodwork at home" she informs me "He is a surveyor and like you works away all the time, mostly in middle east. I know about building" and with that the two teachers have again jumped onto the bench seat in the front with the headmaster, leaving the other three to climb on the back, looking for something to sit on, instead of the rusty bare metal, the usual result of carrying just about anything and everything sliding around loose in the back of a pickup truck. Today Mrs Mutwa comes out with some blanket type material, which may be cleaner than the truck and will, at least provide some padding as they bounce down the dirt track.

I don't expect to see them before lunch, so I leave the cooking crew planning and preparing food. The teaching team are heading for one of the classrooms and I and the remaining members of the DIY group will look and see what we can get started on.

They start by taking the timber and corrugated iron sheets down to the goat field. It's called the goat field, but there aren't any goats in there for the time being, which is probably just as well, as there isn't a thing to eat anywhere. Not any green is visible. The field is a mix of hard rocky compacted ground and loose sandy gravel. There's not a lot of rain here to make everywhere green but they tell me, and I have no reason to disbelieve them that when and if it rains plant life will appear like magic. These people could do with a little magic like that. There life would improve significantly with a water supply that could be used for irrigation as well as survival.

Mrs Mutwa showed us where the store cum shelter was to be sited as she had been informed previously of the location for the building by the headmaster, and in addition to, they now were hoping that a good job may well allow for it to also be used as a crèche and kindergarten. She warned us that leaving good building materials unattended over night was likely to leave us without anything to do the following day, as they wouldn't be there. We took her advice, delivered this time in a friendlier manner, on board, laid it all out and wrote on the parts in a chalk that we'd robbed from one of the classes. I did a quick redesign in my head as to how we would lay out this building now that it had become a kindergarten as well and pleased that I had ordered sufficient insulation boards to cover the inside or anything or anyone in there might rot, explode, die or even worse. Our materials were about to build an oven if the temperature was going to remain like this.

 I was hoping the shoppers would return sooner than later as I needed the new saw and four-inch nails to put it together, but we've had lunch and shortly the classes are finishing. We returned all of the materials to the security of our classroom and come late afternoon we could see the headmaster's vehicle hotly pursued by his dust cloud racing and bouncing along the road. There are more people in the back than went as the headmaster has picked up men from town and given a lift back to the village. I can see supermarket bags and tins of paint, brushes and plastic footballs and unmarked cardboard boxes squeezed between bodies looking like they've spent too long at the theme park rides. They are wide-eyed and dusty and stiff as they try extricating themselves from the goods. I can't find the saw and assume that Alex and Gary have put it inside for safekeeping. Alex looks at me blankly when I ask her for the saw.

 "There wasn't a saw on the list" she says.

 "Yes, there was it was the first thing on it. Where's the list?"

"We left it at the shop."

"Why?"

"We didn't need it."

"Yes, we did. As evidence." She'd aggravated the situation by getting aggressive and bolshie with me and having had a day out on a jolly and not come back with what we needed was not my idea of how we should be performing on what was the students project.

She walked away following the headmaster into his office. Gary didn't want to get involved with me and disappeared after her.

"What are we going to do Rob?" I looked at Richard and laughed because it wasn't his fault and there was nothing else I could think of to do. Nigel was doing his leader duties and Richard had stayed with me. He was keen on remaining on the building programme and I'd much sooner have keen with some skill; that's how we all started.

"I might go into my tent and swear" I said, "but that won't get us a sharp saw before morning. Let's go see if we can find a file or two in the classroom. We don't have a contingency plan but let's keep the fingers crossed. Repetitive strain injury to fingers likely soon"

Sometimes when everything else is going wrong you come up smelling of violets. We found not one but two serviceable triangular files that we could use to sharpen the saw. They weren't proper saw files, but they were better than nothing. We clamped a couple of pieces of wood around the saw to stiffen it while I filed it and once again I was pleased with myself at having watched and worked and learnt from some old hands. These days we buy saws use them and then throw them away as they are not resharpenable. I consequently hadn't sharpened a saw for years, but I managed to get it sharp enough to make a decent cut without burning out my arm muscles. Roll on tomorrow; I think inactivity creates lethargy and stifles productivity and although we are oversubscribed with available man-days getting some momentum into the project will be a fillip for all.

Even after the fresh food shopping the meal was again just edible and the group meeting was brief. It would be eggs for breakfast tomorrow I wasn't certain if I should be looking forward to them or not, but I figured that they should be able to fry us an egg each. The teachers suggested that they may have some news at tomorrow night's meeting but try and persuade as the team did they got no further information so hot chocolate and early bed. Some of the team were playing cards and one had brought a small chess set and just about everyone had books that were going around. Most of which had changed hands at least three or four times. They were doing well considering most had nearly rebelled when they were told that there were to be no mobile phones. Sarcastically I was thinking that some of them were even talking to each other rather than texting. I left them in peace and after a visit to the toilet, no long drop here, which was a pleasant surprise. I went to my tent to do my paperwork by torchlight.

The moon was just on the wane and in ten days we would be in Fish River canyon in almost total darkness perfect for sky at night views, something a lot of the team were hoping to do, and the promise of clear skies and a new moon boded well for stargazing when we were in there.

There's a light wind with an unpleasant aroma coming across the school ground, the sort one gets from a vented long drop, which shouldn't have been happening with their conventional drainage system. But with the tent zippered shut I lost interest in the smell and even though the paperwork wasn't finished I was quickly making my way into dreamland.

Its Saturday. The school is closed, though the secretary will be here most of the children have gone home and only a few remain. A cooking lady will feed them over the weekend and those that have stayed will be allowed to spend their time with our team as they trust us to mind them.

I could hear strange noises coming from the early risers. Sticking my head out of the tent to find out what was happening. Overnight the wind had increased and shifted round and was making the school smell something akin to a sewage works.

Dressed and outside later we moved the cooking into the classroom and kept the door shut whilst the cooking and eating took place. They did the eggs on the Trangias and made a decent job of them. Pans mind you would probably require shot blasting to get rid of the residue. Still one job at a time. The groups organised themselves for their work programmes. They started the swapping and changing at this point. Some were keen to remain on the jobs they had started yesterday. Whilst contact with the Namibian children was limited due to their numbers there was no lessons to attend and therefore lots of opportunities for games and play

"Is this alright Rob"?

"The only time there will be a problem if one of the groups gets undermanned. I keep saying it, it's your programme your expedition take ownership of it and make it work."

"Thanks Rob."

They swapped and changed around, did a body count and got on with it. The cooking crew, most of whom, hadn't been responsible for the fried egg pollution found themselves with the unenviable task of having to clean up before they could start anything else.

I took my team of budding DIYers to pick up from where we left off yesterday hoping for a straightforward day. The aroma wasn't any better and when we crossed into the goat field we realised why.

The addition of twenty-seven extra people had caused an overload on the drainage system, which on investigation, we found only extended to the boundary of the school and into a huge hole in the ground.

We probably had no right to complain about the smell as we'd made it. A cover and maybe some straw would reduce the problem. We would have to see what was available, but we were the lucky ones the wind was coming from our direction and as long as we avoid getting sunburnt, we have the prime location for the day.

We went to work on the goatshed come creche knowing nothing would happen with the sewage problem without the agreement of the headmaster and as he hadn't arrived and was unlikely to do so before Monday it was pointless looking at the problem.

We did establish that straw was a nono as it was too valuable to be wasted on something as trivial as a hygienic and healthy environment, so we gave up on any thoughts of getting our hands on any.

At lunch there is still no improvement with the wind direction, so we have tightly shut the classroom door in an attempt to preserve our environment.

Gerry says there are some tarpaulins in the store-room, where the tools and materials had been kept even without agreement of the head, I decided we should act upon the problem as best we could. I'm not taking care of people if I allow them to live in a sewer and guess what I'm not that keen on it myself.

There had been some attempt at trying to fix the broken sewer pipe sometime previously and the problem as much as anything else was basically they had dug a septic tank which allowed the unwanted stuff to leave the toilets but only travel a short distance to the hole in the ground. This works of course quite successfully and it's not unusual but normally it would have an airtight but vented cover over it. We needed to source something that would provide a solution to our problem. Fortunately, just like in the movies we had found just what we needed in the classroom. Well done Gerry.

Two tarpaulins which were each plenty big enough to cover over our offensive smell and using four lengths of just about serviceable timber in a noughts and crosses game pattern the covers were quickly over and some soil and rocks used to weigh down around the edges finishing the project as quickly as we could. I don't know if it was my imagination, but it wasn't too long, and the air seemed cleaner things were looking up.

We finished the afternoon over at the store building project and later when we got back for the evening meal there was a definite improvement in the environment. The cooks had decided to take advantage and cook outside which was a good sign, but the change of location gave us more sand than we had got used to in the meal. Being inside had spoiled us they had come close to nearly producing edible, digestible meals.

"Hot chocolate for those that wanted it would be in an hour."

I heard a voice saying. I instinctively looked at my watch logged when it was due, and I too headed for my tent, to continue with my paperwork and check over the expedition accounts. I got so involved in the accounts, mostly because I couldn't work out what was going on, missed the hot chocolate and had to settle for teeth cleaning and sleep.

Today is Sunday, It's day thirteen of the expedition. We have been at the school for five days and things are starting to get people too easily irritated with each other. There's a bit of whining and sniping going on which I'll keep an eye on. I'm hoping I don't have to get involved and it either dies off or they resolve the issues themselves. I don't think that any of them have been this isolated before in their lives. They have no phones no computers no place to retreat to and some are homesick. None of this is unusual but it's a nuisance because it will require compromise and they'll need to do that before they get so entrenched in their own personal issues the meaning of compromise becomes long forgotten.

The atmosphere is not improving, and, in the end, I decide to call a meeting for after breakfast. I told the teachers the reason for calling it and to my surprise they readily agreed. They thought that it might be more likely for the students to talk about what`s bothering them if they are not there and have opted out of the meeting. I'm more than happy to agree to this as they've been trying to influence decisions more than they should be. Or at least Alex has, and Gary just goes with the flow.

We have porridge again no salt too much sugar and more than enough sand. Coffee as normal is needed to remove the taste as best it can.

When Alex and Gary are leaving I tell the rest of the team not to rush off after breakfast as there are certain issues that need resolving before they develop into murder and mayhem.

The meeting starts quietly enough. And then develops into a free for all. There's been a lot bubbling under the surface and up until now they've been good at keeping it bottled up. But when one starts they all have a go and as no one is throwing anything other than tantrums or in tears I let it run for a while, so they can all let off a bit of steam. It slows momentarily, and I call a halt to the proceedings to get it under some sort of control. Although Peter should have been leader today he had wanted to swap with Charlotte and I ask her to chair the meeting.

It has worked out well, she is a sweet girl, and everyone likes her, and when she calls it to order, the place does sit and take notice. The seating has been formed into a ring and I ask if I can have the floor. I know no one is going to refuse me but hey this is a democracy after all and it's their expedition. They kindly let me speak without interruption. I didn't want or need to lecture them and for most of them having a good shout and putting forward their arguments had been enough. But there were some grievances that needed resolving. Some of the team felt the work programmes were loaded in favour of different teams and that others were cruising and shirking jobs that needed doing. There was a general feeling of a loss of control and direction feeling that they were just being used. The accounts team had been denied access to the accounts by Paul who had taken it upon himself to run it singlehandedly. Oliver had done the same with the cooking after Lizzie and Maddy had given up the job and where Lizzie and Maddy had attempted to do everything themselves, Oliver was running like he was on a television programme and bossing all who helped. Most were unhappy about work, eat, sleep with nothing else to do.

They agreed that some of the grievances could be solved at another time in smaller groups and now with a lot more of a relaxed atmosphere I suggested that as some of them were attending church this morning some others might be interested in a walk out to stretch their legs. If the church goers want to walk, we can wait until after the service. Either the teachers or I will do the walk.

"You please Rob," asked Charlotte. "If we all get on with any jobs that were needed today, Charlotte and I will come around and speak to anyone who wants to take the issue further or has an idea to improve the situation that maybe could be discussed later at this evening meeting. Tonight, after everyone's had their say either during the day or tonight. We'll see if we can hatch a new plan that keeps everyone happy. If we do it will be as near as we will ever see to a miracle but let's give it a go ok?

The fact that somethings might get better and that their grievances had at least been listened to if not yet acted on had improved the mood wholesale.

We'd just finished the meeting when Alex and Gary returned I filled them in on what had occurred, and they were happy to leave Charlotte and me to sort it out. And yes, they were happy to stay at the school to mind whatever needed minding as they too had paperwork they wanted to get on with.

After church service and a sandwich lunch I took about half of the team out for a couple hours walk. I wanted to check for a mobile phone signal and a better sat phone signal if there were any and I was hoping that higher ground i.e. a hill in the distance might provide them. The hill hadn`t given any mobile signal and the sat phone was telling me that there was no news from home. That`ll do for getting on with for now. This morning a commotion at the shack behind the main classroom's got everyone's attention. I`m not completely sure what had happened in the previous minutes but now their dog was being dragged across their patch of ground. The dog the crossed Rhodesian ridgeback had been a regular visitor to the camp always on the lookout for food never too pushy and never snappy either. I`d insisted on it being kept outside the camp not wishing to either to feed it or make any friends with it. African dogs are not pets but are there to serve or protect. The dog was tied between two posts and a young boy maybe twelve or thirteen proceeded to whip it with a whip normally used to crack above the mule's head s as they pulled the cart. This went on for a couple of minutes the pain of the dog getting louder squeals. The girls wanted me to do something about it. They didn`t want to hear the noise anymore so I sent them inside.

 Unhappy with me they may have been but at least they went inside. After around ten lashes the boy stopped, put the whip inside the shack and walked across to the dog. He undid the ropes that had tied it by the neck between the posts and then turned and walked away. The dog followed immediately and walked beside him with his head pushed against the boy's knee as he walked. Subservient to the last.

An older man stood in the doorway of the shack shouting at me whilst this was going on. I could not understand a word he was saying other than "English" which he snarled in such an aggressive manner I figured it to be less than complimentary. He had a couple of days earlier tried to make a claim from us for new clothes for his boy as he had got paint on his uniform from what we assume was off one of the walls judging by the colour. No one knew how or when this had happened as the painted classrooms were out of bounds and unused until the paint had dried, and all the children had been warned about touching or drawing on the new paintwork. A probable beating for non-compliance from a teacher normally got minds and bodies focussed on blind obedience. I had refused him any payment and he had been hostile towards us since then. I'm not surprised clothes were expensive, but I was unwilling to take responsibility for something that was not our fault nor risk the possibility of a flood of spurious claims when one was seen to be successful.

The whipping of the dog had been witnessed by more than the girls. Not many were in the mood for a discussion and almost as soon as the evening meeting was open it was closed until tomorrow. Quite a few hadn`t joined us preferring to remain in their tents and given the sad mood prevailing they had made the right decision.

The dog was tied back to its frame the following morning and although there wasn't any massive shift in the happiness level at least everyone was up and moving and eating breakfast.

Alex called for quiet for a minute. They, the teachers, were going into town with the headmaster to pick up the presents for the school children and they would be taking Paul the account person and a couple of other volunteers with them. It wasn't for discussion they had made their decision and I was secretly glad to see the back of them. Gary said if they had time he would pick up a saw for me, but they would probably be too busy. I checked with Paul to make sure he knew what was happening, but he knew yesterday as the teachers had told him last night, as he would have needed to pick up funds from some of the other team members. I should have smelt something odd but maybe the broken drain had distorted my nose and my sense of smell was momentarily lost.

I suggested to the guys, who were working on building the store, with that a change onto another job this morning would be a good idea. We have the paint for the outside of the school and today is a good day to get it started as the teachers are not here and if their track record was anything to go by they wouldn't be here until late this afternoon. I left them to see what they could do; promising I'd be with them as quickly as possible. There was little I needed to say to anyone who was going into Keetmanshoop but it's useful to know who's going. I count them out and count them back in again. It would prove difficult to find an excuse for losing someone here believing that they had gone into town.

The advantage to the teachers disappearing into town is that I get them to go up the step ladder to paint the top of the classroom wall and therefore we would be able to complete all of the painting. It was hardly death defying as it involved going up two steps and although it was prudent to have someone keeping a steadying hand on the ladder it did at least give us a chance to complete it in one go rather than leaving an unpainted band around the top for me to finish after as Alex had banned any of the students from using the step ladder on health and safety grounds. The other good thing about painting the walls was the roof extended far enough over the sides to afford protection from the sun throughout most of the day. Which also saved me having to treat sunburn. Today was looking like a good day as I'd asked one of the town team to pick me up some extra rations whilst they were out, the teachers were off the job, everyone was smiling happy days indeed.

As I'd forecast it was late afternoon when the headmaster's pickup could be seen dragging his usual dust storm behind him. The walls had been painted and most of us were washed and cleaned helping the cooks prepare the evening meal. Once again, the guys on the back of the truck were squeezed between numerous cardboard boxes and almost certainly in more pain than they thought they could be. Sand coloured faces and wide eyed, sore behinds and stiff legs. It was above and beyond the call of duty riding in the back of the truck and no one having done it once was in any rush to volunteer for another trip. I believe Paul went rather than give the accounts role to another. Some of the other guys in the team carried the packages over to our storeroom whilst the tortured individuals tried to get dead or stiff body parts back to life by walking up and down the playground, moving not unlike a car with square wheels.

Alex suggested that we have a meeting before the evening meal as they were wanting to pass on the promised news that had been in the offing for the last couple of days. Cooks said sauce could simmer and rice, a welcome but dangerous change from pasta wasn't started yet. There was general agreement for the idea and we proceeded to the classroom in some anticipation for the news. Seated in a circle and Alex had the floor. "We have been talking to the headmaster over the last couple of days and as a special treat we have managed to secure the use of a 28-seater coach to take us on Saturday to a cultural festival in a village about 60 kilometres from here. There was stunned silence. Undaunted she continued. We will be picked up promptly at 6 30 am in the morning and the journey will take between an hour and a half and two hours. We have paid for the coach, as this was the only way to guarantee us getting it. This festival is extremely popular, and we would be unlikely to have transport if we had left it any longer. We will have a good time I'm certain and it's something we can look forward to and probably be discussing amongst ourselves as a highlight of the expedition and saying how good it was. Jacob asked how much it had cost and how we were going to afford it as we were living on the edge already due to under-funding on the project. Alex continued, "We looked at the accounts with Paul and the rest of the accounts team and we can make some future savings that will leave us in the black. Jacob hadn't got his answer but a lot of the team who were starting to get stir crazy were more than happy to get away even for just one day and it gave them something to look forward to. Though they readily accepted the answer. Jacob wasn't happy, and neither was Harry. Paul looked worried when Harry gave him the "you're in trouble pal" look and the remainder of the accounts team were hearing all of this for the first time just as the rest of us were. Alex called the meeting to a close and whilst the cooks returned to finishing the meal and the non-employed searched for something to occupy themselves I figured it would be time to talk to Alex. Alex left Gary as a rear guard to stall me, the predator, and did a runner abandoning him to speak to me.

"You know you are supposed to run anything like this past me first. Have you done a risk assessment have you checked the transport over have you got rock solid confirmation that we will be able to attend this festival. What contingency plan have you made for something going awry?"

Gary was unable to answer any of these questions other than to assure me that it was all arranged by the headmaster who knew the owner of the garage. The coach looked clean and tidy. No, he didn't know if it had seatbelts or not, but the headmaster said it was ok and they were ready to go along with his judgement. Especially as the owner and the headmaster are friends he could not see any problem at all.

"I can. This is Africa Gary. Did you get my saw?" "Didn't have enough money," he said, and he hightailed it off towards his tent and locked himself inside if you can do that in a tent. Alex too was keeping her distance and avoided me during the meal, which given the bombshell news strangely tasted better than was usual or my taste had

had so much immunisation against badly cooked food I had succumbed to accepting that this is what it would always be like. It still had a good portion of windblown grit, but this only served to make it crunch in your mouth like brown rice instead of the boiled white rice that it was. When I`d told them that if they didn`t cook it properly they could poison us all they took me at my word and provided carbs possible to eat even with the grit and a slight taste of burning when it had been singed in the pan.

The headmaster had disappeared shortly after dropping the team off but the following morning he is at the school earlier than normal to let us all know that everything was organised and to collect the balance of the hire for the coach. He also managed to extract I found out later, another day's fuel money for driving the team back and forth to town. Over a barrel is where we were and any possibility of changing the situation was unlikely. This looked like grin and bear it time. There had been minimal money allocated for travelling during the time we were on the project. Not an unreasonable consideration given the fact that it had not been expected for a trip into town on more than one possibly two days.

We on the building team were still awaiting the arrival of building materials that had been ordered and instant delivery promised a few days ago and as usual the promised delivery time and day was well passed. I requested the headmaster to call the builders merchants if he would and try to confirm our delivery date in order that we could finish insulating the building now no longer just a store room, but a kindergarten classroom come crèche as well assuming it got insulated.

We have only been on the job a short time but without the materials we are waiting for the project is grinding to a halt and due to lack of any further available funding we are quite soon likely to run out of work that we can do.

Wishing to keep themselves occupied they asked if they may paint a mural on the gable end of the school. There was enough paint of different colours to achieve this and though it is of no use whatsoever to the local community it kept a good few of the team occupied and entertained; he was happy to let them do it

He tells me that he will do what he can to speed up the materials but, in the meantime, he wishes to officially invite me along with the rest of the team to a Namibian feast which he and our teachers have arranged for Wednesday evening. The details of which Alex and Gary are sorting out with his secretary and the cooking staff. If he does not see us before he will attend the gathering with us. I asked if he is aware that we have a vegetarian with us who under no circumstances will eat meat. Yes, he is, and he has ordered a vegetarian meal to be cooked separately for her.

Late Wednesday afternoon and we have made reasonable attempts at tidying ourselves. Not exactly presentable but clearly an effort made. It's getting towards dark when we lock the classroom and head over to the communal room next to the cooking area.

There would be entertainment from the school choir, hymns and traditional folk songs, with a request that as they were singing for us; then likewise we should be singing for them.

The group had got themselves together and came up with a couple of tunes they figured they could perform successfully. They did have an ace up their sleeve, in one of the girls, with a beautiful voice and a good repertoire, sometime drama queen on occasions but currently the leading lady of this group and a shining light when performing.

This morning the headmaster had bought a goat from one of the local people and most of the team, not realising its destiny, had been over and stroked it while it was tied up behind the classroom. Later in the morning two men arrived and cut its throat and butchered it on a tarpaulin they had brought for the purpose.

Shortly after dark a fire was built in the school grounds near to where we would be eating and where the performances would take place and there the same men, who had butchered the goat, then cooked it on an open fire.

Twenty-four students, two teachers and me. Now I don't do the singing and as you're aware the teachers don't get involved in too many performance related projects. But they gave a good account of themselves; our diva sang her little heart out and though they were short on content no one could fault the quality.

Meal time came around and as we sat down we realised that we were the only ones eating. The feast that we had been invited to was for us only to eat. Neither teachers nor elders or headmaster would be joining us for this meal.

Much to my annoyance and astonishment our vegetarian insisted on being served with fresh goat and did she munch it down. The whole performance was watched from outside the classroom by the school kids. They had watched all our singing and had applauded everything. They then watched us eat. There's nothing like having a starving Namibian kid in ragged nightclothes to give you a healthy appetite I don't think, and I wondered if not for the first time whether these kids were being exploited.

After we had finished eating the little ones filed in. They were shown the presents that we had brought with the promise that they would be for Christmas. Hang on this is August that's a lifetime away for these kids. Then they were given a piece of bread which had been wiped on the inside of the cook pot for some juice and then sent to bed. That makes you feel on top of the world and the feast so much more enjoyable; just pass the brandy and cigars, oh thank you, how kind.

Mrs Mutwa asked for a football for her daughter from the Alex and Gary, but they refused her, and she looked almost heartbroken.

The meal was superb but owing to the arrival of the kids I would in retrospect, have preferred al dente pasta and cold tomato sauce. Surely things can only get better.

Thursday passed with a lack of interest. It could just as easily have been cancelled.

It is Friday and the school will break up part way through the afternoon, normally to allow the ones who stayed here all week to walk home. Today they are finishing early in order for them to do, as we needed to, and get ourselves sorted out for our trip to the cultural festival tomorrow.

They will be travelling there on the back of a tipper trucker not an unusual transport for people throughout Africa. But before they go they must get clean. Getting a wash was a precarious affair; periodically there was water but most times there wasn't and although we were looking forward to getting ourselves spruced up for tomorrows festival it was more importantly the children's clean-up day and they would be in the washroom first.

The little Namibian children piled in got scrubbed were checked by a teacher on the way out and within a short time they were all sorted, clean and playing football and getting dusty and dirty again.

This team were unable to organise themselves into any semblance of order and wanted to go into the shower room on their own without any spectators so whilst all the arguing was taking place Alex typically got in first and almost immediately some screaming, and shouting had let us know that the water was cold and particularly so. For such a supposedly genteel lady she was not averse to some choice language on occasions.

The knowledge that the water was cold and not as expected created the sort of reluctance that a second journey on the back of the pickup had.

 Eventually we got them all into the washroom though I'll swear some of them came out drier than they went in. The water supply hiccupped a couple of times, but I too eventually got myself clean as I could, given the circumstances.

Mealtime. The pasta and tomato sauce came and went with most people carrying off their bowls as usual in order to add some personal goodies into the meal. Hot chocolate and an early night we needed to be up by 5am at the latest. Shortly before shutting down we had a visit from the school secretary; asking if it would be possible for us to take her and her daughter to the festival tomorrow. Personally, I was all for that. We would have a translator with us which was well worth the inconvenience of trying to squeeze another couple of bodies into the coach. Nevertheless, I ran it past the team fairly quickly and they too saw the wisdom of having someone who could act as our intermediary if required. I gave her the good news and she promised to be here at 6.15 in the morning ready to go. Later I could hear what I assumed to be the crossed ridgeback mooching around our tents looking for scraps and then music that would drown an aeroplane noise out came bouncing across the fields. It is Friday night it's party time and guess what; it will go on for hours.

My eyes were stinging when I awoke this morning. Some of the others were up but the sound of snoring was clearly audible coming from more tents than a few. Harry was our waker upper today and he had the unenviable task of getting the sleepyheads up.

6.15 am finds us in the playground waiting for our transport. Most of us look like we've been up all night and I suspect that's not too far from the truth. Mrs Mutwa has arrived promptly with her young daughter. They are both in their best bib and tucker and have dressed to impress. By 6.45 the troops are getting restless and Alex and Gary are out of earshot obviously deep in discussion about what. We think we know but it could be anything given their previous record.

At 7.00am we hear the sound of a vehicle and see the normal dust cloud following it. But it's only a small van and then another following it. Maybe it's the building materials we've been waiting for. That would be par for the course. The two vehicles which we thought would drive past, at the last minute made a sharp right-hand turn into the playground and I realised what I thought had been vans were dusty minibuses. The drivers got out leaving the engines running. Sorry we're a bit late one of the drivers says couldn't get the van started.

"Are you telling me that this is our transport to the festival?

" I am," said a voice from inside the front of the first van. There was a man in the front seat slowly getting his body out of the cab. It was small wonder Africa had a food shortage this guy looks like he's eaten it all. The van rose a fair few inches when his feet hit the ground and he waddled over to me. "I'm Obrien," he offered his hand and we shook it Africa style. "I`m headmaster's friend and it's my duty to get you to the festival today."

"What happened to the coach we were promised?" I asked.

"Double booked," he replied, "so we brought you two mutatues." I wasn't happy. I had to appraise these two vehicles in the space of a few minutes. Now given that a fully trained mechanic gets more than 30 minutes to do an MOT in a purpose-built garage I am faced with the task of establishing the roadworthiness of these two vehicles and I have minutes not hours in which to do it.

I was running over in my mind what the board of enquiry would make of this if anything went wrong. I know who would be to blame. I am expendable in these circumstances, as I've shifted from the standard operating procedure to unilateral decision making. The windscreen is of course cracked. I don`t think I've been in or seen many vehicles in Africa with a full unblemished screen. I look at the tyres. There are four one in each corner with some inkling of tread once again not bad. Both vehicles are in the same sort of condition. They`ve been driven here that`s another plus. Unless I want a rebellion on my hands, I have to go with these two vehicles. "Let's pile in one of the teachers in each vehicle," I tell them "in front seats please." Alex keen to be in the front to see what`s going on has my blessing. She has chosen the vehicle that the big man didn't climb out of, but he has decided to join her in the other one as Gary is so much bigger and the front of the other will not fit them both in. People die in the front seat of these things and as she`s been squeezed between the driver and the man who is the vehicles owner I have little sympathy for her having organised this trip without consultation.

We turned right out of the school gate and proceeded to travel down our sixty kilometres of gravel road. Constant changing of leads as first one vehicle and then the other overshoots a turning and loses the lead the penalty for which is dust eating punishment. The only respite on route is when one of the vehicles a Chrysler has a puncture. We all climb out and the two drivers and our owner between them manage to change the wheel. Our teacher isn`t terribly happy as not only is the owner a fairly big and she`s feeling his weight now and again but his personal hygiene is somewhat lacking. I have to stop myself making any comment, but I really don`t care. The wheel finally changed, and we all climb aboard again in hot dusty pursuit of culture.

More vehicles mostly of the commercial variety are with us and we have reached the festival site.

We are at a village school not dissimilar to the one we have just left and it`s starting to fill up with performers from all over the area.

Trucks carrying maybe thirty or so adults and children have travelled fair distances the travellers having stood up for most of the journey. They tumble out full of enthusiasm ready to do business. They are carrying with them bags and boxes containing their costumes for this cultural festival also has an air of competition about it. Lots of schools are taking part with numerous categories for different age groups.

We wander around the school grounds that are home to this festival saying hello to people here and there trying to make ourselves as friendly as possible. Our drivers have disappeared to find something to eat and we are pretty much left to ourselves. A man smartly dressed in a morning suit comes over and introduces himself. He is the master of ceremonies today.

I explain who we are and that we have come to the festival to watch and to see some of the performances. He shouts instructions to some children and ladies and quite soon a number of benches and seats arrive at the corner of the stage where we are told that we may sit and from this vantage point we should get a good view of the performances.

The stage is about the size of a small five a side football pitch so probably 30 metres by 20 metres and raised up by about half a metre. A band, electric guitar, keyboard and bass are playing some music and Namibian Broadcasting Corporation has sent a camera crew. They are moving around setting up and taking some footage. They don`t seem to be interested in us so we sit and wait for the start of proceedings.

This is of course Africa and in Africa nothing ever starts on time. Our plan had been to arrive after the proposed start knowing that it would be delayed however we hadn`t bargained on quite this much of a delay.

We have been here about an hour or so wondering if anything is ever going to happen when things start to spring into life. Unseen by us down in this bottom corner the guests of honour have arrived, and a small procession of dignitaries are walking slowly across the stage towards a table and chairs set up directly opposite us. They have the benefit of a covered gazebo to keep the sun from cooking them. They are well-dressed proper Sunday clothes making us all look particularly scruffy. The main man is one of the tallest I`ve seen in Namibia; this is possibly accentuated by his top hat but even without that addition an imposing man without a doubt.

The MC introduces the guests at the table. Our man is the minister for culture and tourism and a person from this area.

Now Namibians like speeches and in formal gatherings such as this all the protocols are observed.

The MC reads out a list of speakers and the order in which they will speak. Sorry I`m thinking did I catch that right. Someone from the European delegation will give a speech in answer to ours. Surely, I`ve misheard. No one else in the group seems to have picked up on this so I must have.

Probably due to the recent death of a local man, and a famous freedom fighter from the time of the war for independence with South Africa there is here, an upsurge in nationalism which is reflected in the speeches we hear.

A couple of speeches and our man the minister rises. Thanks to the MC and welcome to this festival and to all the guests and then in a different language he repeats it for the non-English speakers. Then he does another dialect for people who don`t speak either of the first two. 45 minutes later and I have fallen asleep twice but our man is finally coming to an end.

The gist of his speech was about the influences of western European and North American culture and its effects on the young people of Namibia and how all of it was bad and under no circumstances should either of these cultures be entertained. The old Namibian ways were the best ways and the youth of Namibia should forsake all western influences (as they didn`t appear to be doing) and embrace the traditions and culture that was Namibia, which they didn't seem to be doing either. His speech too may well have been influenced by that death of one of his fellow freedom fighters, whose memory was also being celebrated and at the same time capitalised on this day.

I`m almost certain that the minister was a well-informed man but I'm not so certain that the general population were equally so. There was little international news in the local main paper but one article that did catch my eye whilst I was there at that time concerned the number of stabbings that had occurred recently in London. This article had a picture attached to it of two policemen with Alsatian dogs standing outside the law courts in Liverpool. Neither the picture nor the article of course bore any relation to each other, but they did manage to convey a level of lawlessness that doesn't really exist in the way it was graphically described.

Our MC was back on his feet again the lady mayoress I think was next and then the representative from Europe would give a speech. Oh dear, I did hear right. A sudden movement to my right saw the two teachers disappearing way from the group rather akin to a roadrunner cartoon.

Now if we're going to take this logically as we have a student leader today it should be his responsibility to give our guests the full benefit of his worldly experience and reply to our hosts.

Given who our leader was that day, I figured if we were to get out alive, it was not really prudent to give him his moment at that particular time. I'd overheard muttered effin and blindin whilst the minister had been making his speech. Sebastian, our leader today was the one person out of the whole group who could cause a riot in an empty room. His language could make your hair curl and what he called banter the rest of the world found offensive. Armed with this and a selfish desire to get out of here alive I figured to do the speech myself; and especially as Seb was probably the incarnation of the Namibians worst Western European nightmare.

The lady mayoress was brief. When I needed time to prepare I hadn't got it. After the applause had died down the MC called for the European representative to make a speech.

It was very quiet, and I knew I was going to have to make a move. Namibian Broadcasting who had been working throughout the programme thus far, stopped filming, or at least left there camera on its own. I took the stage.

The quiet changed tone, it started like a humming, moved into a loudish murmuring, and became a noisey booing from a lot of people as I walked towards the MC. He was holding out the microphone. I needed time I hadn't like all the other speakers had time to prepare a speech and unlike all the other speakers I wasn't a welcome guest here. The television people are still not near their camera. They don't want any evidence if some guy gets mobbed or shot I was thinking. How much can you make up Rob in a ten second walk? Not a lot. Most don't speak English so keep it brief. And with that in mind. I took the offered microphone from the MC.

"Good morning everyone. My name is Robert Platt. I am the leader of this team of hard-working students. We have come here today to observe your culture and to watch your festival. This group of students I have brought with me are from the East of England and have also come here for this same purpose. We look forward to going home and telling the people back in the UK how friendly and welcoming are the people of Namibia and how much we have enjoyed our stay here. Thank you." I handed back the microphone and started to walk back to my group. I`d forgotten all the protocols not once did I mention the honoured guests, nor did I thank our hosts. You blew that one soft lad. My group raised a cheer and then there was some polite applause I looked back, and the minister was applauding which got everyone else joining in. it wasn`t rapturous but it was a welcome sound after the initial booing. I got back to my seat, the students came and said well-done you did us proud thanks guys the two teachers returned "we just nipped for a coffee when all that happened, I suppose we should have done it, but it went ok". Alex sounded like she didn't give a monkeys how it went and the sentence had been delivered as though she was reading it for the first time off a sheet of paper pinned to Gary's back which she was partially taking refuge behind.

Our standing at the festival changed radically. All sorts of people appeared shook my hand and gave me copies of their school performance. Most spoke to me in language that I did not understand, most of them breathed beer on me and one or two nearly fell on me due to too much beer. It wasn`t yet lunchtime, so I found this somewhat worrying especially when I noticed that our drivers had now found the beer tent and were comfortably ensconced in there. They looked to be drinking from mugs, so hopefully tea or coffee. The bus owner, though, was drinking for the three of them, by the look of it.

It was unnecessary to go and warn them about drinking and driving but I kept an eye on the situation and I advised the teachers to do the same.

We watched the festival for a while. The dancing was unusual and not at all easy to perform. It seemed to be based around a dance called Gwara, which itself is not easy to do, requiring movements that look both uncomfortable and physically demanding as well. Most of the dances told stories that were aids related and part of an aid's awareness programme.

At about twelve thirty, in theory, when the programme should have been halfway through, but was a long way short of that, the MC called a halt to proceedings; insisting that everyone returned from lunch bang on two o`clock to continue.

I got my group together, suggesting that we needed to make a move and retreating now, when everyone else was moving around, wouldn`t be as obvious if we left it until later.

My brief requires me to get all the students off the roads before it goes dark and as it was at least two plus hours back to the school and dark would be before six o`clock, hanging around too long was not a good idea and we still had to find somewhere, other than the bar to get some food.

The drivers knew of a place on our way back where we might get some lunch and having got everyone squeezed back into our minibuses we headed for home. I wasn't sorry to leave as I figured the longer we stayed the more likely something was going to go wrong. We'd survived a number of near misses with boisterous drunks and although nobody was harmed, I thought that it was not if but when. So I moved them all.

We stopped for lunch at a wayside hotel, come restaurant, come guest-house, about 5 miles from the festival and ordered toasted sandwiches. Not because we wanted them, but it was all they could do for us. The owner and one member of staff were all that was here as no one was expected. Suddenly they have 24 students, 2 teachers, 2 taxi drivers, one drunk, one African school secretary and her daughter and me. 32 in total all hungry. The place was deserted. The building a fair distance from the road was well worn and in need of some serious maintenance. The paint peeling from the wooden slatted walls and a general look of neglect, isolated and in an area of scrub desert made it look like part of some wild-west ghost town and they weren't used to 30 people suddenly arriving for lunch. Spaghetti western country. A man in a poncho carrying pistols and smoking a stubby cigar would not have been out of place. Dried brush blew about the grounds and I swear I could hear someone whistling and the sound of a twangy guitar. The people at the café were just about coping our drivers appeared to not have the wherewithal to buy food. Either they had spent it already on refreshments or were prioritising their finances. I bought them lunch and they were grateful and thanked me which always makes doing favours worthwhile. In Namibia there's an expression that goes "come and touch me" and this means when you're ready let me know. The taxi driver has said to Sebastian "Whenever you're ready come and touch me". This has frightened the hell out of him and he rushes over to tell me. I was tempted to tell him he'd pulled but that wouldn't have been a good idea, so I put him right on what he had meant. About an hour later we had all finally eaten and were on our way again. I suggested to Seb it was time to go and touch the taxi driver he laughed but without real amusement or enthusiasm.

We are an hour into the journey when we get another puncture. Sad part about it it's on the same vehicle that had the first one. We are all sitting on the roadside whilst the drivers try to change the wheel. They decide to put the spare wheel from one vehicle onto the other. After a while I went over and explained that a Toyota wheel even if it has five stud holes will not necessarily go on a Chrysler. They eventually see reason and reckon the best course of action is to go to one of the local farms and swap the tyres over.

All three are about to disappear and leave us here whilst they go. I point out that we're not too happy about this and as the boss can't even sit up on his own due to the amount of alcohol he's consumed; he at least should stay in case we need someone to translate for us if we can ever get him to talk. They reluctantly agree and our man, with difficulty climbs into the other vehicle and goes to sleep. They reckon fifteen minutes and they'll be back.

Considering we are currently on a major road for Namibia and it's a Saturday afternoon there is no traffic at all and whilst we were waiting for the drivers to return, only two other vehicles passed by.

Ninety minutes later our heroes did return, change the wheel and off we go again. It's now getting close to 5pm and I'm just a might concerned that if we have another puncture we aren't going to be in before dark or maybe even before tomorrow.

Just before 6pm we arrive back at the school. I get Seb to check one of the vehicles for anything left while I did the other; mine is clear but Seb has found Paul's accounts book which he passes to me shaking his head having established what it was and who it belonged to.

The drivers are expecting a tip. They are not getting one. The fat man is fast asleep, his head lolling on the dash board and as they get the message and leave a bump in the playground bounces his head wake. A row is taking place and clearly audible as the vans depart the school and one can only assume that at some time along the road it was resolved. This may well have involved violence and death. It was the least of my worries and as we did not hear or see any of them again I forgot about it until now.

I spoke to Paul about the lost accounts book which he swore was in his kit bag; until I gave it back to him. He didn't have anything to say and even less when I asked him how it worked given that there was no order to anything and, on some pages, there were cartoon type drawings some of which were more like toilet wall graffiti. "Tidy it up please" I left him, last seen, he was red-faced and heading for his tent.

The following day Sunday was a finish what we can day. In the afternoon when what we could do has been done and before the evening meal is being prepared I call the team to a meeting. I think it will a good idea whilst it is fresh in our minds to think what we have achieved over the last ten days and how we might, given what we know now, have done it differently. It was the gentlest, least demanding meeting we had ever had. The project had gone badly as retrospectively it was seriously underfunded and most of the money was spent on paint and materials which did little for the improvement but just brightened the place up. Too much was spent on unnecessary transport, at which point Alex left the room, followed soon after by Gary. The classrooms had received a new coat of paint on the outside as had the four sets of toilets. What went into the toilets still didn`t travel too far though as the drains had stayed un repaired and even though we'd put a cover over the open cesspit, an unpleasant smell on occasions was still in the air if the wind blew in the wrong direction. The buildings had been painted to maintain the apparent standard of the school. Schools performance and status is measured not by the quality of the teaching but by how nice it looks from the outside. A triumph of style over substance but typical of the area and school headmasters were well aware of the advantages of a highly decorated school meant more pupils more government funding and consequently greater prestige. The education of the learners was at best intimidatory. Punishment for spelling mistakes and incorrect answers resulted in beating with a stick and the whole process of learning was driven by fear.

We could never be certain if the materials would ever get to the school, and the kindergarten finished; or if all the presents made it to the students as was promised. Our relationship with them was at an end whether we changed anyone's life or made anything any better for anyone I will never know. I suspect that our impact will be minimal.

Eddie possibly got the most benefit from our visit and in all honesty, he was probably the one who deserved it. His education of the team far outstripped anything that we managed to give to the Namibian learners.

We are near ending our review when we hear a truck coming down the road. Our transport has arrived and some of the team, in a rush to meet our new driver, hurry across the playground to open the gate and let him in. He stops just inside not knowing exactly where to go, shuts of his engine climbs out and walks across to see me.

We have all gone out to meet him. I shake hands and introduce him to Gary and Alex and Louise who`s boss today. His name is Ephraim and he will be with us until we are at Swakopmund. He is completely the opposite of Eddie quiet and monosyllabic with almost no bounce at all. The team are disappointed and lose interest in him almost immediately. If we wish to use his truck tonight he will park it up for us where we want it and it`s much the same as the one we had with Eddie and will we feed him too please. He seems keen to eat he tells me as its Sunday and he ran out of most of his food yesterday; he has not been able to get anything since breakfast. I wonder how keen he will be to eat after he`s sampled the delights on offer here.

Ephraim ate the evening meal and the porridge the following morning and, with the rest of the team, carefully packed the kit away into his truck. We checked the classroom and the storeroom for any of our kit made certain that all the keys and padlock were returned to Mrs Mutwa thanked everyone more times than we needed to and sorted seating places out in the truck. Alex and Gary had started a damage limitation programme, said little, ate together quietly, not interfered and knowing that I would be sitting as near to the side door as possible took seats at the back out of the way.

There were only a few tears from our team, mostly from the child minders, and the majority seemed happy to be off and as Ephraim started the truck I to climbed aboard and we were on our way. I had told Wendy and Alun that I would take the front with Ephraim until town so that I could sort the details of the next couple of days with him and they could sit in the cab later.

Many of the school waved us off. The secretary, without football, scowled as we left, perhaps she knew, as we thought, that presents were unlikely to be dished out in the way promised. After the transport fiasco on Saturday I would have been surprised to see the headmaster. I wasn't surprised, the headmaster hadn't bothered to attend.

I was not unhappy to leave here behind and get back on the road. The team should have been on a high, tinged with a little sadness at leaving, but they too were desperate to escape. The whole project may have been better had we been able to get on with it for around five days. Boredom and consequent homesickness would not have set in as much, and there would have been a lot more achieved with short quality time rather than a drawn-out slow grind.

Ephraim will start by taking us to Keetmanshoop, to stock up on supplies and to get fuel for his vehicle. For most of us the journey back to the main road was a first trip in that direction for ten days and again we saw the shacks and tin huts of the people with the same children, excited at the sight of the truck, running to the tyre fence and waving. I wonder what they were thinking about as we passed.

FISH RIVER CANYON

Alun directed Ephraim, from the back, through the sliding window to the supermarket at Keetmanshoop that the team had previously shopped at and wished to return to.

It is well stocked, had armed security inside and out, reasonably priced and had everything needed on the list. As there was no reason to go anywhere else we all trooped off inside to do some personal shopping while Ephraim went to a garage that he knew was nearby to fill up his truck.

Around the entrance were groups of young men, who harassed some of the team as they waited outside for Ephraim's return. I was inside at the time and unaware until later when we had the evening meeting. They didn't get physical but were noisy and intimidating and highly entertained when a local drunk tried to urinate on some of them as they sat leaning against the shop wall minding bags of food.

Some of the girls noticed a ladies clothes shop near to the supermarket and though it a good idea to pay a visit. Two of the girls left before the others to be met outside by two guys they reckoned about twenty five years old or thereabouts.

"We don't know where you're from and we don't care so fuck off and don't come back again. We don't want you people here."

I'm not certain if these things would have occurred had I been there and in some ways, it was a life lesson for the team; being blissfully unaware it stopped me thinking I would have had to do something about it, which isn't what I'm there to do. I'm there to keep us out of trouble not get us into it.

Only a short wait for Ephraim with the refuelled truck, and stores loaded we were away quickly from the supermarket and on the road heading for Fish River Canyon; the second largest canyon in the world after the Grand Canyon in the USA.

Out of Keetmanshoop and then it's around a hundred and seventy kilometres of empty main road driving until a turn off onto a minor road with even less gravel.

We pass a number of houses offering accommodation and now we only have a short way to go before we are at our campsite. Driving down here is like a moonscape apart from the actual gravel road wherever you look seems to show little signs of life. We crossed salt flats over a narrow bridge spanning a dried riverbed with just enough room to get the vehicle through, and Alun shouts through the partition to us that it is not far to go now.

I'd made contact a couple of days earlier from the cultural festival site, on one of the few occasions when I could get a signal on my mobile phone and our arrival was expected.

We had been promised access to bunks and showers; in the event we got neither, as a group had overstayed, due to transport issues and would now not be leaving for another couple of days.

This group were in their twenties on a university meet and spent the evening in the bar spending money. We as a school group, would not be drinking in the bar and spending money, and this may well have influenced the decision to send us down to one of the outbuildings, where we could pitch our tents and cook our meals. This was no hardship as far as I was concerned as it made for shutting down early considerably easier to complete.

Nevertheless, we were assured that after the trek we would definitely get bunks and showers and access to the upper lodge and a nicely cooked meal.

The following morning, we breakfasted and were ready to start the trek. We wandered around the site awaiting the arrival of our transport to the start of the trek otherwise we would have a long walk to the start.

Our bags and most of the equipment went onto a Toyota pickup and then we were presented with our transport. What we thought was a derelict farm vehicle parked up near a fence not too far away was our transport to the canyon. It resembled something akin to a second world war, experimental truck; and to be honest although its vintage possibly wasn`t that ancient its design most definitely was. The staff seemed more than happy to take us in this, and though I felt a certain unease about the journey, I was again in a situation where there wasn't another option.

We clambered aboard. This is how a lot of other people travel in Africa standing on the back of a commercial vehicle. We were jammed in like cattle, but the back was open and given the number aboard there was a danger of some of the team falling from out of the back end. I had asked for a rope, but the driver didn't have anything or couldn't be bothered to get anything as he seemed in a hurry to follow his mate, rapidly disappearing into the distance with my ropes on the back of the Toyota. Possibly he didn't know the way and he was very much in a half panic to get going. Certainly, out of the ordinary in our experience thus far.

Two of the boys and myself formed ourselves into a human chain and managed to stop a mass exodus out of the back of the truck as it took off up the first hill. We remained in this uncomfortable chain position thrown forwards and then backwards and it was a testament to the strength and fitness of the two boys that the whole team manged to survive this journey.

The ride was like the waltzers at the fairground and finally after about three-quarters of an hour even this vehicle couldn't go any further and we had arrived at a parking space where our Toyota had been offloaded and our bags and packs were waiting for us.

Our drivers pointed us in the direction we were to go, with the instructions that after a while we would find a rock in the middle of our track pointing to a path off to the side. We were to take this path, and fingers crossed in four days' time we would be back at the lodge. We asked how far to the rock sign, or how long, but it was shrugged shoulders, Africa time, or a country mile, individually or perm as required.

Just hope the stone is where it's supposed to be.

It was a steady undulating ramble not too difficult but might become so if we were out and about as exposed as we were when the sun got to its high point . I was in my normal position near the back better placed to see what was going on at the front. The leaders are always briefed that anything unusual and I must be called up to assess the situation.

About half an hour into our morning walk and I can hear myself being summoned. In the middle of the track is a stone about the size of a shoebox with an arrow painted on it. The arrow pointed off to the right towards what appeared to be the start of a descent into a valley type shape. The top of which was covered in sparse, hardy vegetation with a few tough looking stunted trees dotted about but no obvious sign of a path.

The team are in discussion as to the value of this lump of rock as its easily moved around and could so easily as one insisted on showing us be turned to have the arrow pointing in any direction one wished. Our leader was not happy following the route down into the unknown, but as there was no other obvious, he was going to be overruled. Unfortunately, today our budding explorer and the man in charge is Alun; he is one of the boys who stopped on Dune 45 further along after Lizzie.

I was under the impression at that time, that it was because they were tired but in fact is was due to a fear of heights. I think he is going to have to push himself. I join them at the front, and we head off down the descent.

 I need to keep him in close proximity to steady or encourage him if a problem occurs. The teachers who have been amazingly quiet and out of the way since the cultural festival debacle have taken my place at the rear where they seem to be more than happy to be. They seem to be happy whenever they and I have a buffer of 24 students between us.

We are making good progress and in a steady descent. The question of are we going the right way. "Rob are we going the right way?" "Are we going the right way Rob?"

sounds out from behind me on too many occasions and to be perfectly honest I don't really have a clue. The information I have been given is wholly inadequate and my map sadly resembles something from a childs colouring book. I have to assume that the rock at the top of this canyon was exactly where it was supposed to be and also pointing in the right direction. Turning left at the top would not have sent us downhill but across the open plateau so we definitely had to go the way we're going and I must assume that if we weren't to be going down this canyon we would be going down another to arrive eventually at the Fish River. We have food for five days and we can make shelter this is what I do for a living. We can always turn around and walk back out if necessary.

We have arrived in a cool sheltered area with some trees and a flat rocky shelf well able to accommodate us all, so I suggest lunch time and have no arguments as to whether this is a good idea or not.

"I reckon an hour from now and the sun on here will be too warm so let's have a reasonable lunch break but keep in mind we will certainly be on the go again in less than an hour. Everybody ok with that?"

I don't really care whether they are, or they aren't I'm not allowing them to cook themselves halfway through day one; and Alun going well, given his vertigo, is not going to be bothered, if I make all the decisions on his behalf today.

Good old Richard has carried the sandwiches again, refusing to trust them out of his sight on the luggage truck; how he had managed to keep them mostly intact throughout the hair-raising ride from the lodge to the start of our trek I don't know.

After today we will all responsible for our own lunches, with breakfasts and the evening meal still being a group effort.

After half an hour or so, I suggest that starting to pack up might be a good idea, and well within the hour we are back on the move again and heading down into our valley. The sides are getting steeper and vegetation is becoming sparser; in the near distance there is a split in the side wall were another canyon joins this one and we are presented with a geological fault.

Where the canyon joins there is a drop of maybe twenty feet. Our leader is about to bottle it, but the teachers are way behind deep in conversation. I do a quick risk assessment, find an easy route to the bottom, leave big Harry at the top with the order of play and take Alun down to the bottom. He's smiling when he gets there. That's good.

There's a decent sized platform part way down and I position myself there. Harry is sending them down one at a time, and Phil the first one, has had his brief from Harry that he will mind the bottom. It's only taken a couple of minutes and most of the team are down, when Alex can be heard shouting over the top. She's not happy. Harry is getting an ear bashing when I get to the top. I take the teachers to one side and Harry who's got pissed off good style with the teachers sends the last two of the team down to the bottom and follows them down. Harry's not at the school next year, the teachers need to be a bit more careful.

"There is no problem unless you create one "I say to Alex and Gary. "The team haven't got any worries and even Alun who got scared on dune 45 got down. So, let's get ourselves together and back with the team." I wasn't either interested in or prepared to have an argument. I left them with the choice of following or spending the rest of whatever, where they were; and went over the edge to the place where I had been stationed.

Alex came down first without her pack and once again I felt the trembling fingers as I steadied her down the path. Harry had positioned himself halfway between me and the bottom and took her the rest of the way down. Gary came over the edge carrying both sacks, one on his back and the other over one shoulder. I took her bag from him. Gary didn't need anyone's help in negotiating the descent and quickly we were all back together and on the move.

Another half-hours walking, and a couple of the team are asking for a break and as soon as a bit of shelter from the canyon side, hides us from the sun, we take a rest. The group is getting tired and are still worried that we might be in the wrong canyon, as we can't see any end to it only sheer rock walls, where it twists and turns. We have decent shelter they had a short lunch and the day thus far has been energetic and long; a rest won't do them any harm and I could take anyone who fancies a bit of exploration, on a recce to see what's ahead.

Three of the boys are quite keen. Alex and Gary are happy to mind the rest of the group, so we leave our packs, grab a water bottle each, and head off down to see what we can find. We make quick progress eating up the ground. We are light and quicker, without bags and the downhill gradient allows for speedy travelling without any serious danger of falling over. We have come a fair distance when the canyon we are in suddenly widens out; although the cliff sides are as high as we have seen them, now directly in front of us there is a massive vista and clear space.

We are in Fish river canyon proper. In front of us the river potters quietly past. Maybe 30 feet or so across on the other side is a good sized sandy island with some trees and greenery. This looks like a good stopping place for tonight's camp.

 Back up and down again will take us at least an hour so rather than hanging around enjoying the peace, the quiet and the view, we head back to the team.

The river was easy to cross over when we all got back; a camp was organised a cooking area sorted, evening meal needs to be on the go by 5pm at the latest. it will get dark here and as we don't have either a full moon nor an early moonrise so dark will be the word. And early too. We set the toilet area up in some rocks away from the water and gathered any wood we could find to build a bonfire to sit around in the evening. All the ones not cooking probably a good half of the team and myself went upstream in search of firewood.

The river was quiet and short of water, there would be enough to keep us going for drinks and cooking but unless there was some change the option to take a swim further down was looking unlikely.

However, there was a fine amount of timber available for our fire almost certainly brought down, when the river was carrying more water, and now nicely beached and dry and available for our heating and light. A fire pit has been dug in readiness and the wood already here sorted into size and length. Gary has it organised while Alex is busily writing in her diary. I knew Gary was a seasoned backpacker from the information he had supplied for my reading, but this was the first time he had shown any sign of his talent. The set up for the fire was perfect and it would have been unreasonable of me to start fiddling with any part of it. I gave him two thumbs up, he smiled, no more to say.

Maybe he knew more of what was going on than I was giving him credit for. Dinner tonight had even more sand than usual. No sense in being on this sandbank and not taking full advantage of what's on offer. The coffee washed the grit down and as darkness was coming in to land, we lit the fire and sat ourselves around it. There was no wind, so smoke was going pretty well straight up and conversation which can be frequently interrupted by people rushing away due to stinging eyes was gentle, pleasant, uninteresting and boring. Until a screech and a sound that went sort of ugh ugh ugh rang out from the dark. The sound was repeated, and someone asked timidly 'what was that?' Baboons I said. They're up on the cliffs they were around from about halfway down the canyon.

They all decided that it would be prudent to go the toilet in groups as a minimum of twos seemed less than safe. Although we had brought three four-man tents with us as a just in case we were all sleeping al fresco and we allowed the fire to burn out long before our wood supply was used up.

Some other group would be able to use it in the future in a similar way, to wood collection, we had found on our arrival. The fire has died down there is no moon and above us in the sky sometime in the past a mad artist has thrown a huge pot of white paint around the universe millions of tiny dots surrounding the huge brush stroke of the Milky way. I'd never seen it like that before and I don't think I've ever seen it like that first night in Fish River canyon. We have the advantage of almost no light. The moon is new and not visible; it was the first time I'd seen it without any source of light pollution, and I think it was just lucky to be here, right time, right place.

I could hear Harry talking and giving a lecture on the view. He had with him a star book and a laser pen he was naming the stars as he pointed the laser at them.

Sometime during the night, I awoke to find a baboon sneaking off with one of the Trangia pots presumably missed in the washing up duty but my light and my movement towards getting up caused it to drop the pan and scuttle off. The air outside my sleeping bag was cool and I didn't fancy going for the pot, so I snuggled back down inside my bag and went back to sleep.

There's an inkling of light in the sky I look at my watch and realise nearly 6am it's the start of sunrise it won't be dark much longer, so I set of for the toilet and an early start for my day. I pass the Trangia pot. There are still some obvious signs of last night's meal in it along with some sand. Maybe I did the baboon a favour by stopping it from eating the food we were having to put up with.

The morning air here in the canyon is cool and fresh and as I wander over to the toilet area I can feel stiffness in the back of my left leg probably all that downhill yesterday and bouncing in the truck. No doubt it will walk off this morning. I think I need to get them moving soon, as it will get warm later today and we are exposed here in the canyon.

It was one of the reasons I insisted that they brought the tent outers. If the sun is getting too hot and we can't find enough shelter we can at a pinch, if needs be, get everyone in the tents. We will get warm and sweaty, but we won't burn in the sun which should be enough to keep us all safe.

Porridge is almost grit free this morning, which is brilliant but there's not very much of it because they've miscalculated the number of breakfasts and won't have enough to keep us supplied through the four days.

Gary has organised the clearing and tidying of the campsite; he does know what he's about and the students get on with him better when he's away from Alex. One last check that all is clean, and nothing has been left behind and we are on our way. The stiffness in my thigh isn't in any rush to leave but the walking is on the flat and not at all strenuous.

The trail meanders through patches of thorn bush and there is a possibility that during the morning we may have to cross the river. Simone who took over the leadership today knows that she must not attempt any crossing without my being there first, so it was no surprise to hear that she needed me to come to the front as the path had petered out on the bank at the riverside.

Crossing was a simple affair easily done without anyone getting wet feet a pleasant change from the usual. Though most people only got a soaking on training exercises there was frequently one who slipped and popped a boot into the water. A short break on the other side a quick look at our map for a rough idea where we might be or what more realistically would be described as a guesstimate.

What we do have though is a good description of our campsite tonight and an approximate journey time and distance of 4hours walking and 8 miles distance. Which doesn't seem either very far or very quick but in this case is surprisingly accurate. In the end we went the distance and the journey before our lunch stop which gave us an opportunity for a rest and what I hoped might be a relaxing afternoon.

There is good shelter here but nevertheless I put up a tent as a better before, than after. I was given information by one of the staff at the lodge that a little further down river from our camp was where there might be a couple of pools that could provide an opportunity for some gentle swimming or paddling. Time to see how good that info was.

I took Simone and Henry our leader and deputy for a walk after lunch and after only a short distance, with the camp still visible, we came upon a small rocky pool about fifteen metres long and 5 metres wide. There was a small amount of fill coming in from the river and a slow outflow from the other end. As good a swim opportunity if ever.

Things hadn't been planned this way, it would have been too difficult, but Henry was a qualified lifeguard and county standard swimmer.

"You and I will be the pool attendants" I told him, "and we will watch over a group of 6 at a time. Ok?" He nodded. "The girls will be split into 2 groups as will the boys and therefore we will have a maximum of only six at any one time in the water. Miss Alex will come down with the girls and Mr Gary can do the same with the boys. What do you think.? Simone?"

"Sounds great" she said, "Who's first?"

I took a coin from my pocket "Heads or tails Simone"

"Heads" she called I showed her the coin on the back of my hand tails. "First or second"? I asked Henry.

"First," and Simone smiled

"Worked out nicely" she said, "I would have gone second as the girls will need more time to get ready."

When we got back to the camp I let Simone and Henry sort out the announcement and the split for the teams. Another tent was put up to act as an additional changing room while I had a chat to the teachers about what we'd organised. "Did you know about this?" Asked Alex.

"I knew before I came" I said, "that's one of the reasons why there was swimming costume on the kit list; but I didn't know until we got here whether the pools would have any water in or if they were safe to swim in, even though I'd had a nod from the staff back at the lodge".

 She looked like her winning lottery ticket had got lost and didn't know what else to do. "Boys are going first if you will be good enough to come with them Gary." I explained how we were going to run it and left them to mumble to each other.

Henry and I spent the afternoon making certain no one did anything stupid or drowned which might have been difficult to justify in any report. They'd all had around half an hour each when the last of the girls team had left, I found myself thinking about a swim myself; all I needed was Alex to return to camp and I could give it a go.

She had spent most of the time on her duty watch's taking shelter under the overhanging branches of a tree out of the sun. Blondes don't have more fun when its cooking time and she was well aware of how easily she could burn. She made a move and I thought good she's off but instead of disappearing back to camp she came down to the edge of the pool. "I'll have a swim" she said. "I should have gone in before, but I didn't bring a costume." She started to remove her shirt and shorts and I looked away before my mouth fell open.

I don't know if you could call what she was wearing a thong. Its design had certainly been influenced by the boot lace and the on the front something the size and shape of Hitler's moustache or a Victorian penny black. It failed miserably to hide her blonde Brazilian. A case of less is more I suspected. The less material the more it cost and calling it underwear constituted a stretch of interpretation of the word underwear.

She had the body of a supermodel and swam like a fish. She was doing somersault turns and going from one end of the pool to the other for about five minutes. She came out in one single movement and went straight for her towel. I looked away again to give her some privacy. She had seen me look away on her exit

"You are a gentleman" she said, "are you not having a swim?"

"No, I'll head back up to the camp shortly and I didn't bring a towel down." If I went in the water now she might not think me the gentleman she currently did.

"I can loan you mine I've hardly wet it. And it will dry quickly enough in this heat. Thank you for the swim didn't think I would ever swim in a river, in a canyon, miles from anywhere. Something to look back on. Sure, you don't want the towel. Gary and I can organise the meal."

I changed my mind. "Yes. Please. I will have a swim if you and Gary will get them started. Before it gets dark and too late."

She threw the towel to me and walked off back to camp. The swim was enjoyable drying myself on a towel that smelt of expensive perfume was even better.

Gary had organised a fire again the sun was close to going down, but time was still on our side and as it was still warm Alex's towel would be dry before darkness took over, and the chill joined us for the evening.

Food was on the go and there was a buzz about the camp. They were a happy group and all of the friction that had been developing on the project was long gone into forgotten history. We were camped on a rocky shelf where groups had camped before. Again, there was sign still visible of where a camp fire had been, and we plumped for the same site as there was still plenty of sand about which we would need to kill off the fire before sleep.

Gary, who was successfully proving that he had at least two sides; again, he'd organised a firewood collection and what was there looked well able to see us through the evening. They cooked rice again with some of it stuck to the bottom of the pan and burnt. If nothing else this team proved that they knew how to destroy carbs and spoil a good meal. The burning put a smoked flavouring on the rice and tomato-based sauce and caused mayhem for the ones washing the dishes. Most annoyingly, we were back on the vegetarian meals again; the team were catering for our guilt-ridden lapsed vegetarian with most of us glad that we had brought our own lunches. The evening meal had turned into something that made us look forward to breakfast.

The walk followed by the swim had left many of the team tired and less than a couple of hours after dark quite a few were in their sleeping bags and nodding off. Harry was doing his Patrick Moore night job and talking a few of the team through the night sky.

Screams from the other side of the camp fire and I can see the problem a red coloured frog has hopped between the few remaining students and is bouncing its way towards the fire. I drop my bush hat on it which stops it going on the cooked side of the supper menu. Two of the boys are quaking although it was one of the girls that screamed these two weren't keen on frogs and were disappearing as fast as they could away from the fire. A plastic dinner plate slid under the sand and I have my hat some sand and the frog still trying to extricate itself.

I wander off away from the fire towards our toilet area when voices start pleading with me to take it away from there as they need to go later. I don't know why they.re worried so much about a frog but I'm glad I didn't show them the cat paw mark that I'd spotted in the sand when we got here. The two boys had disappeared into one of the tents much to everyone's amusement. Harry had finished his lecture tour he and a couple of others joined us for hot chocolate.

Like last night we had heated a pan of water on the remains of the fire. Any hot water left over I used for teeth cleaning saves using any I've purified with chlorine. Both the fire and the stars are out the air as expected has cooled down; I have been to the toilet and I am looking forward to bed. It's not too long and I have drifted into a deep sleep. I'm dreaming about screaming and shouting and panic until I realise it's not a dream but real.

"They're fuckin wild animals and they were watching me" The shouting is coming from behind Gary. Screaming sobbing and a multitude of swear words and I eventually establish that Alex has gone for a wee and whilst there her head torch has showed her two baboons within close enough proximity to turn a simple wee into something substantially more. Gary has managed to calm her down he's got hold of her, but she is still visibly shaken. She comes to realise that half the camp is now awake, and embarrassment is about to set in. She storms off grabs her sleeping bag and heads for the spare tent instructing Gary to stay on guard outside. Gary has nothing to say to us but meekly takes the order and parks his sleep mat and bag outside her tent door.

We can hear her inside and she is going to sob herself to sleep. She has turned from a sweet gentle lady into a wild bad-tempered hooligan with a vocabulary that would make anyone blush. I think I should feel sorry for her but somehow, I can't quite find it in my heart to do so, even though she had loaned me her sweet-smelling towel.

The morning of day three the team are up and ready to go in super quick time they have got themselves into a smooth-running group now. Everyone knows what they have to do and what order to do it in. Their speed and efficiency has given me a bit of a surprise; I am ready but not as far ahead of them as normal. My thigh is irritating a bit which is another surprise as I'd figured the swimming yesterday would have eased it. Maybe I'd overstretched on the project and it had been slow to show itself. Whatever it doesn't matter I can still walk this route without any problems. We have to cross the river a couple of times and Henry who has taken over the leadership from Simone is well aware that he doesn't cross without my say so.

The route wanders in and out of stunted bush the river is not running as high as it can do but it has its moments in some parts with substantial amounts of water with both depth and width. I think we were lucky yesterday finding the pool with water and only a small outflow, today what was deep enough to swim in was flowing way too quickly. We have made a couple of easy crossings and everything is going as normal.

Too late my sixth sense should have warned me grief was in sight. Henry had stopped the team and called me to the front whilst I was on my way two of the boys jumped across the river to land on a rocky islet towards the middle of the river. Peter tried to follow just as I was getting there. Missed his footing on the other side and twisted around trying to get back to the bank. Given that he couldn't get it right one way I don't know why he thought he could turn through 180 degrees and get back to the bank with his full pack on his back. He was wet when we got him out and in pain. Wearing shorts may have made the impact damage worse but it at least saved us the problem of getting his trousers down to watch his very red knee swelling.

I told the two boys to stay where they were and had Gary and Alex move everyone else back from the riverside and find a spot to rest and chill out for a bit. Alex was happy to stay out of everything this morning after last nights unwanted interlude, but Gary came back to see if he could help. He was a Jekyll and Hyde character. Super-efficient and then almost ingratiating around Alex like a private personal assistant.

"I'm glad you're here" I said, "It will stop me killing those two". Peter was making more noise than Alex had last night and if his knee did not stop swelling soon it wouldn't be long before it was the size of his head. He was in pain, but he wasn't about to die so I left Henry and Gary sitting with him and went to see what life had in store for me next.

The two boys on the islet were both well over six feet and had no problem getting across the first part of the water. I doubt that more than half of them would not make the crossing and stay dry. I took my boots off, unzipped the legs off my trousers and carefully tried to wade across to the boys. It was way above my knees and what was left of my trousers was well soaked I ignored them and there "sorrys" told them to go sit and wait. There was plenty of water on the other side, but it was slow and shallow and an easy walk from there. I needed to find a safer and better way to get the others over and, in the end, it took nearly half an hour to find a suitable crossing further upstream where it was safe to cross for everyone.

Peter, with a couple of borrowed walking poles had little trouble crossing, and even with only one good working leg, he hopped and limped across the river. Everyone had taken their boots off and crossed without any difficulty; I sent the two boys across from where they were. The only problem had been getting Peter's boot off and on again. This did however provide another painful and noisy, but sadistically entertaining experience. We put a support bandage around it and with the use of the walking poles he moved reasonably steadily along. We asked him to report any problems immediately and that we would check it over every half hour or so to start with. I gave the other two the responsibility, for minding him and making certain no further damage occurred. The short walk remaining would likely turn into a long drawn out hobble for Peter and the other boys. Gary had a first aid qualification as do all the teachers and mentors on an expedition, so I left him plodding along with the boys while I took the remainder of the team with Alex on to our camp.

I said I would wait if there was another river crossing but if there wasn't they would stay on this side until the campsite. I promised to backtrack as soon as we got there and settled the team in.

It was a while until we arrived but there was no mistaking that we were at the campsite. It was a tip. Whoever had been through here last had left their rubbish and debris all over the area. As the walk from here tomorrow was no more than a couple of hours they presumably had decided that there was no need to carry anything back. Or am I being unreasonable and making it all up. I didn't care it was a tip and I asked the team to photograph the mess and be kind enough to have a litter pick before they sorted out our camp. I would be going back to Gary and the boys to make certain they too were ok.

Before I left Peter, I'd swapped the walking poles for mine and I took a confidence rope with me to make a stretcher with just in case we had to carry him at any time. If we were going to accidently break a pole it better be mine. They were making reasonable time. He was using the poles like mini crutches and with them under his armpits; he was now bouncing along quite quickly. "As long as my leg don't hit the ground I'm fine" he said. Gary had used a

Sam splint, which is a lightweight foam-covered piece of aluminium about 3-foot-long and 4 inches wide and strapped it around his leg which provided support and protection. "One of yours?" I asked Gary. He told me he now carried one since a friend broke his ankle in the Lakes years ago. "Glad you had it. There isn't one in our kit to be honest or I'd have done the same. Thank you."

The ground was a lot easier to negotiate at the end; Peter had got the knack of using the poles, and it wasn't too long before we joined the rest of the team at there. It was now clean and tidy with the food on the go. The two tents had been put up a fair distance apart. The two boys frightened of frogs would probably be in one the other was certainly Alex's home for the night she was sitting in the doorway looking through her camera pictures and ready to repel all borders.

"I have the pictures of the site" she told me "what should I do with them?"

"Hang on to them and we'll find out from the staff who's been through here. If it's one of our schools, we'll take it back to the UK with us and I'll get our people to sort it. If it's another group, we'll play it by ear. But whoever it was we will take credit from the park for what we've done.

It was our last night on expedition; tomorrow we would stay at the lodge and then make our journey back up North with our R and R on the way. The food was awful. If nothing else, they were consistent when it came to cooking. The evening wandered out into disinterest. They knew that tomorrow was the end of the trek and a couple of hours walking should have seen them back at the lodge. Peter's knee will dictate our speed tomorrow and my suspicion, having had a look at it, was that we needed an early start to avoid the sun when it was at its hottest.

They were looking forward to their promised meal, hot showers and a bed. I tried to get them to reflect on the expedition and have a team talk but none were interested and even Harry's stargazing programme couldn't get any takers. Though Gary and Harry did have a short discussion around the night sky there didn't appear to be much enthusiasm for anything but sleep and earlier than usual most were in their sleeping bags and off to the land of nod. Gary Harry and I had a last hot chocolate Peter was in his sleeping bag with some Paracetamol inside him and snoring rather noisily. Gary parked himself outside Alex's tent Harry followed soon after and after I checked the fire was out I did the same and slept a proper sleep.

Peter was as stiff as a board when he woke up although the swelling had gone down appreciably he was unsurprisingly sore. We had little to do after the first quarter of a mile of rough ground other than to walk along an undulating 4x4 track for a few hours. It's a disappointing anti-climax to the finish of what is an entertaining and delightful walk. Before leaving we made doubly certain the site and area were clean and then made our way back to the lodge where we arrived just before lunch. The view has little to offer of interest and due to the continuous up and down most of the time there is no view at all other than the seemingly endless blue sky and the person in front of you. We had not seen a cloud since we had left Heathrow some 24 days earlier. Then from a hilltop the windmill sails can be seen and after that one more small hill and the whole of the lodge is in view and its downhill all the way now.

"I was worried I expected you hours ago" said Ephraim "but you are still in good time, I have made you a chicken soup for lunch with rice and fresh bread."

"You are a saviour" I told him, "what about our vegetarian?"

"I've done a pan of vegetable soup as well and any left over I will put into the chicken soup to bulk it up." You'll be sainted" I said, and he just smiled. "There is bad news" he added. "There is no showers the water system is kaput and not likely to be working before the weekend. You can all still get washed but it will only be in the sinks."

"I'll give them the good news thanks Ephraim. Will you join us for lunch?

"Yes."

Time to tell the troops what's happening. They were a sorry looking bunch now, adrenalin had probably managed to get them through the morning along with the prospect of a hot shower. When they had all got together, sitting around the tables. Obviously tired, the trek had certainly taken more out of them than it should have done.

A lack of stamina and a poor choice of food was not a good recipe for a successful expedition, but they had managed well considering the conditions and I felt it only right of me to congratulate them on a job well done, which was what they were entitled, to but I thought it also might cushion the blow of the no shower situation. I was wrong I had a mini riot on my hands, a case of the messenger being shot, and it was only Ephraim's soup rice and bread that probably stopped a lynching.

I know I'm almost certainly exaggerating but I didn't expect that much hostility from what was an inconvenience of no shower but no problems of either a water shortage or a worst case no washing at all. I have been in that situation on numerous occasions and the reaction has been a lot less aggressive than this team were. Maybe their blood sugar levels were at a low and hunger had driven the aggression for as soon as they had eaten lunch their demeanour improved no end and after a civilised discussion they organised a rota for washing bodies and clothes and the menu for our evening meal.

Not surprisingly, all of the lunch was eaten and the chances of saving any for my dinner had long disappeared into other stomachs. Why anyone thought that we might be eating anything other than pasta and tomato-based sauce was delusional so with nothing other to do than sitting around sorting equipment and chilling out the afternoon was spent in a relaxed and untroubled mood.

The evening meal had a hand from Ephraim and was potentially a fitting end to our stay in fish river canyon. It was the first time without grit, but el dente was almost reaching new heights as an adjective. "You're lucky it's even warm" said Ephraim. "They count the 20 minutes cooking time from when they put the pasta into the cold water and turn on the heat. "

No wonder they're all losing weight. I expect to lose anything from 7 to 14 lbs. when I'm away I told him. Ephraim who looked to weigh somewhere around 17 to 18 stone reckoned he'd die if he lost as much as 7 lbs. He was being serious, so I left him with his fears and went to see if the bathroom was clear now, so I could get myself clean again. Ongoing tiredness, the lure of a night in a bed and the fact that no one was allowed alcohol, and darkness established, and the team are drifting off to bed.

It is latish compared with the time in the canyon and with some prompting from Alex and Gary most of them are in their rooms and ready for bed before the generator is switched off.

Ephraim and I have a last hot chocolate and although he's had a few beers whilst we been away on the trek he knows the drill and isn't seen to be drinking anything other than soft drinks from the bar. I can hear Alex telling them to settle down and shortly the generator shuts down and quiet takes over.

The walls aren't soundproofed here, they have the same quality of sound insulation as a tent and everything that happens on one side is clearly audible on the other. I think Alex was thanking Gary for taking care of her during the trek and a good time was had by them both. There wasn't a peep from anywhere else in the lodge and I doubt that anyone missed a thing.

The following morning as usual they took a table separate from the kids and this morning it's quite handy as I can give them a heads up on what the group are up to today. I sit down opposite them and they are all over each other like a rash. I quietly whispered to them the good news that not one person missed any part of last night's performance. It was unsurprisingly providing the major source of conversation at the breakfast table. This didn't seem to bother them too much and I couldn't see why I should be worrying about it either, unless it turned into a problem. Alex and Gary looked at each other a question unspoken and answered without any words. They walked over to the two tables where the group were eating. Alex starts' We would like to let you know that Mr Gary and I are shortly to be engaged and sometime in the future we expect to be married. It went very quiet. One girl started bubbling over with Oh miss I'm so pleased tears just about holding back whilst just about everyone else sat opened mouthed at the news. It was too quiet. "I think we should congratulate Miss Alex and Mr Gary on their engagement and wish them all the best for their future." I offered.

That got them started talking and I slipped off to get some coffee and food happy in the knowledge that whatever happened hereafter was not going to get any worse. Just in case though I crossed my fingers.

The journey to our next camp was via Keetmanshoop again which would be a good couple of hours driving then add in the shopping to buy supplies for the next couple of days which could probably take another couple of hours. We were starting our journey just after nine; which was likely to make it a late lunch at Quiver tree forest which is just a twenty-minute drive out of Keetmanshoop. We have a plan for the day. It is Saturday, but we had checked when we were last there that the supermarket would be open today. No one minded what day it was, the supermarket would be open, and a happy relaxed group left the lodge and headed off on the next part of the trip for the start of our R and R. The best laid plans of mice and men required us to have a puncture.

It was in one of the double wheels on the back of the truck. The road was narrow with rock walls tight in part to the wheels. Probably a pinch between the rock and a wheel rim was the cause of the puncture but fortunately we were able to continue on a bit further until we could stop and change the wheel.

Ephraim cannot get the wheel off. He will not accept my advice that the near side of the truck probably has left hand thread nuts and therefore all his huffing and grunting is only serving to tighten the wheel further. I suggest he has a good look, but he won't accept that it may be possible, and he decides to travel very slowly until he can get to a garage in Keetmanshoop. Even though it was a long time in the making, the journey was at least accomplished without any further problems. I was living with the fear that we would have a repeat of the cultural festival. But he dropped us all at the supermarket albeit later than planned but we were here in one piece.

He knew where he had refuelled his vehicle before we left for fish river did punctures and as he needed to refill again he would head for there. In the supermarkets you have to leave any personal kit bags at the door as walking around with a pack on your back is not permitted to stop people stealing stock. We've never lost a pack doing this, as most times there is a guard type reception person like a cloakroom attendant who will mind everything for you until you are ready to leave. There wasn't a problem for us this time as most of our bags had stayed in the truck. But in the end the lack of our own bags found us an hour or so later standing outside the shop with a considerable number of overfilled plastic bags, with goodies on display, which has now attracted probably the same large band of late teen early twenties locals who once again are trying to make our waiting outside on the pavement as uncomfortable as possible.

I am standing in between my group and the locals and I'm hoping Ephraim is going to arrive back as quickly as possible before I'm thinking of my options as the situation is coming up to simmer. The armed security guard is avoiding getting involved, wise man, and I get the feeling that this is a regular meeting place for this group. Although I've got some big lads in my team a show of force from me is not going to be backed up and I'm really more than happy to avoid any serious confrontation. Sometimes I have bluffed it but the unpredictability of the outcome here is a dangerous game to be playing. The truck's arrival has the locals losing interest and they amble away though we are told once more by one of them to "fuck off and never come back again". His parting shot is from a distance but still attempting to provoke some sort of reaction. "Sounds like my last boss" I said and the team in earshot laughed and the guy with the attitude realised he was wasting his time and did exactly as he suggested we do.

It was later than expected when we reached the Quiver Tree Forest campsite we grabbed a quick lunch first before they started on the tents. Even though they hadn't put the inner and outer tents up for a while they had no problems and fairly quickly we were off to visit rock formations, not far along the road. It's now late afternoon and this is when the black mambas like to take the rabbits for dinner. They hide under rock near to pathways and care must be taken when walking around to keep a careful eye on the ground in front especially, but all around as well.

The rocks were not interesting enough for a group that has just spent four solid days in the Fish River canyon, and most were disappointed not to have found any snakes killing any rabbits which they didn't see either.

It would need to be either a domesticated or a stupid wild animal that would go near 24 teenagers making the sort of noise one would expect to hear at a football match. And it wasn't long before they got bored with the view and the lack of gladiatorial contest so much so that they were asking if they could go back to the camp to get on with the evening meal.

There was little point in attempting anything else; Ephraim drove us all back to the camp. They came close to getting the meal right, but by the time I got to the serving table there was very little remaining, and Ephraim and I shared what might have made a poor sized portion between us.

We have a couple of nights here leaving early on the Monday morning as our next stop is Swakopmund, something over 860 km and is a nine plus hour drive not including stops, which is where Ephraim is due to leave us. He will stay there with us for a couple of days, as our emergency transport, and as we should not need him, he will get a couple of days rest before he starts his next job.

Our original plan had been to split this journey into two, staying over at Hardap Dam, one of the parks, halfway to Windhoek, but they are full and also short of drinking water and when phoning them to confirm our booking we were told we couldn't stay. Being here was no great hardship and the team opted to stay as Ephraim said doing the whole journey in one goes was no problem for him.

Shirley and her friend Jan have come to see me after the evening meal. Shirley is crying and has apparently been avoiding me for a couple of days. Instead of changing her contact lenses for her glasses as I suggest to everyone going into the desert, she pretended she didn't need to wear her glasses and left her lenses in. Looking at her eye she has conjunctivitis and according to Jan she has been hurting since we left the canyon and sitting in the truck whilst were on the move is causing a lot of pain.

Vanity is what stops her having her glasses on and we have decisions to make. We have another day here which may well be enough but looking at her eye I don't think it's going to improve before the 36 hours we have before we leave. It's fairly easy to change our plan, as we have not yet booked into any accommodation in Swakopmund and our journey will take us via potential stops at Maltahohe and Windhoek. We will wait and see. She has her glasses with her now and Jan has been watching her movement as she can't see without either the contacts or her glasses. I have bathed her eyes with saline solution and put some cream into them. All we can do now is wait and see what tomorrow brings. Jan has been instructed to tell me if anything further develops and I've given her the cream to put in her eyes if needed.

 They have gone to bed and I need to get my paperwork out to find the nearest hospital. I'm convinced that its conjunctivitis and it's probably due to sand behind the contact lens but with eyes I prefer a qualified medical opinion by someone with the right equipment. My head torch, limited knowledge and peering into the problem is not a good basis for a diagnosis. If there is no significant improvement, then I think I may need to redirect to the hospital.

I needed to compensate for the shortfall in my evening meal, so I doubled up on the hot chocolate later before hauling myself off to bed. The showers and toilet were a decent walk away, so I think no one had checked out the showers. But they looked clean and tidy and unused. I settled for a quick wash and a good teeth clean and went back to my tent to work my way through our options for the next few days in case we have to change our plans.

Midnight nearly and I can't sleep. Too much caffeine possibly is now depriving me of my rest maybe my body needs a proper wash so as the only sound coming from the tents is some gentle snoring I grabbed my towel and soap bag and head off for a shower. The showers have come out of the sort of magazines dedicated to beautiful homes. Clean smelling like they have a season ticket from a French perfume house. The team haven't bothered coming here so the it's even more immaculate than one might expect if it had had 24 previous visitors. Warm clean and beautifully built with hot water, heaven is here on earth at Quiver Tree farm. I almost felt like I was about to commit a criminal act, but I needed more than a good wash. My hands were dirty so using body parts as a loofah I gave them a good scrubbing. Everything got clean, but my other plan went wrong. Stimulation was missing and even the thought of blonde Brazilian could do nothing in the way of providing the answer. I had no plan b, so I got myself dry and not for the first time thought I must get a medical opinion on this. But possibly not at the same time as checking out the eye problem, if we needed to visit the hospital.

Doing what I set out to do might have been a criminal act in showers as nice as those, but tiredness beckoned now, and I wandered off back to my tent, cleaner, but somewhat unfulfilled in my ambitions. Thwarted but sanctimonious as if there had been no thoughts and nothing had happened. I put possible thoughts of guilt to the back of my mind and I slept like I needed it.

It's early Sunday morning for the first time in a long time I have heard a lorry moving noisily down the road.

My watch says 5 am, too early to get out of my bag, but I can hear voices in other tents.

Later I hear the cooking crew doing breakfast and as it's the best meal of the day I join them for porridge.

They have a cheetah sanctuary come animal hospital here and with a number of other animals this will provide something akin to a visit to a small zoo there is insufficient entertainment for a much beyond a half day which will allow for a decent chill out for all. Many were glad of the opportunity just to do nothing take some time to themselves read (like they needed to?) and relax. This is after all r and r time. This will be one of the last times we need to use the tents. The zips on the group tents have mostly been replaced now by a system of laces. The time in the sandy area in the school caused the problem. When they had been serviced and checked in our stores the zips had been lubricated which had caused the windblown sand to stick in the zip and making the opening and closing difficult until they finally broke. We were obliged to take them back so that we would not be charged for them even though we knew they would be thrown away. Our make do and mend day saw most of the clothing washed and dried, rubbish disposed of and Ephraim's truck smartened up. My paperwork was up to date, food was back to its usual standard of poor and inedible and now we can look forward to tomorrow and being stuck in the truck for an indeterminate length of time as we head, avoiding bumps where possible, for a hospital in Windhoek.

We left the campsite as early as we could; the drive to Windhoek was going to be slow and careful. Shirley was still in pain and all Jan's efforts as Florence Nightingale were in vain, as she sobbed and cried her way to the Catholic Hospital in Windhoek. They knew that they needed to book accommodation for tonight and tried their best option, which didn't happen. We were unable to stay at the cardboard box, but the team had, with their help found a different hostel for tonight which though more expensive was within our spend capacity so we booked in there.

After, Ephraim had dropped Shirley, Jan and Alex, who had come to supervise, and myself at the hospital; he took the others to the new lodge promising to return as soon as possible. We had each other's telephone numbers so communication was possible as parking his truck up handy was not going to be easy.

The service at the hospital was excellent the bill not unreasonable and the doctor who spoke perfect English had a good look confirmed conjunctivitis gave us cream saline wash and some antibiotics and a bill, which we paid in cash. He gave us a receipt we shook hands and the whole episode was over in double quick time. Before Ephraim arrived back we were standing on the pavement where he was able to easily pick us up and take us to our lodgings. The hospital visit had been a psychological boost to Shirley and the following morning having paid the bill for a night's accommodation which came with the use of a kitchen which had little effect on the standard of cooking we were on our way to Swakopmund the adrenaline capital of Namibia.

We had managed to book accommodation at the Dunes backpackers hostel which we found without any difficulty and four hours after we left Windhoek with one stop on the way we were in Swakopmund. We saw something on the way we hadn't seen for 28 days, a cloud. It didn't last very long but shortly after we arrived mist could be seen rolling in off the sea a short distance down the road from us.

As part of their R and R the team had booked to go dune boarding with a company called Alter-Action on our last day here so when we had settled in at the Dunes Lodge, our leader and a couple of the team with myself, went to their offices round a couple of corners to check on the arrangements.

When I got back I checked through some of my paperwork to see if I could give them any more money. My sac had been put in my room but no matter how hard I looked the answer stayed at no. The robbery had been sorted by the extra income from the favourable exchange rate and the dune boarding for me was free being the expedition leader.

Gary and I were sharing a 4-bunk room and Alex had a similar four bunk room to herself. The team were split into three dormitories boys and girls separated. More finger crossing.

We have comfortable accommodation and access to an indoor swimming pool and a soft drinks and coffee bar. There is a pool table, indoor and outdoor seating areas and the main gates are kept locked which makes the place as secure as one can hope for. We have easy entry through a front door, which is accessed by bell. Originally, we had three nights here but the stay over in Windhoek has reduced this to two.

Because I have compensated the team for any unforeseen overspends where I can they are now left with a limited budget, some of which is earmarked for the celebratory meal which consequently allows for just the dune boarding as our only R and R activity. This leaves them one and a couple of half days to walk around the town, soak up some atmosphere and chill out together. Most will leave the school on their return and unless they organise a get reunion in the future this may well be the last time they are all together.

When I had done my original group meeting at the school some six months back I suggested to the team that a good idea was to bring any old designer label clothes to work on the project in as they would be a good trade in the markets with the stall holders. As they no longer needed them it could be a win win all round. Some of the team were still wearing the project clothes complete with paint stains and holes and my suggestion to thinking about trading at the market fell on deaf ears. They were saving their clean clothing for our last night in Windhoek at Joe's beer house and were unwilling to risk the clean clothes on the few days we had left before home time.

They split themselves up into four mixed groups expecting to return to compare notes in time for the evening meal. Darkness was around 6pm and I wanted them in by 5.30, which still gave them a decent look around the immediate area, which included a fine selection of local shops and cafes.

Alex and Gary had kept themselves separated from the decisions concerning the last couple of days, finally leaving the team to take responsibility for it all themselves and were more than happy just to go with the flow. They hoped they would find a good vantage point to keep an eye on proceedings. They were out of my way and that suited me more than anything else. These students were seventeen and eighteen years of age they didn't need mothering in this part of the city in broad daylight. I found myself a small café with outside seating from where I might be able to chat with some of the locals to get any up to the minute news or information that might provide us with some options for tomorrow. I didn't strike lucky and after touring the immediate area and spotting a few of the teams I headed into one of the supermarkets on the main street.

New and nearly new 4x4's were parked up outside. A couple of guys were operating security there and minding the cars for a small fee. There was a Toyota Hilux with two men inside and rifles hung in the back window. "Rapid Response Armed Security" sign written on the doors just in case anyone misunderstood what their purpose might be.

I had noticed that most of the expensive housing had cameras, dogs, high walls and barbed wire to deter the criminal element. When one person gets this sort of security it creates a snowball effect as anyone not taking as much care in their property protection will certainly look like an easy target and consequently likely to suffer accordingly. Most of the public buildings seemed to have some sort of guards some of which were quite discreet but if you watched carefully for a short while they could be spotted.

In the supermarket I picked up some snacks and spotted a few of the team in there. They all appeared to have been doing similar snack buying while some of them had shopping trollies loaded for tonight's meal. Half an hour later and the whole of the team apart from the teachers are back at the lodge. Charlie has spent what remains of his money which was fairly substantial and amongst other things is the proud possessor of two wooden giraffes. When I asked him how he was going to get them back to the UK given that they were taller than his rucsac and not as robust as luggage travel might require. He figured he would come up with a plan before Thursday when we're due to fly home. I hoped so too, but I wasn't too certain that he would.

The evening was spent around the pool. The food was the normal rubbish. Nobody really cared anymore as most had eaten out during the day.

Ephraim was leaving tomorrow, and I asked them if they would be giving him a tip. The look on team faces gave me my answer. They hadn't got on with him as well they had with Eddie as he hadn't entertained them as much so although they had given Eddie probably the best tip he'd ever had, they weren't going to give Ephraim anything more than thank you and a handshake. I set my alarm for 7am to give me peace and quiet over my porridge.

Gary had been with Alex when we had all gone to bed last night and I assume unless he had been whisked away by spaceship that he was still there now. The kitchen allowed me to make porridge with salt which made the start of the day so much better Ephraim was leaving around ten am for Windhoek so after breakfast I walked up to an ATM in the shopping centre.

It was 8 am the security guard on the hotel on the first corner wished me good morning I wished him a good day as well thinking once again how pleasant it can be to be friendly and civilised to one's fellow man and at no cost. I took one of my day's wages from my account and carefully put the money into an envelope that the receptionist at the Dunes had given me.

Sylvia was our leader today and on getting back to lodge I went and found her. "Please give this to Ephraim on behalf of the team and wish him Bon voyage and many thanks." She said she would and I had no reason not to believe her and after I said my goodbyes and thanks to Ephraim and it was just a coincidence of timing that I watched a little deputation hand over the envelope and speak with him as I had suggested. The teachers still weren't about I wasn't even certain if they had had breakfast.

After he had left the morning was spent pretty much as yesterday afternoon. The team had worked out a food budget for the next couple of days and decided that lunches would be up to ourselves by splitting up the money allocated for lunches and leaving us to our own devices. Everyone was happy with this as it left everyone on r and r and not having to do shopping. Takeaway pizza was proposed and accepted as tonight's evening meal. Late morning found most of us out on walkabout. I had spoken to Gary to see if everything was alright. Apparently, Alex had got frightened being on her own and so he stayed in one of the other bunks. Any comment I thought about making was avoided. I knew it would have been misunderstood.

I'd let the team know the area where I was likely to be and headed off to what was becoming my coffee house of choice. Two coffees and a meat sandwich later and I think I've stayed here and people watched as long as I should have and go see about some serious window-shopping.

There is an abundance of Nazi memorabilia in addition to some fine shops and I happily spend a good part of the afternoon admiring a lot of the African craftsmanship on display. A lot of which I can't afford, and much would have the same problem of transport as Charlie's giraffes, but I spot a couple of nicely made enamelled bangles that will be perfect presents one each for my wife and my daughter. The team have stayed fairly close to our lodge and I periodically see odd groups as I walk around.

Swakopmund is a big city for Namibia but with shops close to our lodge and also being near to the sea we have all that we need for the short time we are here.

I'm ambling along on my way back to the lodge when I spot quite a few of the team down a side street at an outdoor market. They are having a good laugh at something and curiosity demands that I go and see. From the edge of the group I can see Charlie in his underpants negotiating with one of the stallholders for his work clothes. The sight is bordering on old English theatre farce. Either the market man has had enough of the dealing or the sight of Charlie down to his underwear and he finally agrees to the deal and Charlie gets himself a pair of Bermuda shorts and a new pair of trousers and a shirt. They shake hands on the deal and he has a big smile on his face as he heads off up the road. "You were right Rob it's good trading here think I've got more trading than I got with my money yesterday."

"You haven't got any more giraffes I hope"

"No but I got something like a shillelagh that I think will use to protect them when I wrap them up and some new clothes which you can see" All I could do was hope his plan worked and I spent a short time walking around the small market before heading back to the lodge myself.

Some of the team came up with the good news, that during the journey at one of the stops, robbers were getting on the overnight train to Windhoek and robbing the passengers at knife point before getting off at a later stop. To suggest that this created anything short of hysteria would be an understatement. I promised them I would find out what the situation was and under no circumstances would I put them at risk. You have to trust me this is my part of the job ok.

This possibly didn't slow down all the fast beating hearts but at least we managed to eat the pizzas in quiet. Either they were the best pizzas I've ever eaten, or I'd eaten so much undercooked pasta anything cooked would have tasted good.

Gary had left me with the whole of what was a small dormitory to myself. He had spent the evening with Alex, almost completely out of the group and this morning wasn't a great deal different. They had shut themselves away from the rest of the team and other than check that there were no major problems I was quite happy to leave them to each other, as it gave the students that breathing space that teachers aren't permitted to.

Today is Dune boarding day. At 9 am we have breakfasted and are awaiting our transport we have been warned about cameras, phones and body parts. Peter's knee after his Fish River incident is as fixed as it's going to get and my only advice to him and the rest of the team is; "listen to the briefing". If there is any opening sand will get in it. The warning was not to be taken lightly. There will be a video of the boarding shot by a cameraman who has his very obviously expensive piece of equipment in an underwater housing, which reinforces the warning about sand.

Dune boarding is the most fun you can have without taking your clothes off. Its steeper than snow-boarding to get the speed up and getting your balance and body position right may be just as easy for a novice as someone who snowboards.

We are given instruction by professional boarders and as we trudge up a ridge of the dune we can see our cameraman is around halfway up the slope that we will shortly be boarding down. He is out to one side and ready for the start. We have been given helmets boots elbow pads and boards all of which we have carried to the top of a dune we grease the boards and hey ho off we go. Crash, crash, crash, I think there may have even been a fourth tumble before I got to the bottom. I did have sand in just about everything, but I couldn't wait to get to the top and have another blast back down again. The number of times you could go down was only limited by your ability to walk back up again and after three goes I was knackered and going up that Dune a lot slower than the first time.

This time I walked up to have a go down the other side, which was sledging down on a piece of shiny greased hardboard. Speeds were exhilarating. The finish over bumps as about as uncomfortable as it gets before pain.

The finale is on the board side and is a small jump off a wooden ramp set into the sand not too far down the hill. I was elected to go first, which gave me a chance to show how not to do it. Nothing ventured nothing gained last time down the dune flying a short distance but far enough the landing was good the downward route perfect for about half a second and then I was doing a couple of cartwheels I got to the bottom and I swear my smile was becoming a permanent feature.

Going first I found later that the photographer had got me a great shot as I left the jump. Sadly, that was our last time and not one person wanted to leave or had had enough. The session was finished with a desanding ritual followed with a make yourself sandwiches and soft drinks and I was pleased to see Alex was enjoying herself too. I had checked with Gary that everything was ok as she had become a worry in isolation but as long as she kept smiling without interfering the last couple of days should go well.

Our journey back to the lodge had everyone full of buzzing excitement. We had returned to the lodge to pick up our baggage and have a final shower before checking out. I don't think we blocked the showers as even though we brushed ourselves down and left our clothes outside the shower tray had to cleaned as we changed over. Probably only a token gesture but we had put a flannel over each of the outlets to stop any large quantities of sand leaving though I'm sure some must have done so. I checked the showers were emptying before we left, and it didn't seem to be any worse than when we first started.

I had spoken to the people at Alter-Action and they weren't aware of any on-going problems vis a vis the train robbery. There had been a while back a minor incident when a passenger had been robbed and the robber had made their escape at a stop further down the line. I passed the good news onto the team and they settled down for their last walk around town. Personally, I didn't leave it there, but further enquiries didn't provide any more information than I already had.

Alter had allowed us to leave our bags at their base. We would be given a DVD of today's dune boarding and we would be able to buy stills from the day's shoot as well. After we had left our kit in the safe hands of Alta we split up into small groups to have a final couple of hours in Swakopmund before we started our journey back to Windhoek on tonight's train.

We are due back at the outdoor offices at 3pm to see our DVD and if we wished to buy any stills of the day, which we were promised, would be burnt onto CD and available for us before we were due at the railway station. I returned to the café with the outside seating, sat myself down and checked through the itinerary for the final couple of days; but with particular attention to today's programme and our train journey tonight. As it had accidently worked out our leader today was Tommy and he had been responsible for minding the train tickets that we had bought on our first day from the train station in Windhoek.

 I'd spoken to Tommy earlier to confirm that he still had the tickets as we had all done throughout the month away. Visions of them blowing away whilst we were dune boarding had been in more thoughts than mine alone.

DVD watched, and cd's of stills and we are making our way to the station. We have eaten as it suited us the new accountants have split up some funds for meals. (Paul having got the sack which he'd not been too unhappy about.) I have checked they've got the sums right and haven't missed anything like transport to the airport or something equally as important. Thankfully they are on the ball and all my checking time was wasted and my fears were groundless. It's not a long walk probably around a kilometre and around twenty minutes later we are sitting on the station a quarter of an hour before our appointed time. The evening is still pleasantly warm and a soft wind is blowing. We pile our bags all together and sit and wait for the train. We are the only people on the platform; there is no one in any official capacity. We were told that we must arrive at the station by 8 pm and at that exact time a couple of taxis arrive and drop what must be other passengers off in the road outside. Suitcase wheels rattling along the platform and a couple of families with small children pass us by. I suppose if the locals turn up the train must be due. Well not quite we are still sitting there 30 minutes later others have arrived at the station and they too are finding something to sit on whilst they wait. The pleasant evening has cooled down. The gentle wind now has a bit of bite to it and most of us have got coats and warm clothing on.

We have been sitting here for an hour. We are taking turns walking up and down the platform and minding bags and its getting dark. Somewhere in the distance we can hear a whistle. If it had got any darker we would not have seen it but a long way away down the line, we can just make out a huge snake of a train crawling along. It is a long time coming. A massive engine pulling dozens and dozens of cargo carriers. It probably wasn't but I'd swear it was a quarter of a mile past when the train came to a slow halt and in the middle of all these cargo carriers were two passenger coaches. It was a good piece of driving to have stopped where he did. I can only assume that he'd been told to or that he had a marker some distance off.

There was a guard on the train who told us all to get on. No reserved seating or anything like that just get on and grab what you can. You'll be on this for ten plus hours a bit of everyone for themselves see what you can do. That had been my advice to the team figuring trading places and seating arrangements could always be refined if and when you had something to trade. I'd got everyone aboard and I was pleased to see that Charlie had got me the front seat of the first coach which should let me spot anyone getting on later in the night.

The journey to Windhoek is 200 kilometres and the journey time is given as ten hours. So, with an average speed of 20 k per hour; when the dawn breaks opportunities to do some sightseeing should be possible. Ten hours on a wooden seat wasn't much fun. Nobody was any better off than me except possibly Alex who was fast asleep with her head on Gary's shoulder; and most of the team spent the journey trying to sleep the night away.

The day had been long and adding the extra hours onto the dune boarding had left them devoid of any semblance of energy. Though the journey slow noisy and bumpy most got a half decent night's sleep and early in the morning as dawn was breaking I spotted giraffe and antelope by the side of the track. No one had any interest in seeing anything at all. This was their first opportunity in 28 days to see wildlife in the raw and they preferred sleep.

I spent a couple of hours watching just about everything that we could have spotted had they not been so noisy whilst trekking and I think I was the only one. They started to awaken as we came into Windhoek and I figured I was going to have some fractious teenagers to deal with once again. Just get to the cardboard box was my thought as we had accommodation there and all will be fine when the still tired ones can get back to sleep. We couldn't get hold of any minibuses. I suggested we should walk. We had done the journey when we first got here and as it was only a kilometre or so it shouldn't take us too long. It was a bit uphill I knew but the longer they stayed here doing nothing the more likely that the harmony that had developed over the last couple of days would very quickly disappear.

I told Gary what I was doing and asked him if he wanted front or back. He and Alex set off at a gentle pace at the front, which I was pleased about, as I don't like not knowing what's happening behind me. 30 minutes saw us at the Cardboard Box with our plans going out of the window.

When the team had confirmed our reservation that they had booked in the company's name what no one realised until this morning that there were two groups almost the same number of students, teachers and leader and they had arrived last night again booked in under the company name. This was becoming an unwelcome happening. Unfortunately, the school names on the booking form had not been recorded and the result was we'd lost? Have we? No, we haven't, the Cardboard box are going to book us in in another hostel for the last two nights of our stay, and not only that they will ship us there and pay the extra over cost.

They are going to send us to the hostel we stayed in a few days ago when we had our dealings with the Catholic hospital and the conjunctivitis. A bunch of sad looking emojis has suddenly become super smilies. They get buzzy and noisy again and they all head back outside to wait for the minibuses that have been ordered to ship us to the other hostel. Our leader had gallantly led the team without stopping to thank the staff at the hostel for sorting out our problem. Under the circumstances it was the least I could do.

We have rooms and beds and access to a kitchen. I have promised them that I will cook the meal tonight. They will be going to Joes Beer house tomorrow so therefore they won't have to cook an evening meal again. I have asked for a couple of helpers and Alex and Gary have surprisingly volunteered. The team have asked for a vegetable curry and rice and this afternoon I and a couple of boys from the team, have been to the supermarket and picked up the food. The walk to the supermarket is a lot further from here than it is from the cardboard box and loaded up with provisions we consider it as prudent to get a taxi back. The transport costs about £2 for the three of us for the mile or so, which adds little to the cost of the meal. Whilst we were out another school has arrived just a small group of eight plus one teacher and an ex-army NCO whom I had previously met at one of our expedition meetings. They were eating out tonight so weren't bothered about access to the kitchen. My leg was hurting again after the walk and having got warm and sweaty doing the shopping I considered it only proper to have a decent shower before I started the cooking.

I cooked rice two curry sauces one mild and one hotter and some pans of vegetables that are now mixed up on a huge tray in the middle of our al fresco dining table. Some chapatti like flat breads made with just flour and water and some salt, that they weren't aware of, completed the meal. Embarrassingly there wasn't anything left at the end. There was a lot of complaints as to why I hadn't done the cooking during the whole of the month as quite a few of them had lost quite a bit of weight though none of them seriously enough to cause any worry. There was only humour in their complaint and when I blamed the teachers for the quality of the meal and shifted the responsibility of the good cooking on to them everyone had a laugh. I felt that we were almost a complete team in harmony. It had taken most of the 28 days to get there. But finally, I think we had. The next 24 hours passed in gentle relaxation kit was cleaned and sorted, Trangias scrubbed and polished.

Most of the tents had sustained damage in the desert to their zips; what was left of the tents we put into bags with a repair list attached. Our penultimate day was spent getting cleaned and preparing for our final group dinner at Joes Beer House. My leg was still sore after the trek in the fish river canyon and when I was washing I could feel like a scab just below my crotch. The good thing about digital cameras is you can see instantly the picture you've just taken. Wow I've got a tick right at the top of my leg near my scrotum.

I think it might be a good idea to see the leader on the other team; ex-military, shouldn't have a problem getting the tick off me. Having just met the man a short while back I did consider it a bit of a cheek to ask him to do what he did, and I have to admit it might have been a lot more difficult if I'd had to ask Gary or a lady leader. Had the circumstances been different I'd have done it for another person which gave me the nerve to ask. We put the tick into a plastic bag having pulled it off me with a pair of tweezers. It wasn't a lot of fun having it removed; in fact, it was extremely painful for me, and it too looked annoyed and was walking up and down, inside the bag, still alive. I suppose I'd have been annoyed if someone had removed me from some of my body parts as well. I figured to take it home with me just in case my system became infected and maybe someone would know about it and able to treat it accordingly. I told Gerry not to worry about the prongs my body would eject them over time. I dosed myself with some Antibiotics and then notified ops room of what I'd done. We'd be back in the UK if I asked for advice and waited for an answer. As I wasn't sticking pills down someone else's throat no one was going to protest. I made Gerry a cup of coffee as a thank you and my lasting memory of him is of a smiling face and a shaking head in disbelief as to what he had actually just done.

We are ready to go out. Alex and Gary have spent the day in town where it seems Alex has indulged herself in the beauty parlour and the dress shop. Gary's had a haircut but not much else by the look of him. He'd almost made me look smart but not quite. He lost that by having his hair done.

The rest of the team look like they're going to the school dance; a few of the boys are wearing the clothes they traded in Swakopmund, but where the stiletto heels and proper going out shoes have come from that most of the girls seem to have, is anyone's guess. I should be worried for them it's a long walk to the restaurant as I have been unable to get minibuses to take us there and back we are having to walk both ways but telling the ladies that perhaps their hiking boots would be a better bet for footwear is likely to get a reaction that even I'm not equipped to deal with.

Although it's still early evening dusk has well been and gone and most of Windhoek have left and the streets are empty save for the odd person walking home. We are 27 people and I have suggested that they stick together as a group and not split up into small groups that possibly lose contact with each other. The herd instinct works successfully with a group this size and single persons and small groups have crossed the road to avoid any contact with us. My job as I've said is to keep them out of trouble I don't for one-minute think that anything is likely to happen but to make sure I'll do what I need to do.

From the cardboard box it would be around 30 minutes to walk to the restaurant from United Backpackers its around 45 minutes with high heels we are just on an hour when we get to Joes beer house and the ladies are not terribly happy. They want taxis to get back. I tell them that we have been unable to get any minibuses to take us back and forth. The school requires that there must be an adult on every journey. One, if I could have got one, could have done two journeys but I don't have enough adults even though 4 of them are over 18 they are on a school trip and still subject to local education rules and so I can't let them travel in a vehicle without an adult present my hands are unfortunately tied. Alex had laid down these rules and when I'd suggested a convoy the answer was "no way".

Our vegetarian is eating kebabs with everything that is not an endangered species on the skewer. I wonder if some of the team are thinking that a skewer and kebabing would be a good way to deal with her selfishness. I'm getting a feeling that some of the team "going to the toilet" are using the time to partake of alcoholic refreshment whilst not at the table. A couple of them are getting just a bit louder and a tad looser than one would expect. Gary has noticed too, and I suggest that he has a word next time someone makes a move towards the toilets. They were to do what he asks, or they would have to deal with me, which allowed him to threaten them without involving himself in being anything other than the messenger. It worked the word went around the table and unnecessary toilet trips stopped almost immediately.

Later with full stomachs and sleep beckoning we made our snail-like journey back to the hostel. Alex and Gary were hanging way back possibly discussing their late-night entertainment choices and sometime over an hour later we arrived back at the hostel. Most of the girls had removed their shoes during the walk and I must admit I felt quite sorry for them. They had all gone to great effort to look the business this evening but after 28 days in boots they told me that walking for an hour in heels was bad enough, but another hour was way too much.

We had a last chocolate together as a team. Tomorrow our transport would arrive after lunch around 2pm to pick us up and take us to the airport. The hostel checkout time was 10am but we were to be allowed to stay in the grounds until our pick up arrived. We had a last group discussion confirmed our times and plans for tomorrow ran through any complaints or grievances. Apart from still not getting through to Air Namibia there were none. Happy days indeed.

Then someone felt a need to make a speech. We've had a great time Rob we haven't always agreed with you or got along but we couldn't have done it without you. Thank you. They started to applaud and then Harry made a "thanks Rob" speech and thrust a parcel into my hand.

When Eddie had left us at the school project one of the team a keen photographer who'd taken the job of photo recorder had used a timer and a tripod and taken a team photo with everyone in it. They had been into Windhoek today and had the photo printed and finished in a nice wooden frame. I got close to nearly being emotional. I managed to get out of the danger and control of myself, just. I Thanked them in return and said I would always treasure the picture and the memory. I kept my promise and I still have that picture and its memories.

There was nothing left to do now but go to bed and sleep as much as we could; tomorrow would be a long day, we needed to be at the airport 3 plus hours before our flight was due to leave and because of the mix up at the start over flight times we were unsure as to whether the flight was leaving an hour early as our original e mail had suggested.

As we had been unable to get in touch with Air Namibia to clarify the situation we had booked the minibuses for the earlier time; having settled to get there too early rather than too late, as had happened at Heathrow a month back.

In the end, we arrived at the airport nearly 5 hours before our flight was due to depart. To be honest there wasn't a great deal we could have done differently without the risk of missing a plane and once in the terminal and then through customs the pressure would be off, and for us, it was.

Our seating got most of us together, or in easy reach of each other, and after food, sleep and more food the flight was over, and we were in Heathrow again. The sky was overcast we dumped the company gear with our rep who picked it up and the emergency funds left over, along with the account from the Catholic hospital which he gave me a receipt for. They could claim this back on the medical insurance if they chose to do so but that's someone else's department. Our coach has arrived, and we were on our way back to the school via the A1M. It was 10am and although most had slept on the plane the reality was that a month away had left them drawn and tired. They slept again on the coach. I knew that an opportunity to speak to them all again would disappear as we arrive at the school and stopped at a set of traffic lights.

"Hey, everyone, one more thing before we say goodbye. You've been a great team I hope you've all had a good time whilst you've been away it's been a pleasure to be with you all. And as every day is a learning day did anyone notice anything unusual about the pasta salad we had with last night's meal? No one said anything until Harry's voice, doing his best star trek impersonation, could be heard from the back. "It was cooked Jim but not as we know it" I couldn't have said it better myself and we all had a laugh "thank you guys it's been a pleasure." They were still laughing, and I'd just managed to get finished when we arrived back at the school we were greeted by anxious parents, some of the laughter turned to tears. They seemed to be coming from just about every direction.

Young Caroline's dad gave me a smile and mouthed a thank you and saluted me before walking away with one arm around her and her bag in his other hand. I've seen that somewhere before I thought to myself.

Alex and Gary were talking to an older man. Gary left them and wandered over to me. "Thanks again Rob for everything. Alex's dad sends his thanks too. He's the guy talking to her at the mo. He asked me to take care of her not that she knows of course but her dad thought she might be out of her depth. It's why I followed her around and minded her".

"Any thoughts about when you will be getting married?"

"Probably not ever" said Gary "I think that now she's back where she belongs we will drift apart like just another holiday romance I suspect."

"I can only wish you well and thank you for your support too." We shook hands one more time and he returned to Alex and her father. They waved to me and then left. I was standing alone in the schoolyard just me and the caretaker and in the rubbish bin Alex's walking poles. A statement of intent if there ever was one. I took them out and put them with my sac.

The caretaker came over "Will you be off soon then sir?"

"I'll get away now" I said, "are you waiting to lock up again?"

"I am sir."

My beat up old Mondeo was parked on the edge of the yard I put my bags in the boot and then it did what it always did. Started up and took me home.

Addendum

After every expedition we write a report for information
purposes to give a heads up on any difficulties encountered
any changes from our original plans. The robbery took
pride of place I suppose then along with many other minor
things I remembered the truck in Fish River canyon the
hostility in Keetmanshoop the excellent hospital in
Windhoek and the lady giving out confidential company
information.

I write a sheet of A4 on the individual performance of the
team personnel. It's a good idea to find something nice to
say about each of them. Most of the report will be copy
and paste and even though some have appeared to come
along for the ride and offered little in the way of input into
the time away, the fact that they managed to keep the
enthusiasm going for the 18 months or thereabouts whilst
the expedition was being put together is a testament to
them in itself. My paperwork was completed and emailed
to HQ. A couple of days later I get a phone call from
Duncan one of our H and R people. Rob thank you a good
exped kids loved you. Teachers were fine except the lady
teacher said you used group money without consulting
them. I've been through the accounts because I have to,
but I can't find anything out of place. Do you know what
she's talking about? I haven't got a clue Duncan. "

Any way I'll go back and find out what she's on about and
I'll get back to you. He said "And in the meantime, think
about where you want to go next I'll send you a list and
see if anything takes your fancy."

 A couple of hours later Duncan got back to me having
spoken to Alex. Seems you gave the driver a tip without

consulting the team. I explained what had happened and that the money had come from me, but I gave the team the chance to appear generous when they hadn't been.

"You won't hear any more about this Rob thanks again and let me know about where next." Duncan hung up and I continued to work my way through the list of available expeditions for next season. I should have been irritated but it didn't seem out of character and in the end came as no surprise. What surprised me was that someone had gone and told her what they suspected, as neither she nor Gary had come out of their room when Ephraim was leaving. I did wonder though who that might have been.

When the chance comes you sometimes need to grab it because you want to and you think it'll be right. And only in retrospect do you question how different things might have been if you hadn't.

I'd not managed to get a late season expedition so end of the year was spent on D of E training, some mountain leading, and the remainder of my time would be spent back on the woodwork to keep myself solvent.

I'd sent Duncan a request for a Mt Kenya expedition and he had pencilled me in subject to it going ahead with an option to go to Tanzania and Mt Meru should it not happen. I was quite happy with either of the options and in the meantime, he was looking to find me others that would fit in the time window. Most of the expeditions take place during the school summer holidays the six weeks off give the opportunity to spend 4 weeks away with sufficient leeway all around so that ten schools don't all land at say Nairobi airport on the same day leaving a logistical nightmare for the in-country agent to deal with and the possibility of our travel team trying to buy 250 seats on one aeroplane. The d of e training expeditions were coming to an end when in early October I got a phone call from HQ. Maisie, one of the management team I recognised her voice.

"Duncan has asked me to ask you if you can do 9 days in Morocco?"

"When?

"Leaving this weekend."

"Whereabouts"

"Jebel Toubkal." I knew I was clear not having any work for the next three weeks, so the chance was an opportunity to be grabbed.

"Why the short notice?"

"Leaders got appendicitis. We will pay an extra £300 due to it being short notice."

"Deal done" I said possibly too quickly I probably could have got more though in fact I'd have gone for the standard fee. Apparently only one in four people who visit Morocco ever go back. This would be my third trip in the last 18 months.

"Good I'll send the paperwork over thankyou Rob"

It was Wednesday afternoon. I had to be in Gatwick airport at 9 am Sunday morning to pick up my team. I needed to get myself organised and let my wife know I wouldn't be home for dinner for a while.

Morocco

So near the Topic of Cancer

Apart from the trip to Tunisia which turned out to be the only time it was tried the only job I do that is North of the tropic of cancer is in Morocco. Some of the leaders do eastern Europe and upto Norway but I've been dealt mostly the Africa hand and again like Bob Hope et al and Websters dictionary I am Morocco bound. I have driven down from home for the first time without a Friday traffic jam and now after a pleasant meal and a decent sleep in my hotel near Gatwick airport I am ready for what Saturday has to throw at me.

My company will pay for accommodation but not my parking fees. This hotel will allow me to park my car for the time away at no extra cost over my night's stay. Staying here is even more of a no brainer, as they will also provide transport to the airport when I'm due to travel. An early breakfast and I am in the airport it`s shortly before 9am and I can hear my phone ringing. We have found each other sort of. We are on different floors but as long as they stay where they are I will come to them.

There are three teachers two ladies one man and 12 boys. According to Melissa, one of the lady teachers, the boys are as fit as any group she has ever taken away. This is a regular trip from their school. Melissa, Jo and Martin, are all regular climbers, mountaineers and skiers with shed loads of Alpine experience between them. However, as none of them, experienced as they are, have any recognised qualifications, the local education authority, as usual has demanded a qualified leader to be with them. Melissa and Jo are quite happy with this, but Martin seems to resent anyone else being "in charge" and is consequently reluctant to get involved in the group discussion.

The team, as Melissa has said, look to be the fittest bunch of guys I have ever taken away. The talk is a quick one they're up to speed having spoken already to the original leader and as is usual on these short expeds apart from the time at the refuge they won't be doing any cooking. I tell them about "its cooking Jim but not as we know it". They don't quite get it but we're not going to fret over it.

They are friendly enough and they`re all keen to get on the plane and off to Marrakech. Melissa swapped with one of the boys and sat next to me on the flight in order to gen. me up on what the situation was, and how it had all come together, before we got to Marrakech.

The person who was due to lead had had a run in with Martin at their first meeting and again on the training exercise, mostly over how the expedition was to be run and she was not surprised to find that he was now not going to be with them.

I wondered when she was telling me all this how much the H and R team were aware of, when they offered me the job. This trip was a regular one for them all and on just about every trip Martin and the leader didn't get on. "Don't worry about it, get thick skinned if you're not already, and ignore him and his attitude. He will generally toe the line," was the advice.

Apparently, he'd had a poor season and been benighted twice in the summer, once in the alps and again on Gran Paradiso when an argument with a fellow climber on which way the route went then found him sleeping rough in the cold whilst the other climber was back in town at a bar enjoying the evening.

Jo will mind him she has a soft spot for him, and her mothering instincts will watch over him.

Melissa it would appear had had more jobs than I had, and though she enjoyed teaching she reckoned the best job she'd ever had was as a chalet maid and amateur ski instructor in Chamonix.

"I did some cooking, cleaning and minding I got paid, fed and spent all my spare time skiing at no cost. Best job ever. I think I'm too old for the chalet maid job now, so I teach. I have an honours degree in maths and so I didn't have much of a problem getting a job after I'd done my teacher training. The best part is I only teach AS and A level students. They don't cause any trouble at all, as they all need to be there. She told me a lot about herself and was interesting to listen to. I've spent a lot of time on planes on my own and sitting next to the wrong person on a daytime flight can be a nightmare. I suspect that it will be the same for them when they get sat next to some boring person who doesn't want to talk endlessly about world politics religion or sport. Melissa was something different though, assured and positive but at the same time easy going, relaxed, someone comfortable in their skin and with their life. She sounded like she didn't have a care in the world and the flight was too soon over and we have landed and still chatting, a rarity for me.

Marrakech was still warm the airport is modern and interesting in its design.

It costs around 30 dirhams to get from the airport into town on the shuttle bus which is about £2.50, and this will drop you near the Fjeema, but this was unnecessary today as we were to be met at the airport by a minibus driver to take us to our pre-booked hotel for tonight.

Morocco is a popular destination for us and pick up drop and into the hotel Ali is all as slick and smooth as any movie script could make it. We walk from where our bus drops us at the top of the road. Police are on duty and have as usual blocked off access to all transport. Across the park, cars, coaches, buses with trailers, stagecoach and horses, motor cycles often with trailers attached, multiple passengers on scooters, families on mopeds, carts made from old vans towed by skinny mules. A cacophony of noise everything crossing junctions and each other without aggression or contact.

Nothing has changed other than the date since I was last here.

That time, I was sitting on the park wall by the bus and when in Rome do as the Romans do. Or in Morocco as the Moroccans do. Quietly like I was waiting for a bus 35 degrees c and I'm wearing a fleece. No one is taking any notice of the guy with the beard sitting on the wall. You can learn a lot people watching and as its cheap and easy enough until someone is asking questions in Berber.

Je ne sais pas. Je ne comprend pas. Waving arm and more Berber and I am dismissed. Today is not for people watching though, I have a job to get on with and we head for the Hotel Ali, just up from the Fjeema. the world heritage site, where tonight, we will have our evening meal. The rooms are sorted, Martin and myself in one, Melissa and Joe are next door and on the floor above the twelve boys have got a dormitory to themselves.

Our contact here tells me that he is unable to supply transport to Imlil.

Imlil is where we will start walking from and where we are to meet our guide for the mountain.   He can only get us to Asni, which is about halfway. From there we will then have to arrange transport the rest of the way ourselves.

The bus that would normally transport us all the way is unable to negotiate a recent rock fall as it's too big to get through. We decide that it's best to negotiate a deal here to take us all the way rather than trusting to luck in finding suitable transport to take us the rest of the way from Asni. We need to do a deal with some Grand taxis, the ubiquitous brown coloured Mercedes that are out of town taxis. Our rep says he can organise it, and we leave it with him, to make the arrangements, for a pick up at nine the following morning. There will be four cars, four persons and sacs per car and an ops room unhappy about me spending some extra over budget money on day one. He comes back to me in less than half an hour with the deal sorted.

The meal in the square has to be done if you are in Marrakech. I have eaten there on numerous occasions and whenever I take others who have not been before they are never disappointed. There's only me who's been here before so sticking together and a gentle walk around is the best option. Martin seems to think he could wander around without getting lost and as far as he's concerned Two teachers and a leader is enough to mind twelve boys and he will see us later. I'm reluctant to advise him about where he might not be welcome, but my suspicions are that would be his immediate destination; so, I say nothing and trust that he will arrive back in one piece and breathing. We meet up again later, as we had arranged, in the square ready to eat, and although some of the cafes are filling with people, all of them are keen and able to squeeze in sixteen extra guests.

Filled with chicken and rice olives dips and bread we head back to the hotel Ali for some mint tea and an early night and shortly after we are in the room Martin has put out the light and is snoring soundly. Perhaps I should do the same thing though I was tempted to do otherwise. There was no 'goodnight' or 'have you finished with the light'. Pig ignorant git.

We had breakfast at the hotel as it had been paid for in advance as part of the deal and just before 9am we are standing outside the hotel waiting for our taxis to arrive. Loaded as we had worked out, and drivers instructed about staying together and no racing. "We have already been told by my cousin who is your agent" I am politely informed. Do for me rock and roll time.

The journey to Imlil is only a couple of hours. It's not inconvenient then to include a short stop on the way at Asni and this we do. The town is in full swing and oozing energy and noise as its market day. We stop here for a quick look around, pick up some refreshments and stretch our legs and let our bodies expand back to their normal size. The team will have a wander around and I tell them I shall wait here for them. I'm expected to share some mint tea with our drivers as they have invited me to join them for a sit down at an al fresco café, trestle tables and benches packed, friendly and accommodating. I would like to make a deal with them for our return journey but as I can't give them an exact time we realise that it's not a good idea. They tell me that we will always be able to hire taxis from Imlil and more so now because of the rock fall.

Our journey continues to Imlil. Our arrangement was to be dropped off near some shops and cafes, and it's here, our guide and host, Mohammad meets us. He has a house in Aroumd a short walk up the road. We will be staying with him there tonight, before making our way up to the refuge on Toubkal tomorrow morning. His house is on the side of a steep hill with one room on top of another that in effect makes his house around 5 stories high some of the rooms are only shells and are being worked on as an ongoing development as a gite cum climber's hostel. Having a boys only team makes the sleeping arrangements easy in that you put them all in one big room with mattresses and sleeping bags and trust them to behave and get some rest. We four were in another room on the next floor smaller but with the same type of mattresses and our own sleeping bags. Mohammed would be with us tomorrow and would also be with us to the top of Toubkal. He had confirmed our reservations with the refuge, that is at 3000 metres, for two nights and also organised some mules to carry extra food and supplies to the refuge for us.

The rest of the day should have been spent walking around and enjoying the scenery, but the weather has closed in and a cold wind was turning the light rain into sleet, which was sticking for longer than we would have liked. Mohammad tells me that he has lived here all his 35 years and has never seen snow here or known it get this cold this early. It's as though we have lost a month he said. I would not expect this weather until late November or early December. The forecast isn't terribly promising either as we are experiencing a cold front coming at us for the next few days.

I let the teachers know what was happening.

"Not frightened of a bit of snow are you Rob?" asked Martin he had a sneer in his voice and given that this was day 2 of 9 I had a feeling that it was going to get worse before this exped was over. I gave him a smile when I really wanted to tell him to go away and said I'd keep them posted of any further info. I went back to Mohammad who I needed to plan the next couple of days with to make sure nothing was going to go wrong. Melissa found me later. I was talking with the boys going through their kit and making sure that what needed to stay dry did so, and that they weren't carrying anything they didn't have to.

Mohammad had said we could use a store room to keep anything in that we didn't need to carry, and I suggested to everyone that this bit of generosity should be grabbed with both hands. We were here for extra days after Toubkal so cold in the mountains was one set of clothes and hot in Marrakech required another and the option to leave the surplus here should be taken.

Melissa made polite conversation with me for a short while. I got the feeling she was sussing me out in some way maybe to see how I was going to react to Martin's sniping. There is a small fire in a portable stove, which has attracted our group into conversation when all we were after was its warmth. The boys were well adjusted to this sort of environment; they were all part of a Combined Cadet Force group in the school, so, roughing it and outdoors was not a new thing for them. They were polite and respectful courteous almost to a fault and getting to know each other wasn't going to do any of us any harm.

As the fire slowly died down people wandered off to bed and after one final check out side to see if there had been any change in the weather I did the same myself. We slept well. Someone in our room snores. I am told I snore as well, but you don't hear yourself snoring so there's definitely another. Melissa says, "good morning and you snore Rob."

"There's oboe and bassoon," says Jo and we're all having a laugh except Martin who looks like he's lost his house keys.

Its breakfast time we have coffee and pancakes and after I do a run through with everyone re their kit, medication if they take any, water, snacks for during the walk up to the refuge, wet weather gear, sleeping bags, hats and gloves and spare batteries and head torches, passports and wallets. Always keep your passport with you at all times. When asked why? Identity emergencies whatever happens even getting lost with your passport you can get help. Martin isn't interested in the kit check and disappears outside to inspect the weather.

I have already been out, and the situation is too finely balanced almost on a knife-edge. It could go one-way or another. There is still a cold wind albeit not as strong as last night but at the moment there isn't any rain though the sky is leaden and threatening. We have decided to go for it the chances are it could go well but should it deteriorate we can always turn back. Our journey time will be about 6 hours to the refuge, which could get us there and back in a day if we had to make a hasty retreat. A couple of mules and their drivers are waiting patiently for us to leave. Mohammed has given them the extra baggage with our food and they have lashed it on to the mules back. I am ambivalent about using pack animals one side of me says that if you can't carry it you shouldn't be here and expect the mule to be pushed and possibly whipped up the hill. But the other side of me says if the driver takes good care of his mule then between them they will make enough for both of them to eat and survive. I will never reconcile those thoughts and it is not for me to tell others what they should do for work or to feed themselves.

This team does not readily embrace the leadership and team work ethos that would normally be on an expedition. They are all in it together they don't need anyone in command and they don't need to vote on anything either. If it needs doing, get it done. You'll do for me gentlemen.

From Aroumd to the refuge on Jbel Toubkal is around 12 kilometres. Just as we were entering the park we met some ladies carrying decent sized loads down the hill. The interesting thing was their footwear. They were wearing opened toed sandals with plastic shopping bags as socks to keep their feet dry. I couldn't tell if they had proper socks underneath though I presumed not. Just looking at them made my feet cold.

Shortly after, we passed Sidi Chamharouch, there was a hint of snow just flying around in the air and a little further on the remains of last night's fall was still evident. Though we are following a well-trodden mule track in parts the snow is thickening and though not dangerous at this time we will have to maintain a watchful eye just in case. We could see a way behind us a couple of other groups making their way up the mountain. The snow that's falling now is not causing any further problems and the path to the refuge is clearly visible and Martin has taken off out front and is stretching the group out. I get Mohammed to slow some of the guys in front down as they are in hot pursuit and to leave Martin to go on his own. Whatever he felt he needed to prove he could prove it to others I wasn't interested.

"Are we going to try and catch Martin up?" asked Jo.

"No"

"Pardon"

"No. This is a team effort this is their expedition I pointed to the boys and we will pace ourselves with the idea that we reach the refuge in reasonable time but importantly not burnt out because they felt a need to go quicker than is necessary."

"I think you're splitting the group up" she seemed worried

"Don't be silly he's split the group up and personally I don't miss him."

She was worried, and she wasn't happy. I didn't care, my responsibility was to the team not to some egocentric teacher. We stopped a couple of times over the next hour or so. The muleteers had decided that the snow was possibly going to give them problems later on. If it persisted they would have to return to Aroumd today.

It got worse. Yesterday's snow was still sitting mostly where it landed after it had been blown around. Mostly loose powder unconsolidated like polystyrene balls a bloody nuisance at best. Neve which is good for walking on it was not.

A short time later and we have offloaded the packs and shared the kit out between us, said hello to a young French alpine team who were moving very quickly with their guides; who were followed a little later by another couple of Brits who had decided to just "nip up Toubkal" before they went home. They had been climbing down in the gorges, but they figured they might not go past the refuge as their clothing and boots were inadequate for the snow. They too had seen the ladies wearing plastic bags and they were keeping that in mind as an option.

Martin was outside drinking coffee when we arrived I gave him a nod as we passed and went with Mohamed to see the man in charge. I had nothing to say to him and no interest in speaking to him. Ignoring him got him irritated but Jo started to talk to him as soon as he was about to start and that shut him up for the time being but I got the feeling it wouldn't stay like that for long. Mohammed and the boys cooked a good meal in the refuge kitchen I figured we'd need it as shortly after we got here the snow started to come down heavier and now there was a steady build up and looking down the valley although we were in darkness there was a clear view for miles due to the reflected light the whole area now coloured in white.

The guides had their mobile phones balanced on the window cill pointing down the valley trying to pick up a signal and any news on the weather. Mohammed was talking to the other guides picking up what information he could and what their plans might be.

The consensus of opinion amongst them was that if the snow continued to fall as it was then it would take a good-sized team of maybe a dozen experienced climbers to get up and down again and that they would be lucky if they got it done in 12 plus hours. They would have to break trail up and down and possibly risking life was a stupid idea and the likelihood was that if this continued as it looked like it might then tomorrow morning they would all be heading down. The French alpinists were not even thinking of going up if it stayed snowing and they had been out a short while back on the hill and their guesstimate was that there might be anything up to a metre of fresh powder in parts by the morning.

I got the team together and passed on the news that we could possibly be going back down in the morning if all the others were going too. There would be the added safety in numbers and following the others would be easier as they would probably break trail for us. We will make the decision in the morning but the general thoughts here, amongst the guides is to return to Imlil or in our case Aroumd first thing tomorrow morning. Mohammed confirmed what I had to say and although they were disappointed they knew that what we were telling them was the truth and that the health and safety decision is mine alone.

I left Mohammed with the other guides who were sleeping in the lounge tonight, partly for warmth but mostly for company and hauled myself off to bed.

Its six am and voices and footsteps are clearly heard. I got myself out of bed and peered out through the window. Except I couldn't see a thing. Snow had completely covered it in and so I grabbed my jacket and went to have a look outside. A metre of fresh powder snow in parts, was about a good guess. The morning was crisp, bright, clear and cold. I heard Mohammed behind me. There is no chance of getting to the top. We need to make an early start in case anything else blows in. I'll get them up I said "We need to eat something first. I have porridge on the stove two of the boys are watching it and making sandwiches as we talk. Good man I'll get the others up. Jo and Melissa were awake when I got back in the room but there was no sign of Martin. His sleeping bag was where he had been, but his sac had gone, and I started to get worried.

Mohammed had asked if anyone had seen him and he had left just after 4am according to one of the guides to make a summit attempt.

I did think about leaving him there and letting him get to safety on his own, but they could get down from here without me. The boys were well capable and with Mohammed Jo and Melissa and all the others, there should not be any problems. It was a decision I didn't want to make but I knew that with everyone but the staff going down there was great safety in numbers. I figured if Martin had the sort of problems that were expected he was going to need all the help he could get to make it down to Aroumd.

Mohammed knew what was needed and after seeing everyone off I spent the rest of the morning with the two staff left at the refuge. We had a language problem in that it was difficult to work out who spoke French worst. Their French, which was almost certainly better than mine, became distorted by their heavy accent which made it more difficult for me to understand and they probably thought exactly the same.

We understood coffee and they were as happy to drink my coffee, as I was to share it with them. We could see the sky suggesting that the weather was deteriorating higher up the mountain even though outside conditions here hadn't worsened at all and the long train of descending climbers had long disappeared from sight. There was some wind that was blowing the powder around come mid-morning I got the feeling it would get worse before it would get better. It's now late morning and Martin has just arrived back at the refuge. He was irritated miserable cold and surly the personification of bad temper.

"That's the third time this year I've not summited" he snarled at me like he'd carried the grudge back looking to start an argument with someone or anyone for that matter. Perhaps he considered it to be my fault he certainly wasn't prepared to accept any responsibility for his problems himself.

The refuge staff sensibly had decided to avoid him. Unable maybe to understand exactly what he was saying his tone left no uncertainty as to his demeanour.

My bag was packed, and I was ready to go I told him to get his sleeping bag and let's get on our way. I decided to stand outside for a bit to think beautiful thoughts rather than whether I could get away with killing him. The wind is getting up a bit now and whipping up the powder into little flurries. I went back inside to see where he was up to, to find him in the kitchen cooking.

"I haven't had breakfast Jimmy so I'm cooking myself a meal before we go. It's alright for you you've eaten."

It was an hour later when we started down the hill. The path that was well worn into the ground and visible on the way up had all but disappeared. The wind hadn't wasted any time in filling up the hollows and although we could make out approximately where the route went we had to break trail again through the snow. Then as expected the weather closed in again and visibility was reducing. We had lost the path completely even going at right angles to the way down we couldn't find the path again.

The river on our right-hand side gave us direction down but without a path we were walking almost blind. Boulders would block our route then without warning we would drop into a hole to our waist. We knew that we had ascended in around six hours quite easily, but we had left the refuge over six hours ago now and we were not even halfway down. He had hardly spoken to me for the last couple of hours and he just allowed himself to be shepherded and directed wherever I needed him to go. He needed rest before he turned into a zombie. It was getting close to eight o clock; energy was going quickly, we needed to find some shelter, as there was no way we were going to get down to Aroumd tonight. Up way beyond where we were guessing the path might be we could see a band of rocks and heading towards it pretty well drained the last of our energy reserves. It wasn't perfect in fact it wasn't even good, but it was all we had now. The loose powder wouldn't provide anything to build a shelter with, but the rock would protect us from the worst of the wind.

We got ourselves established on the leeside of the rock and tried to find somewhere flat to lie down on. We were on a slight slope, but it was all we had. I hadn't eaten for around 12 hours and all I had to drink was water from my bottles. One of these was empty and I changed it for the full one from my sac. We had sleeping bags and I had a Gore-Tex bivi bag with me. I told Martin to get into the bag with me at least he would be out of the snow but for whatever reason he refused my offer and dug himself down as low as could into the ground. I rattled my way through the night and as good as my equipment was it was a hard night under real harsh conditions.

Tiredness eventually forced me to sleep until the early morning light woke me up. Sunshine it wasn`t; we were too low down in the valley but only morning light nevertheless I was pleased to see it and pleased to have survived. The snow had stopped and the wind as well.

I couldn't feel my fingers and my feet weren't a great deal better. My Nalgene bottle filled with water was now solid ice. It had been in the sleeping bag with me throughout the night. Martin was awake. He looked like a bag of shite. I think and hoped that he'd had a bad night too and his snarling disposition unsurprisingly still did little to endear him to me. Getting going was hard. Boots which had been removed and taken inside the sleeping bags, were as stiff and as frozen as my water bottle. it took a good half hour to get them on tied and able to walk in them. The sun had still not shown itself but was on its way into the morning and around 8am we were loaded and moving again.

A couple of hours later and we have passed people on their way up to the refuge. We wished them well, which was all we could do and hoped that they fared better than we had done. Martin became even more morose as climbers passed us on the way up as we were slowly limping down. I knew his feet had suffered during the night. They had been grey when he had been trying to get his boots on this morning and the way he was walking suggested that he had as much feeling in his feet as I had in my hands and they still didn't appear to have any colour in them when I checked them periodically even though they were in two pairs of high performance gloves.

Late morning; we have taken a break. The sun is warming my body I am getting small amounts of water from my bottle. and a beautiful sight in the distance, 12 boys and two lady teachers walking towards us I don't think I've ever been more pleased to see anyone. Melissa smiled as she got near me.

"God you look rough" she said. She took a picture and showed me what she meant. My cheekbones were black, and my lips were cracked and looked as sore as they were. There were black bags under my eyes and my skin looked drawn and tight. "Who's a pretty boy then?" was all I could think to say when she showed me the picture. One of the boys came over and took my bag from me "I'll carry that sir" I really didn't want to argue with him, so I gave him the bag. Melissa gave me a drink of coffee from a flask she had borrowed from Mohammed, and I could see Jo doing the same with Martin. "His feet are maybe in a mess" I said to Melissa "if Jo could have a look later and if you need some advice come and ask me."

"I'll pass the message on."

"To be honest I said if his feet fall off it might keep the idiot out of the mountains, he's a liability." Melissa sensibly avoided the discussion which was a smart diplomatic move cos it shut me up and we spent most of the journey back to Aroumd in a comfortable silence. Mohammed served us mint tea and he was so obviously pleased to see us. We had almost nearly walked past his house having come in a different way when a shout from behind us had shown us our error.

Chicken tagine piles of cous cous and spiced oranges and sweet black coffee and the world is back on an even keel. I slept like a log the sleep of the innocent Jo told me that Melissa had checked on me a couple of times in the night just to make sure I didn't drop dead on them. "She was taking your pulse and checking you were still warm and breathing. I am not supposed to say anything", said Jo, "but I thought I'd let you know. And thank you for bringing Martin down He won't thank you but looking at him he wouldn't have got down without you and his feet will get better. I've seen worse, but I will watch him. That was the longest conversation I 'd had with Jo and afterwards she reverted back to her just say enough self. Maybe when you teach art you don't need to say much though I thought that must be wrong.

Food and sleep and let your body do the rest is my standby healing medical advice when you don't feel good but this morning I was on the mend and so was Martin. The team were ready to go and shortly after an early lunch we walked down to Imlil to pick up our taxis to Marrakech. The bags go in the boot and one adult and three boys per taxi and we are on our way back to Marrakech. Again, the drivers have been instructed not to race, or use their phones and to stay together on pain of death. Thankfully they stuck to the brief and a little less than two hours driving and we are back in Marrakech.

We managed to get ourselves into a hotel for the night. We have a hotel booking in the hotel Ali for our expected return, but they are fully booked for the next two nights and as we have come back one day early they are unable to accommodate us.

We have booked in to the hotel Afrique, where I have stayed when I have been here on previous occasions. It provides rooms and washing facilities its clean and friendly and well within budget. The rooms are on numerous floors in a square around a courtyard. The roof is flat with sitting and sunbathing opportunities the walls and seating decorated with ceramic tiles in a haphazard fashion creating an abstract mosaic look. The rooms sleep two three or four at a time with some juggling about we managed to get all the boys onto the same floor. Then two, two bed rooms for Martin and I and Jo and Melissa.

Martin didn't want to stay in a room with me and wished to sleep on his own. The hotel did not have another room. As all the beds were single beds Jo offered to swap with me she would sleep in Martin's room and I should sleep in with Melissa. Martin was quite happy with this arrangement and I couldn't see any good reason to rock the boat any further. Melissa shrugged her shoulders she had no problems with the arrangement when asked and so it was decided. Martin hadn't spoken to me since we had come down off the mountain. Apparently, he figured I was going to hit him and so was avoiding me as best he could, according, to Mel.

I wasn't bothered that this was wrong as it kept him away from me. We would have to find somewhere to eat for the next couple of days and when I explained about how we could go to the Fjeema and get different meals every night even if you ordered the same thing; everyone was keen to give it a try except Martin of course who was wishing his life away and waiting to go home. The boys had decided to split themselves in to two groups six a side and attached themselves to Melissa and Jo. It would be a lot easier to operate in two teams and most seemed happy with this arrangement Martin wasn't consulted but as he didn't raise any objections it was decided that he too was happy with the plan. I'm never completely happy when I lose contact with part of my team but now for the second time this week I'm getting myself in to a situation that I don't want to be in. "Relax" says Mel. "Jo's a big girl, she can handle the boys and Martin without any problems. They have been in a platonic sort of relationship for a while. She will mind him and wind his neck in. So, stop worrying ok? She was speaking into my chest so that no one else could hear, "These boys don't even need us they're well capable of taking care of themselves. These are "A" level students 17 plus and far from being either naive or stupid. I do this with this school twice a year and we don't allow idiots along and before you say anything he's not an idiot she said looking at the back of Martins head, but I'm not getting involved in a discussion with you about him." She fired this statement off at me and before I could speak she turned and was away towards the boys who were waiting patiently just a short distance from us. I followed along behind for a short distance mulling over what she had said and unable to find anything wrong with it, I decided to go with the flow and quickly caught them up. "Good" she said and then hooked the crook of my arm. "God I'm sorry" she said, "I was lost in a different world." She'd dragged her hand out almost as quickly as she had put it in and stuffed it into her coat pocket. When she'd put her arm through mine it had been like an electric shock and I was disappointed when she had immediately taken it out. This lady was only a few years older than my daughter and I think it was caused by a bad night on Toubkal, but she was causing a problem with my emotions. We walked around the square in silence it was still early, and the stalls were just starting to set themselves up for the evening. I took them down to the souk told the boys to stay in contact if they wanted to stop or see something. Fine just let us know, so we don't leave you behind. Mel had avoided conversation I was certain that she felt she had embarrassed herself and I figured it was easier to let her sort out how she was going to deal with it on her own as I didn't believe I had any help to offer. The time in the souk provided a fillip to the days enjoyment and as it had got dark when we left there the cafes were in full swing and serving food. I've eaten in the square more than twenty times and like I told the boys I order chicken and rice every time and I have never had the same meal twice. The basic meal comes with dips olives bread and various combinations at different cafes make a different meal each time. The evening walking around the square provided a pleasant end to the day we saw the others walking around as most people do. It's like a promenade all sorts of walkers going to places that don't exist. You see the same people going up that you saw going down the road. Beggars sitting patiently crossed legged wrapped in a shawl. A blind man walking the same route most of the day hand held out. Feeling the coin and thanking you relative to the amount you have handed him. The permanent street cafes still open. Tomorrow I will take my team to one I normally use when on my own. I show it to them as we pass. Here they will get coffee and a pancake that will fill them for four hours they will not need to eat again until lunchtime at the earliest. If we go there tomorrow, we will take over the place it is small like a front room shop. I could see the others at some tables at one of the cafes, so we disappeared around the other side to avoid them. There is a continuous sales pitch from the guys in the square insisting that theirs is the best café in Marrakech that you look like you need food best food best prices. When I tell them, we have eaten they insist we look too skinny and should eat again. They call me the chief when they realise that we are eight in total.

On my own here I have been offered ladies, of various sizes, boys, hashish, and alcohol but with the group I am not bothered by anyone. There are I am told a number of scams some operated by petty criminals and others by undercover police who aren't too friendly when you are in the local gaol. On your own you need to make certain you aren't compromised and although we are all together I have given the boys a "heads up" just in case. We have tonight at this hotel and tomorrow we will relocate to our first one booked as part of our original programme.

 I have drunk too much coffee too late and I am lying awake in my bed. Melissa is asleep I can just hear her breathing across the small space between our beds. I need to sleep but my mind keeps wandering back to an electric shock I got in the whilst on walkabout this afternoon. I came awake did I hear the door shut? Melissa is not in her bed there is enough light coming through the window to tell me that its nearly 7am I feel like I've had no sleep at all; but I need to be up ideally before the others to get them organised before we leave.

The door opens, and Melissa comes back in "Good morning" with a big smile. She is not far from me and I can smell the toothpaste on her breath. "You snore" she reminded me. "Didn't think I'd even been asleep." "You slept like a log again. That night out didn't do you any good." I was sitting on my bed still in my sleeping bag my legs dangling down, my feet on the floor. I wasn't wearing any clothes.

"I need to get dressed "I said

"The boys are getting their act together and I reckon they'll be ready for breakfast soon. "I'll leave you to sort yourself out then" and she disappeared again.

I took them all to breakfast we over spilled into the street, but no one complained. The waiter was rushing around when he spotted me and remembered me from my last visit.

The mobile phone man he shouts you trade me your phone now no I said not trading any mobile phones. He made a gesture a flourish of dismissal with his hand and continued with his job.

"What was that about?" Asked Mel.

"He wanted to trade phones with me a couple of months back. I was trying to explain that my phone was on contract and not pay as you go. He believed that I got my I phone for what amounted to one month and as he'd paid more than that for his he thought he would do me a good turn and save me money. It was either lost in translation or he was taking me for a ride or trying to. Needless to say, he didn't get my phone."

After breakfast we went for a walk. We dropped the bags off for safe keeping at the hotel Ali as I had told them about the Yves St Laurent gardens being worth a visit. It's a good walk and a pleasant couple of hours wandering around. Martin wanted to stay around the hotel and I was happy to let him do so. Jo had told me his feet were bothering him and the walk wouldn't do him any good.

Not that he would admit to anything, but he probably wasn't up to it. The rest of us headed to the gardens. We left the boys to get on with it whist I walked around with Jo and Melissa.

"Sir, Sir look at this. There's a frog getting carried by another frog what are they doing sir?"

"Breeding" I said, "breeding is a slow process with frogs". There was a bit of almost childish giggling going on and I figured they probably knew more than I did about the breeding habits of frogs. Later back at the square we split up into two teams again to finish the day in the smaller groups. Martin had been sitting outside the hotel and spotted us as we arrived back and joined Jo and her boys. In the late afternoon we took a last look around the souk; they bought a few presents for back home and drunk a lot of freshly squeezed orange juice from the sellers around the edge of the square.

I had to apologise to one stall when after the oranges had been squeezed and put in a glass they tried to renegotiate the price. I paid the man he still wasn't happy and was quite prepared to do some damage to what he considered to be a cheeky kid. I calmed him down and having paid for the orange juice, we shared between us.

 "When I said you could barter with the dealers in the souk I meant the dealers in the souk, not order an orange drink then try to get it cheaper. You have been warned." They readily accepted this, and we continued on our walk around the Fjeema before heading back to our hotel for the final night. We had left our bags in a locked room earlier on and now they were ready to sort out our beds for the night. We had ordered 3 four-bed rooms and two twin bed rooms. The boys were on the second floor and we had the next floor up. Martin who hadn't spoken to me for two days disappeared into one of the rooms and Mel went to check out the other. Jo was standing outside talking to me when Mel came out.

"It's not a twin" she said "it's a double. Will you sleep with me"? she asked.

I said "no" too quickly and I'll swear the whole of Marrakech heard the door slam. "You blew that" said. Jo. I didn't know what to say so I said nothing I didn't know where to look or what to do. "You could've spent the whole night making tadpoles" said Jo. "What are you going to do?"

"There's a bench on the next floor up if the reception can't give me another room I'll sleep there."

 "As you wish. I still think you're stupid. But I think it's also too late to change it now"

"Probably" I said and headed down to reception to try for another room.

My alarm is calling me its 5.30 am and the hotel has promised us an early breakfast as we need to leave at 6.30 for the airport.

There is toast, eggs, pancakes coffee and mint tea. I have woken everyone up as quietly as I can so as not to disturb the other guests. And soon we have the whole crew in the dining room tucking into their food. There was a frosty good morning from Mel. Jo was friendlier "Did you get a room?" "Nearer the stars" I said, "next floor up." Martin was happy he was going home but most importantly the boys were buzzing and ready. Our buses arrived 15 minutes early to give us time to load our bags and half an hour early we arrived at the airport.

I have never missed a flight yet and nor do I ever intend to do so and later that morning we have cleared customs at Gatwick. One phone call from Jo and shortly 2 school buses arrive at the pick-up point. Goodbyes are quick Martin gets straight into a bus we have nothing to say to each other. The boys all shake hands and thank me for being there. I never really got to know them or even their names properly. I don't think it mattered as I'd been told, they were well capable of looking after themselves and if they hadn't tried orange juice trading I don't think they needed me at any time other than to send them back down the mountain.

Jo shakes my hand and says, "Thank you."

It's time to say goodbye to Mel. She gave me a hug, which lasted longer than it needed to and ended it with a kiss on my forehead.

I wondered if I had made a mistake and if given the choice or the chance again whether I would make a different decision. I didn't really know either what I was talking to myself about or even thinking. I'm a happily married man who spends too long away from home. Maybe it was the right outcome lack of confidence and practice would have blown my cover and I had been so long out of the mating game I had forgotten what the rules were and how to play. Maybe I needed to see a psychiatrist or at the very least seek medical help.

My feet sorted themselves quite soon after getting home but it was three months later before the ends of my fingers finally came back to life; it was almost in a flood like a dam bursting. The capillaries or the nerve system or whatever it was in the ring finger and little finger on my right hand just opened up properly and feeling suddenly came back. They finally got rid of the white Raynaud's look that I'd been successfully cultivating since that night on the mountain.

The following week and I'm in the Cairngorms digging in the snow and the fingers have gone dead again. My pal and I dug a snow hole and climbed inside. It was comparatively warm and we were snug out of the elements. The memories of my time on Toubkal came back to me and then Melissa came into my head. The fact I thought of seeing a psychiatrist made me smile but I spoke to my doctor and he suggested that I needed to see a urologist. I saw a urologist, passed some water and gave some blood and went to Botswana.

Botswana

I'm a great believer in "things happen for a reason". The butterfly flapping its wings in South America and a storm developing in a chain reaction over Scandinavia.
Sometimes I think someone's watching over me. Then the cynic says, "Or maybe everyone who'd been asked before me couldn't go.".

When an apprentice completes their training they become an improver, not yet able to class themselves as a master they must expand their knowledge, done in days of yore by travelling to different places in order to gain greater experience. For myself I consider everyday as a learning day and have always considered myself as a leader still in development. This particular company I am freelancing for has its own development scale and as a result of the number of expeditions I have completed for them I am now on maximum wages for a month away. The HR team may consider that I am now a master however I still see myself as a journeyman and almost certainly in more ways than one.

If you're only sitting in one game then whatever cards you get dealt by the dealer, then they're the ones you have to play with.

My phone is ringing.

 "A little job for you Rob if you're interested. A month in Botswana and Zambia be about 2 weeks in each" Gift horse and mouth sprung to mind but "Why not? Yes".

"Good they need someone who knows the area and we thought of you."

"Well thankyou send me the details." They did, gift horse and mouth sprang to mind again when the email with the spec. my now increased fee and the contract came through.

11 in the team 6 boys 4 girls and one lady teacher. Then I looked at the dates and phoned Duncan in H and R.

I realised no one was watching or if they were they were having a laugh. I explained what was on offer regarding

Botswana and asked what happened to Mount Kenya and Mount Meru.

"Well, we let Meru go because we figured you'd go for Kenya and then last minute it fell through, so we put you onto Botswana as a sort of compensation. It should be straight forward for you. You're one of our Africa hands and Botswana is a lot easier to deal with than some places I can think of."

I think he was bullshitting me but the only thing I could do about it was turn Botswana down and that was going to leave my face without a nose. I sent back the signed contract and waited to see when I was going to have to give the team talk.

I drove 290 miles. I met some of the team and the teacher, Mrs Lynn Jones, her husband is a chartered engineer and she has two sons at university. She has a loud laugh coming from deep inside a body that didn't look like it was built for speed. I gave a five-minute talk and answered a few questions all in the space of less than an hour and then started the 290 miles drive back home.

I stopped in the Brecon beacons for a quiet nights camping. It's safer than a nap on the motorway at seventy miles per hour. My friend proved that to me.

I had six weeks to fill when my brother in law turned a job up converting an empty house into bedsit type student accommodation. We finished after a final week of twelve-hour days on the Friday night before I was due to leave. For once I was going to be going away with some money in the bank.

The school had nowhere for me to leave my car, whilst we were on expedition. Even though I normally leave my keys with the caretaker he and the other staff were away on holiday meaning no one was available to come and open up for me when we got back.

Public transport like mileage allowance is reimbursed by the company. I would normally on a journey like this one make another hundred and twenty pounds or so out of the allowance which goes towards my time for driving 600 miles and a couple of trains and a taxi ride each way isn't any easier than the drive down and back.

I get a fixed fee whether I do a meeting prior to going or not the only way I can get the extra money is on my expenses claim. The claim's checked but I don't need to be creative and put in spurious additions. My Mondeo owes me nothing and I have spare wheel and tyres in abundance at home from when my wife had the same model car; so cost is only diesel, my mileage allowance is a welcome addition to my income.

I am waiting patiently at the school. Today is our first day proper. A day when meeting the team again, all the hopes and aspirations can be talked about, a day for making certain that the passports are in order and in pockets. I am early, and fortunately so is the teacher, Mrs Jones. She has been dropped off by her husband and quite soon after, a couple of the students arrive too.

Mrs Jones has disappeared into the staff room to make some coffee, a person after my own heart. I wait outside for the other students. I'm not certain why as they've been coming to the school longer than I have and should know the way by now. One of the girls comes out and takes me to the staff room for my coffee. Lynn Jones has a loud and unembarrassed laugh. She tells jokes a lot and finds all of them funny. I think we're going to get on fine.

After coffee we make our way to the classroom we have been allocated. It's a Sunday and they who have arrived so far don't appear to be in any condition to do anything other than giggle.

They have sat themselves down at a table in the classroom where we will spend the rest of the time until our minibus will take us to the airport tomorrow morning. Over the next fifteen minutes or so the rest of the team arrive. I think that Lynn Jones, and I are the only ones not hungover. Given that we are also the only ones over 18 it's a sorry start to the expedition.

It appears that they all went on a caravan week away in Cornwall, which consisted of sun-bathing, alcohol consumption and sexual experimentation. Probably as near to a dangerous sports holiday as you can get. It would seem a good time was had by all and most had arrived back only yesterday. We gave them a few minutes to have a laugh together and then asked for the talk to cease and the day's business to begin. I think they thought it would be boring here after, but they did get themselves sorted out.

Given their condition I was even more careful than normal, if that were possible, in checking them and their kit over. Everyone was fine. I think parents had taken responsibility for packing which meant everyone who got to the airport checkout would have been telling lies when they said that they alone had packed their bag. We sent out for Pizza and relaxed our way through the evening.

A last drink in the staffroom and Lynn jones tells me of a game that the staff here have got.

Although they are part of the school her position as head of year limits her almost exclusively to the sixth form college that is attached to the school. As a college they take other pupils from other schools to do AS and A levels. She reminded me of this as not all of the students going had been here for the six years.

She then tells me, "We have an 'adopt a pupil game'. At the beginning of term, we pick a pupil we think we would want to adopt. There is no criteria for this other than you need to provide a reason for doing so. There's no prizes as there are no winners and the students know nothing about it. You can adopt one because you think they need taking care of because they need reining in because they remind you of you when you were their age. Basically, any reason you want. We are away for 32 days so when you've had time to meet them properly you can pick one and so will I and in a couple of weeks' time we'll review our choices keep going change our minds or whatever. Ok?"

"Sounds like an interesting game"

"We have been doing it here for a number of years now with some unusual results. We've always done it within the school because this is the first time we've ever gone away on an expedition. So, it's a slightly different format for me too. Sometimes I think it can tell me more about the teacher than anything written on their CV."

At that, I had to smile, but nevertheless I promised I would join her game. and having organised sleeping areas, we settled down for the night. Day one disappeared in the sound of snoring and I wasn't sorry to get it over. It's always better when we're on the road and that won't be until we're on the plane.

Our bus has arrived Lynn has handed the keys back to the caretaker. As it's Monday he is in school for the maintenance work that typically takes place during the school holidays. As usual small group of tearful parents are waving the students off. Given that they are now away for just over a month and spent the first week of the six-week school holiday in Cornwall they aren't going to see much of them at all this summer. Three hours along a couple of motorways and a short stint on the M25 as well and we are in Heathrow.

The team have sobered up and we are flying to Johannesburg via Charles de Gaulle. Today they are totally different bunch. Clever articulate friendly on the ball maybe yesterday was just put there to frighten me. It did. We have a long wait in France and it's too expensive to buy a lot of coffee there. The time is well spent though running through the itinerary for the month and how they're going to run the different jobs whilst they are away.

Typically, there would be more team members on an expedition and the rest days would be easier to fit in and problems easier to resolve but correspondingly they have less mouths to feed. They are all carnivores and with no vegans or vegetarians it makes cooking and food purchase a lot less of a problem. As it does if everyone is either a vegan or a vegetarian. Unless of course you are in Tunisia or Morocco, where even a plain salad seems to come with both egg and fish. I digress because it amuses me to.

At Jo'burg we have cleared customs and are waiting for our lift. We will travel by minibus to Gabarone the capital of Botswana and there we will stay at Mokolodi Backpackers tonight. There is a certain amount of unwelcome hassle from some of the people at the airport who are trying to capitalise on our group's search for transport. They think we are lost and still persist with this even after the co-driver finds us. He's receiving a similar sort of hassle until I lose it and we get left alone then and head out for the minibus. It's waiting not too far away with the driver inside, doors locked, and worry written on his face. He will be happy he tells me to be moving and, as soon as he is, as promised, he becomes a happy smiling man.

We have about 350 kilometres to do and when we are out of the city, this will take us with a stop on the way around 6 hours under normal conditions. As is usual, conditions aren't normal as there is an industrial dispute on our way and road blocks of burning cars and tyres have necessitated a small diversion. Probably about a couple of extra hours our driver reckons, and fingers crossed there aren't any more issues en route.

Luckily there aren't and slightly later than planned we arrive at Mokolodi backpackers a short distance, we are informed, outside Gabarone. It's still light and quite quickly they have their tents erected and are looking to cook some of the food they picked up on the journey over. The six boys have found the pool table and while they play doubles last two playing the winners, the four girls are left to get on with the cooking. Something that will have to change if we can only get them to integrate. They slipped into two separate groups on the Sunday and have remained the same since. Lynn and I will have to come up with a plan but I'm not certain what yet, as currently, no one appears to be unhappy with this arrangement. The team has organised a rota for leading, an accounts team, cooking and food preparation, transport, shopping and medical and risk assessment, figuring the last two could go together as neither had any immediate requirement. The fact that there was only ten of them made getting together and coming to a decision was considerably easier than a large group and they were making good use of this and getting things sorted very quickly. They knew they could change ideas if they proved unsatisfactory when it came to making them work and suddenly I found myself in a situation at the end of day 2 when there was the sort of peace and harmony that normally took at least half an expedition to develop and on some never did.

Day 3 involves us going shopping for our acclimatisation phase, which I have been told will be like a walk in the peak district but not as hilly. I'm not certain what they mean by that, but that's not unusual when my itinerary and information sheet has been written by someone who hasn't been here. They will also make a visit to the British embassy. This will all happen after a short bus ride into Gabarone where we will also meet our trekking guide and our in-country agent.

The team had phoned him yesterday and made the arrangements. They are on the ball and organised better than Sunday morning would have had me believe and I am happy enough to let them get on with it. Not impressed enough to let tell them so yet, but nevertheless impressed.

There is a bus stop around a couple of hundred yards down the road. The bus is every half hour and we are waiting there around ten minutes before its due. There is a mackerel sky this morning and the air is cool. It's more like the UK than the UK and our breath holds in the air. It's too cold to stand around too long and we keep the chill away by jogging.

Lynn is a substantial lady but has little problems in jogging up and down the road and I think her size hides a level of fitness not always apparent in bigger people. It's like rugby players and netball players no one could accuse them of not being fit and I think she falls into that category. We don't venture too far; it would be silly to miss our lift.

The bus arrives and on we get.

"Dumela dumela," voices from passengers inside and laughter and smiles. We have been warned that the people of Botswana are the friendliest and happiest people when they meet and greet you and though this sudden outburst of welcome is at first a little alarming the friendliness with which we are received reassures us of their gentleness. Heaven only knows what they would make of the London tube.

When you are British it appears to be even more friendly. We are still considered to be the saviours of the country from the time when it was called Bechuanaland and then became the Bechuana protectorate when we took them under the wing of Britain to keep out the Germans.

We settle into our journey sharing seats with the other travellers and as the journey is around ten kilometres we stop on a few more occasions and witness the "dumela dumela". We are joining in much to the amusement of the locals and all still on board at the end get off at the bus terminal which is near to the shops that are just across the railway bridge.

We are to meet Charles, our company man in Botswana, and he is aware that we will be on this bus arriving at this time. We hope. We are looking out for him. He is described as white small slim and with too much hair for an older person. He shouldn't be too difficult to spot and eventually we see him crossing the bus parking and on his way over to us. We are significantly more conspicuous than he is being a group of 12 lost looking, white people standing in a bus station in Gabarone. He introduces our guide a young man slight with the build of an underfed youth. He smiles nicely his name is Brian. He will be with us for 5 days from tomorrow morning and will meet us here at the bus station at the same time.

Brian leaves us; and Charles fills us in on where to shop. He shows us where the British embassy is so that we can drop off our copy passports and details in case of a worst-case scenario of anyone losing theirs. We pick up some maps as well of the whole country and specifically as well for the areas we will be visiting. We'll not need a huge amount of food with us over the next few days as our acclimatisation phase is from village to village where we will be fed; and our only need will be for snacks and to supplement our lunches. Charles along with his advice re customs, do's and don'ts gives us telephone numbers and local information for doctors, hospitals etc.

The shopping area is clean and modern. We pick up a couple of sim cards for our two emergency phones and I pick up one for my phone too, much to the irritation of some of the team who are getting withdrawal symptoms from the no access to mobiles programme that we always have.

Shopping completed; and we return to the bus station to get our bus back to Mokolodi backpackers. We are lucky in that seats are available together and we sit and wait. The bus is around half full when a number of street sellers board. Hot pies, cold pies various foods and soft drinks newspaper and haberdashery toys and anything else easily carried and sold. A quick trip around the bus and then they away again to try their luck at one of the other buses waiting patiently at the station for passengers.

The bus fares are reasonably cheap by UK. standards but as there are no subsidies for providing a bus service the economics demand that the bus leaves the station when it's as near full as possible. Fortunately, today we have timed it about right and shortly, after some more passengers have boarded, the bus driver gets ready to roll.

We get off the bus at our stop, bye byes all round.

The road back up towards Mokolodi passes by a G4 security base. There is a sliding gate bolted and two barking Dobermans are warning any potential visitors of their presence. Perhaps the dogs had a lie in this morning, as they weren't out when we passed by earlier on. Or perhaps they were still feasting on last night's intruder.

 We settle down for lunch, but we have to be constantly aware of the location of a blue monkey which has taken up residence in the trees around the site. We have seen him drop down from the trees to the roof of the building then onto the ground to rob food from the pigs that wander around the yard.

After lunch, the afternoon is spent sorting out kit and food for tomorrow's journey. Far enough away from the tents our host has set up some tin cans as targets and is supervising a shooting competition with an air rifle.

In the yard, near the office, on one of the trestle tables is a glass tank with a scorpion inside.

There are two known nasty scorpions in south west Africa. One in Namibia is a pale flesh coloured and the one in Botswana is black. In the tank we have the black one. He has ventilation, but he doesn't look too keen to remain in there.

The shooting competition is in full swing the teacher and I have gone through the itinerary for the next couple of days. The sun is providing just the right amount of heat to make life comfortable and relaxed. We are sheltered inside from any wind by the same boundary wall that's keeping the lead pellets from the air rifle within and the trees will provide enough shade should the sun get too warm. Life was too sweet. So, something needs to happen to spoil it. Guess what? The lid is off the scorpion tank and the scorpion is nowhere to be seen. Our host isn't alarmed he's pretty certain that what's happened is the blue monkey has caught the scorpion and eaten it. They grab them so that they can't sting and then scrape the sting off by using the branch of a tree like a blunt cutting tool. There hasn't been enough wind to blow the lid off and we're all certain that no one has knocked either the tank or the table and dislodged the top thereby letting the scorpion loose "but what if I'm wrong?" says the man. The only thing we can do is search through everything that is on the camp and literally look at anything that might hide the scorpion. The blue monkey is sitting in the tree. He isn't telling us if he's eaten the scorpion or not. Our host has a friend staying here and with everyone all out of harm's way on a raised part of the site Heinrich his friend and I start methodically working our way through the tents, the bags and the spare clothing. Fortunately, the scorpion is not tiny and is easier to find than some I have had to pursue that could easily drop unnoticed into a pocket.

After we've emptied the tents we take them down and move them in case the scorpion has got underneath. I feel like Arnold Layne rooting through the clothing having emptied the rucksacks to make certain there is nothing in there. The whole process takes the three of us over an hour and at the end we have found nothing. Heinrich is extremely sorry and as compensation and to make certain it doesn't wander back into a tent, he has offered all of the team the option should they wish at no extra charge the chance to sleep in the huts that he has around the site.

The group is only too happy to accept his generosity and they will sleep safe in the knowledge that if the scorpion is still around its unlikely to wander into the huts. I didn't feel a need to tell them that the last time we caught a scorpion was in a hut in Namibia. Once we emptied a room and four rucksacks and all but given up on finding a scorpion believing that the students were mistaken it suddenly appeared from out of a jacket sleeve it was small but with small pincers and a big tail it was returned to the outside to go hunting somewhere else in the dark.

Chapter 2

Heinrich's generosity last night made life this morning considerably easier. Tents were already packed away and the only things still to sort before we left were the breakfast dishes and any washing still hanging on our makeshift line. Toby is our leader today and he and Shirley our accountant have sorted out our bill with Heinrich and booked us back in five days' time after our acclimatisation trek.

We knew the time of our bus, so made a move as we had done yesterday; bang on time again and then not too long after we are saying good morning to Brian who is waiting for us at the bus station.

We are starting with a visit to a village called Ranaka, which is around 80 kilometres south of Gabarone; a journey which should take around an hour and a quarter but probably longer with stops. And then we will have a short walk to the house where we will spend the night, but before that we must meet the village elders.

The journey has been thankfully uneventful it's not like these guys have never done it before and at the house of the retired teacher we are enthusiastically welcomed in a way that we are having to get used to, here in Botswana.

Our bags are unpacked to get access to our clothing. We have been warned that there is a dress code which must be strictly adhered to. Ladies will wear a sarong or wrap around skirt over trousers and also a shawl or similar to cover the shoulders. Males will wear long trouser no shorts ever and will look smart to show that they have made an effort.

Our small group walks from our lodgings up to a walled area in the village. We are not allowed to enter via the first gate but must walk around to the far side and enter through a gate there. We are directed through this process by our host for the night, a one-time schoolmaster and respected village elder. We are outside in the garden come courtyard.

The area is out of the sun under the shelter of some trees. A number of rows of seats have been set out in front of the table, where the village elders, their chief and two policemen are sitting waiting for us. Other people join us on the seats. This is a council meeting and we are not the only business today.

The usual formalities are observed we are very welcome prayers are said for us and we do the same for our hosts. Most of this has been conducted by a man whom we assumed is the chief. We are mistaken when he introduces the chief he is sitting halfway between one end and the centre where our spokesman was, and we have now had a change of speaker and the chief introduces the chief of police who introduces his lieutenant. The baton is shifting continuously but it finally stops with the young policeman who stands up welcomes us again wishes us well on our visit to Ranaka and the whole of Botswana and assures us that whist we are here in Ranaka nothing will happen to us and we are safe to walk around and enjoy the hospitality of the village. I got the feeling that should there be any problems retribution on anyone stupid enough to give us grief would be swift and painful. As I've said before Brits are popular in Botswana. The history as is taught might not be as accurate as one might expect or if it ever is, but the end result is satisfactory from our point of view as we are always on the A list. There are a lot of places we most certainly are not.

We are fed well, have interesting discussions with our learned landlord and reluctantly we eventually turn in for the night. We have some clean dry outhouses which we sleep in tonight. Our tents have been left at Mokolodi backpackers in a store-room as we will have somewhere clean and dry, we hope, to sleep every night we are away.

Brian joins us after breakfast; he has a friend in Ranaka and has spent the night at their house. We set off after prayers that our host has demanded that I say. I'm reluctant to get into an argument with him this morning about my being a humanist so a respectful short prayer and we are then properly on the road to our next village.

Soon we are off the road and onto a narrow footpath. The path is dried mud and wanders around and gently up and down odd patches cleared maybe for firewood or coppicing. We work our way through narrow gaps in sharp thorned trees. Brian even with a small pack on his back is still smaller than most of the team and we're hoping that it's not too long before we are out of the woods, so to speak, and into open country. One last push through a dense copse and we are in the clear. The rest of the day is spent in a gentle amble.

The lunch break taken on an elevated section gave an excellent view of the surrounding area and the route we had just walked. It wasn't a long walk after lunch and soon after starting we arrived at our next village and met our new host for the night.

We had missed some of the days planned activities, but we were in plenty of time to help in bringing in the cattle, milking the goats and boiling up the corn on the cob in a cauldron not out of place in a scene from Macbeth. We were treated to some fresh corn on the cob. To be honest I've never liked corn on the cob and todays treat did little to change my opinion. Some unlucky chickens provided the evening meal with corn, sweet potato, rice and flat bread. There was another bread about the size and shape of a tennis ball, called a Magwinya that tasted like heaven on earth it had been fried in hot fat, was probably unhealthy as you can get, and I was nearly killed in a rush from the boys when second helpings arrived.

The accommodation was again in clean dry and Spartan huts. A single toilet made from concrete in the general shape of a wc pan. Was for our use today. Fortunately, the top had been smooth finished which made it comfortable if you were brave enough to put your bottom on it. I wouldn't suggest for one minute that there was anything dirty or unhygienic about our host, but a fixed concrete top does not lend itself to easy cleaning or monitoring of nasty germs and bacteria.

There is no obvious sign of wildlife in the huts and sleep was quiet and peaceful until around 3am, when what started with a single cockerel crowing turned into a cacophony of sound that destroyed that once perfect sleep. Most of us were up by five o'clock and at eight am the racket was still going on. Our host it would appear was so used to the noise she sleeps right through it. A breakfast of fried eggs and Magwinya and we are reluctantly on our way again. We have been gifted some extra fat breads just one each and no! no one will do a deal for theirs. Apart from the pesky cockerels our first couple of days are a fine start to the acclimatisation expedition. The team are well organised there is no friction, that I'm aware of, between any of them. They have sorted out jobs, leadership and thought about future days. They have planned meals, had thoughts about organising a different transport and have tried to foresee any potential problems. They are monitoring the budget as they have a plan for their finishing days, which as of this time I am not yet privy to.

Day 3 of our acclimatisation phase finds us on a similar walking schedule as happened yesterday and again shortly after lunch we are at a house where we will spend this evening. The facilities here are less basic and we all take advantage of the offer of hot water showers often a luxury on African expeditions. More chickens have died to provide us with our evening meal and though the food is similar as last night the meal is pleasantly different. It would be an easy task to bloat out here in Botswana apart from the corn I have yet to experience any inedible cooking.

We are lucky in this instance we are catered for every day and fed by people who know how to cook to start with. Given previous experiences on African expeditions this is a welcome bonus.

Lynn joins me after the meal for a tete a tete over coffee. You've had a while to think about your choice she said so who is the lucky or unlucky choice?

"It's surprisingly difficult most of them are at least ten years younger than my daughter and I'm not sure if I'm being influenced by her and what she was like at seventeen and how stupid her besotted boyfriends were. But I've had a good think and I think I'm going to have to decide between Charlotte and Alistair." "Mmmm I might allow you two" she said.

"If I can have two I will have those two please. If you were going to pick one of them for yourself I would take the other."

"Why those two?"

"Alistair is like me when I was his age I think. Neither lost nor directionless not needing pushing any way but helped in which direction to show him how to get the best out of his life. I think he could do something with the right help and if he doesn't get it he will be like me and consistently underachieve"

And Charlotte. She needs taking care of because she's totally the opposite of Alistair but if she fails it will devastate her and destroy what talent and ambition she has.

Lynn was smiling

"I told you I could learn more about a teacher in this game than is on their CV and you have certainly given me information about how you tick than I was aware of five minutes ago."

"Maybe I'm playing your game to suit my end purpose to point you in one direction when I'm actually secretly heading in another."

"If I've only learnt one thing about you from our first meeting and the last couple of days is you are open and too honest probably for your own good. You wear your heart on your sleeve Robert" and unbelievably my thoughts went back to Marrakech and I think that maybe she was right.

"Ok your turn" then wondering who she'd gone with.

"Charlotte too. different reasons. I think she's probably more vulnerable than you think she is as the case with you and Alistair you were once a seventeen year old boy and understand what you think he may be going through I was once a fragile seventeen year old girl. We all are or the majority are there aren't really many other types."

"Ok so pick a boy as well."

"Toby"

"Why?"

"He's quiet functional deep and stronger than I think we know."

The good thing about this expedition is that with only ten we have a better chance than usual to closely watch how they're developing as the month progresses and it's going to be an interesting time for both of us methinks.

Lynn wished me goodnight I shall take my new-found knowledge to bed with me and sleep on it. And she too left me with my thoughts. Maybe I'd just seen my psychiatrist I was thinking, but only for a short time before I nodded off in fear of being awakened again by a cockerel choir.

We were late getting up today the previous night's disturbances had taken its toll on some of our reserves but it's of little importance as we only have a short half day walk to the village of Manyana where amongst other delights we will be visiting some ancient rock paintings, and, in the evening, we have lessons in African drumming.

Once again the best laid plans of mice and men. I should have seen it coming everything was going too well. After our short visit to the rock paintings and before our evening meal two of the team have got wall to wall chunda. Unfortunately for Lynn its two girls. We have been allocated two huts in the village the girls and Lynn have one, whilst the boys, who have made to promise me faithfully, that they won't be sick, and I have the other. There is hot water here too so getting themselves cleaned and refreshed isn't a big problem. Lynn has sorted them, but neither is interested in food and are looking to stay out of our drumming programme and get some sleep.

I'm certain it has had nothing to do with the food in general but maybe the corn that they ate yesterday was the culprit. I'm always keen to blame the corn but realistically if it was the corn I think it would have made them sick long before it passed out of their stomach. Lynn is keeping an eye on them while I try and monitor whatever else is happening. When she is ready to eat I sit outside the hut. The girls are aware that I'm outside and as they are not sleeping yet they can monitor each other knowing that I will come in if they call me.

There is an offensive aroma from inside the room. They have been provided with a bucket each and both have probably used them. Some ventilation is needed, as the smell is enough to start everyone else off if they're going to spend the night in there.

I've forgone the drumming tuition, which is a bit of a disappointment, but primarily I'm here to work not to enjoy myself and I stay outside the door to the hut to allow Lynn the chance to sit and relax. She did after all have a fair old mess to clean up.

The girls are rocky this morning they're still reluctant to eat and so I've got Brian to find out about transport back to Mokolodi backpackers a day early. The staff there can easily accommodate us as we are the only ones camping and there is plenty of space available for us. We need to contact the people where we would be staying tonight, and

I have asked Brian to do the honours and let them know that we will not be arriving.

Fortunately, they won't be out of pocket, as our visit is paid in advance, and it is us who will have to absorb the extra over cost. Give our accountants a little juggling to do. Better to have the problem early when the chances to save money are still available. We get two buses back to our stop near Mokolodi and although the girls are starting to feel better continuing with the trek for another day would have likely made them worse.

I am more than happy to be back here. I've made certain that Brian too is not out of pocket having lost a day's work and Charles, our agent, has promised that all will be done as it was planned, as the money has been paid into the business account.

The tents are up and sorted there was no mention of the scorpion. The blue monkey is still dropping in from the trees and stealing food from the pigs and anywhere else it can get it from. We have access to a kitchen and a team of cooks that take pride in what they serve. Apart from the girls being sick for an unknown reason the first week has gone well. I have had a substantial pay rise, the teams organised, the foods good, everyone is friends, I should be worried, but I'm not if it ain't broke don't fix it and certainly don't break it.

Chapter 3

This team is proving to be always on the ball. This time the accountants have had a word with the staff at Mokolodi and between them have come up with a plan to hire a minibus to take us up north. There are twelve of us in total, so a minibus is big enough for us all as long as we have storage for our bags.

With a small group a decent roof rack is a problem solved. This is even better the driver who owns this bus also has an enclosed trailer to carry all of the bags in a safe and secure way.

When we left here our original plan required us to take a bus to Francistown. Then after spending the night, there we would travel onto Maun and the Okavango delta and then after the delta to Kasane, where we cross the Zambezi river and into Zambia. The itinerary was dictated by the availability and times of the public transport. Although the minibus won't be needed when we are in the National Parks, the bus and driver are based in Maun which means that he's happy to return and pick us up part way through our programme. Our original plan was to use public bus service and we needed to go that route due to the services and timetables.

As we have no accommodation booked in Francistown and would have to sort that either before we left or when we arrived an even worse idea. Therefore, travelling straight to Maun and leaving out Francistown is a better plan altogether.

So, juggling with our itinerary allows an extra night at Mokolodi which would give the girls, already on the mend, an extra day to recuperate.

They got themselves together as a group talked it through then ran it past me. I couldn't see anything to worry about as, an added bonus, we would be back within our original budget as well. We had a plan and it was better than the original one and worth adopting.

That was Monday. Tuesday, we did a shop in Gabarone and come Wednesday at 8am we were ready to roll when our driver with wife, and minibus with trailer arrived at the gate. The minibus is brand new as is the trailer the inside even smells like a new vehicle straight from the showroom. The windscreen has a crack in it. Low down out of the drivers view but a crack, nevertheless. I often think that they come off the production line cracked; full windscreen may only come as an extra or on the deluxe version.

850 K and 10 hours and we are in Audi camp about 10 k outside of Maun where we will spend the night.

The campsite had been pre-booked by our company as part of their admin programme. It was safer to book this in advance to be certain of our accommodation rather than leave it to chance and booking it when we were in country.

We will travel from here into the Okavango delta tomorrow morning using transport supplied by the camp. Our minibus driver will pick us up again in a couple of days, but today has been a long one and we grab some food at the onsite restaurant and head for bed. The two days saved from the original programme have allowed Ellen and Simone to recuperate and they are well enough now for us not to be concerned about them any longer.

Though the girls are not quite super fit yet they are eating properly again and well on the mend. We will never know what it was that caused the problem, but it was just those two and just the one night. We shall keep our fingers crossed.

It's early in the morning. We have slept well; everyone is fit and raring to go. Last night I got a heads up from some backpackers who had just come back from a couple of days in the delta and they told me there was a shortage of water suitable for purification. Given that we'd just got the girls sorted after the previous problem I was reluctant to risk trusting to boiling or chlorine or iodine to purify the water. We were lucky the campsite managed to sell us enough bottled water to keep us going for the time we are away.

We have breakfasted packed our gear and are waiting for our transport to take us on our Okavango adventure. Tony is our leader today and he has managed to get everyone up and ready; a minor miracle given the timescale of yesterday. Lunch is sandwiches cheese or jam or both if that's how your taste goes. Never quite got that combination myself, but surprisingly to me, most in this group seem to favour the flavour.

Our truck arrives open backed as the canvas cover has been taken off. Typical go anywhere do anything vehicle that's done it all looking at its bruises and dents. Once again we have a happy smiling driver and it's my privilege to join him in the cab. The team are safe in the back with Lynn and a number of other adventure seekers and I can from here, if needs be, slow him down or stop him texting or phoning should I need to do so. We are on the way and before long we are off road and following a dirt track.

 Up ahead another vehicle has stopped on the track. A puncture and there is no way around it, so we settle for a wait as they change the tyre. Its position is awkward for the task and it takes a lot longer than normal but there is no shortage of help as it's carrying either army personnel or heavily armed park rangers.

Job done, and we are back on our way now and crossing wet areas were the water comes into the cab on the odd occasion. My driver has managed to keep his feet dry, as he is aware of the problem; his English isn't good enough to let me know about the ingress, but it doesn't get me a second time.

We arrive at the side of an expanse of water; green islands dotted within we have reached the start of our Makoro journey. We will travel now in dugout canoes called Makoros made from the sausage tree. We will be two to a canoe with a poler who will hopefully propel us gently to our campsite. Lynn Jones and I are in a mokoro together. Her bag is in the bow and mine is behind me as we set off. There are no seats as such and we are sitting on pads of straw. It's probably the most relaxed time I have ever spent journeying in Africa. The sun is high now and its pleasantly warm without being excessive. A sun hat stops my head burning and I'm pleased to see that the rest of the guys have taken my advice and done the same. There is an unusual collection of hats and one of the boys is sporting a turban that he's created from a pale blue scarf he's been wearing most of the time he has been here.

Sometimes animals will come to the water to drink but it's quiet; bird noise is just about the only sound but now my bottom is wet from the boat seeping and my relaxed position is needing to shift to escape the irritation. Lynn has a distinct advantage over me in that her ample hips have kept her bottom out of the water as they're squeezed higher up on the mokoro sides.

My tent is in its bag and is strapped to the outside of my rucksack. I get my tent and stick it underneath me and although I am still wet the problem is not getting any worse and tranquillity is once again in house and the enjoyment of my journey continues.

I have lost track of time and almost nodding off when calls from the polers let us know we have arrived at our camp for the night. The area where we are to camp is around 100 metres from the water. I have reminded the team that there is a possibility that Bilharzia is present in the water here. This infection is caused by a worm that gets into the water from freshwater snails. It isn't user friendly and although the jury is still out on whether it's present in the Okavango my brief is to air on the side of caution. We have as a result of the heads up brought enough bottled water from Audi camp to keep us going for the couple of days we are to be here. We will behave as if we are in the desert. Water is for drinking and cooking not for washing body parts. Wet wipes if you have them and need to clean anything important.

The polers as you would expect, have been here many times before and their tents though big heavy and old fashioned are quickly erected and their gear stowed away. We fit in around them and try to stay together as a big group, rather than spreading ourselves about in search of privacy. It is not unknown for animals to wander around at night and creating a mass of people into a lump on the ground will hopefully deter any intruders from wandering through but encourage them to go around.

The afternoon was spent on a walking safari. Giraffe, zebra, wildebeest, lots of birds all reasonably close for the troops to take pictures but not close enough to see their eyes. The meal was simple and functional it even had meat in it. Hot dog sausages can taste great when you're hungry. I suppose anything can taste great when you're hungry but for a change our cooks on this team are good at making simple food into something near delicious and that's a bonus on any expedition.

The polers and our guides have made a decent sized fire and the evening is spent enjoying what warmth it has to offer. Away from the fire the air is cooler and as the fire starts to reduce people are making a move to bed. The only concession to using water for hygiene is teeth cleaning and shortly after I too am off to sleep. But before I've even got my boots off "Rob Rob" I can hear someone whispering. "Come look see" It's one of the guides outside my tent. "Cobra "he whispers, "You want to take picture?" I grab my camera and follow him quietly.

One of the other guides is standing by a bush. He has a pole inside the bush forcing the branches apart to expose the inside. I look inside but can see nothing. Arthur our guide shines his torch into the bush. "Sorry Rob no cobra." Not a worry thanks anyway." And I haul myself back off to my tent. Make certain zip tight. Sleep.

Sometime in the middle of the night I can hear more noise. It's the sound of something big coming through the bushes not too far behind me. I don't want to put my torch on to look at the time and I'm hoping that whatever it is stays far enough behind me to avoid some serious damage. Later when it's all gone quiet again I settle down to sleep. Whatever it was too big for me to negotiate with and I figured it was not a good idea to let it know I was there.

"Hippo" says Arthur when I stick my head out of the tent at daybreak. "Come look" Even though they were in my tent with me, I shook my boots out to check nothing was sleeping in them and followed Arthur into the bushes. Maybe twenty feet behind was a channel flattened through the bushes. It looked like someone had taken a Landrover through it. The bushes were destroyed, and the ground had obviously had something substantial go through it.

Arthur shrugged his shoulders and walked off. Not a lot else to do or say I assume. Later today we will be returning to Audi camp but first after breakfast we will have another walking safari; a lot of this was almost a repeat of yesterday afternoon; as time was the deciding factor and unable to take advantage of anymore we regrettably broke camp and were poled back to the truck waiting to take us back to Maun.

The Okavango had a lot to offer but sadly we didn't have the time to explore even a small part of it. That night back at camp we all promised ourselves that we would make another trip back sometime in the future. I don't know if anyone ever did.

We are sitting in the al fresco bar. Soft drinks bottled water and we should all be happy. They are quiet, and I ask "Why? after such an interesting couple of days in the delta. I know it wasn't long enough but what you got was better than you look like you thought it was"

"We're a bit bothered about the trek in the gorge came the answer. We've all been a bit under the weather. Not as bad as Ellen or Simone but we've had the runs for a few days and we're not feeling great and except for Toby no one's looking forward to it because we don't think we can do it."

"Yes, you can" I said. "What's on telly on Tuesday night that you need to see?" "Don't know here we've not seen any television since we've been here"

"Right what homework have you got. Who's coming around to get you to do a job. The only thing you've got to do is the Botoka gorge walk"

"But it's the hardest trek around here."

"We can do it. We will do it as a team. We will take care of each other we will share the loads; so, we carry what we can when we can. We will help each other and really learn what teamwork is. We are not in a hurry and all we have to do is concentrate and apply ourselves. Pain is temporary giving up is forever. You have worked together for 18 months in order to fly 5000 miles to do the Botoka gorge and you are thinking of giving up before you start. This is your only chance in this team. You may comeback like you think to the delta, but it won't be as you are in this group at this time. If you don't take your opportunity now you will live to regret it. We are a team and the only people we need to convince is ourselves. Like I said pain is temporary giving up is forever. It's a metaphor for life in every way. So! are we all in this together?"

I got a 'yes' almost in unison and a smile from Lynn that made my day. Later over a late hot chocolate "I told you It's on your sleeve Robert."

"No. it's not I said and pulled my sleeve up. Its tattooed on the inside of my arm."

"I'd notice the script" she said "but I hadn't seen what it said, and you'd never volunteered the info until now. does the other arm have anything on it?

I showed her the other arm. "Nothing as yet but when I get home I've booked a date with the tattooist and he will put on it "one life one chance live it love it" then I will have the philosophy as well as the mantra."

You must send me a picture when it's done and thank you for the talk it's lifted them better than anything else could have done.

Our driver arrived nice and early. It's Sunday morning. We are at the halfway point in our expedition. Today we will head north stopping for lunch en route where tomorrow morning we will be going on another Safari.

We pick up some sandwich makings in a roadside shop and later on stop to make them in a layby on the road. Without warning out of the undergrowth a man carrying two spears suddenly appears and proceeds to join us for lunch. He is not about to make a contribution but feels that we should feed him as he is here. Our driver and his wife are in the vehicle and don't seem too keen on translating or getting into conversation with our new-found friend. We have just enough food to feed us, but I share mine with him and he seems more than happy until I tell him we have no alcohol but only a drink of water. He takes the bottle I give him, and I suggest that if everyone has finished eating they should get themselves back into the truck and ready to get away.

They have picked up their rubbish and put it all into a plastic shopping bag. I shake hands with our luncheon companion and wish him well. The team are in their seats and our driver is on his way as I shut the side door and before I can sit down. He seems quite relieved to be departing and I must admit I was more than happy myself to be leaving the scene. I'm not bothered by unusual dinner guests but gladiators with spears can bother me a bit.

The driver's wife calls for the rubbish bag. She puts paper and the remains of their lunch in it, ties it up, winds down the window and chucks it out onto the road. Maybe I have spent too long in Africa as I am no longer surprised by this sort of thing.

We camp at the park that night a couple of the team feel a bit sick which they think was to do with the bumpy road and indigestion caused by our spear man's appearance. The programme is hopefully to see lion. I have often suggested to groups that if they want to see lion guaranteed they should go to London zoo. This visit to Chobe national park which started at 6.30 am which at that time of the day is about as cold as it could get turned into a pursuit with other vehicles in search of the elusive cats.

Lions are not stupid they have an instinct for survival which if it suits them to do so means they often disappear when four-wheel drives loaded with tourists are teararsing over the front lawn. If there's nothing for the lion to eat it doesn't get its body fed by tourists taking pictures unless of course it gets a chance to eat a tourist. Either the tourists were tasty elsewhere this morning or wildebeest or antelope are on the menu at another venue. The end result was the team got cold, very cold and didn't see anything that they hadn't seen two days before in the Okavango.

A sad bunch of faces were at our camp trying to stop the cold rattle whilst cooking then eating breakfast. It was a downer and the first of the expedition I kept my fingers crossed it would be the last. I must stop doing this crossed fingers thing it seems to be the kiss of death to good omens.

I'm ok as are Lynn and Toby. Everyone else has the shits good style. And what isn't coming out of their rear end isn't getting that far and coming back the way it just went in. All I can do is try and find what the cause was and, in the meantime, keep them hydrated and away from the food and cooking.

Toby and Lynn will do all of the cooking while in the meantime I will organise the next couple of days as we are shortly going to Zambia. The end of our travels in Botswana finds us at Kasane. We will get the ferry across the river Zambezi to Zambia. Slightly further up river from the ferry, near to where the Chobe river joins the Zambezi, is a dot on the water which is the point on the border between Namibia, Zambia, Botswana and Zimbabwe. It is apparently the only place in the world where four borders cross each other.

Before we can cross we need to go through customs which this time goes smoothly, and we then wait with the other foot passengers, to travel over. We have said goodbye to our driver and his wife. He has been of good service to us. We haven't crashed or broken down and has been on time always a plus in Africa.

Zambia

We are waiting for the ferry, which will carry us over. The ferry just goes back and forth in a straight line all day. It makes its money from carrying commercial vehicles. These are loaded on first and then the foot passengers find somewhere to stand. The crossing is over quickly. There was in the past been a charge for travelling over and "gullible tourists" have been charged by more than one person for the journey even though they have nothing to do with ferry itself but have seen an opportunity to make a quick dollar from the unsuspecting.

Our arrival and walk towards the buses has numerous traders trying to buy shoes from us. This was totally unexpected. We are normally bombarded by traders trying to sell us things not by ones who want to buy what we might have.

Most of the African travellers and the dealers are wearing plastic sandals or have bare feet; few have typical European footwear such as trainers or boots.

I spot a driver holding a written sign with our school name just about legible and soon we are en route to our base at Jollyboys backpackers in Livingstone, disappointingly for the traders with all of our footwear.

The bus was good value and the team were happier than yesterday the weather had cheered up a bit it was warm and though most of them had got over whatever bug had decided to evacuate their bodies they were a long way from feeling on top of the world. Just as well said Lynn "cos they're halfway down and in Africa." She started giggling I didn't mind the joke, but I'd missed what she said at first, got half of it and when it was repeated it lost some of its impact. This didn't bother Mrs Jones and she proceeded to laugh a second time.

They'd kept themselves hydrated and even though they had eaten, some were still hungry, and ready for anything available to eat. I'd advised them not to bloat out and I could only hope they would take some notice. I would avoid crossing my fingers for a while just in case.

There was a small problem. We weren't staying at Jollyboys backpackers but Jollyboys camping, same ownership different site, fifteen minutes-walk away down the road. They had a vehicle going down there shortly they would be able to take four or five of the team and a couple of extra bags in the back.

Lynn took the worst of the walking wounded and I, having got directions from reception to where we were supposed to be, took the remainder of the team. Our map, sadly, we found out much later, had a turning missing and what should have been fifteen minutes found us courtesy of some further inaccurate advice from some locals, way off course and having to retrace our steps as the only sure way of finding our campsite. We stopped at the local police station that sent us back to our original starting point. We knew this was wrong but figured that eventually we would find someone who knew where our camp was and probably the best place would be where we started from.

I got another map. The left turn we had in front of the police station should have been right and then immediately left and twenty minutes after leaving one Jollyboys for the second time we were at the other in Chipembi Road behind the golf course. When we explained what happened all the team were blaming me for us getting lost " You should have known it was by the golf course"

"Par for the course" says Lynn "be careful" she continues "don't want any hole in one jokes here" she says and quickly wanders off before I can say anything. One of the girls looks at me. "You're disgusting" she said, and she too quickly vacated. I wasn't really able to say anything at this stage not only was I on my own with no one to complain to but as I'd said nothing untoward in the first place I reckoned any further talk would only get me in deeper than I already was.

Not far from our campsite was a Shoprite supermarket and as soon as tents and kit was sorted we got a team of shoppers together to do a quick sortie for tonight's meal. There is a guard on the gate, and we need to be let in and out. Security can often be an issue, but if there was a problem here then it had already been taken care of. I took the shoppers whilst Lynn got the team planning the next few days meals that we would need for our main trek. Before we left I whispered in her ear. "You dropped me in the shit Ellen thinks I'm disgusting." "Don't worry about Ellen" she replied "She's been shacked up in her boyfriend's house since she was sixteen. She's probably getting more than you and I put together. Haha." Lynn Jones was bothering me I was beginning to feel unsafe on my own with her.

Shopping done, and we are back at Jollyboys. We have access to a kitchen; cookers and fridges are here for our use and the evening meal again is well worth a wait. Its early enough after the meal and as it's still light we take a walk back up into this part of Livingstone where we are staying. Most of the businesses have closed for the day but we have located a bank, as tomorrow we need to change our money into Kwacha the Zambian currency.

We'd been lucky shopping at the supermarket. I thought I might have to pay on my card and then juggle about later trying to see what it had cost but here in Livingstone and a big supermarket I paid in US dollars and it was easy for the guys to pay me back from group funds.

A look into a shop window tells us why the dealers wanted to buy shoes. It is cheaper to buy footwear in the UK than it is here and given the relative incomes the likelihood is that most people will be unable to afford decent ones.

We all slept well thankfully, and most are refreshed and back on the mend after their body fluid evacuations. They're feeling a bit fragile, but today is a shopping day to prepare for our main trek in the Botoka gorge which is along the bank of the Zambezi river on the Zambia side.

They have little that they need to do but prepare for the trip which shouldn't take too long and relax and chill out, go walkabout, window shop, in point of fact anything that takes their fancy, as long as it's legal and definitely doesn't involve drugs or alcohol.

Lynn and I will be basing ourselves in the area and we expect the group to try and stick together as much as possible as their number doesn't allow anything more than a split into two groups. "if we are sticking with the minimum of four in a group I would prefer it if you split at least two boys into each group" Lynn was being Mrs Jones and was emphasising the ground rules and making sure they understood and agreed to this. They are a good bunch of students and I'm happy with their performance. They should make writing a good report easy.

A voice from inside the lodge lets us know that the internet is back on and access is available albeit slow. Phil is first in there. He's desperate to get on to Facebook and tell everyone what they're up to. I hate the internet on these expeditions and Phil is about to prove why once again. Ten minutes later and Phil is sitting with the other boys at the picnic table and he looks like he's had bad news.

Lynn is with the girls who are having a giggle inside, so they seem happy enough, so I stay outside just to be available in case. Tony is our leader to day and when he notices me I beckon him over.

"What's wrong with Phil?

"His girlfriend Julie is now seeing his best mate Charlie back home. They were together at a party on the Sunday we left. Seems like it was going to happen if it hadn't already been planned."

"Ok keep an eye on him let me know if you need a hand"

"We'll need a hand when we get home to stop Phil battering Charlie. And he will".

"I'll leave it with you." Tony wandered back to the picnic bench and I needed to get Lynn to make sure that the girls didn't make it any worse by bringing it up or winding him up.

From Phil's point of view the damage was already done and when the Internet signal disappeared the girls were more than happy with their news and without any casualties; and so, we only had one possible problem to deal with. Banning mobile phones to avoid issues you always hope will be enough, but Internet access is something we've found we can't ban at all. Someone always finds an Internet café when they're on walkabout. In point of fact they go looking for them and all you need is a couple of whatever the local currency is and away you go.

Their bonding over the time of Cornwall caravanning and now two weeks here has stood them in good stead and, apart from lonely Phil, it was a happy bunch of students that we followed out of the camp and up to the shops. We pass a local market selling everything that one would expect. It was called locally the Zimbabwe market by some, as a lot of the stalls belonged to Zimbabweans, who traded here from across the border. We are heading to Barclays bank.

 The bank like all the other buildings is set back on the pavement. From the road across the pavement and up a flight of steps puts you on a squash court sized pavement that leads into the bank there are two security guards one male with stick and holstered pistol and one young lady, boots combat jacket and trousers and an AK47.

It was all friendly enough, but they didn't want to let twelve of us into the bank at one time. We got half of us in whilst the remainder waited outside with me. After Lynn brought the first group out she took the second group in and I took the first group down to Shoprite to start picking up the food for our trek.

We had a comprehensive list for the shopping the only part that was not confirmed was chocolate. The chocolate wasn't quite under lock and key but what there was of it was quite obviously watched. It wasn't cheap by Zambia standards and embarrassingly they emptied the rack and that was all there was in the shop. We had spent a while in here and our shopping trolleys full and the job near complete when the rest of the group arrived. We hadn't seen her arrive but the lady from the bank was doing her shopping along with another girl same age same clothing and the only time in my life when I have watched two ladies pushing a couple of trollies and each is carrying an AK47 assault rifle slung over their shoulder. Today was not a good day for a robbery and we watched as they paid for their shopping and loaded it all into one bag each. One bag one hand and AK47 in the other ready just in case. Certain habits die hard.

Paid for and bagged we made our way back to camp. "You're not carrying anything Rob." No, I never do I keep my hands empty just in case I need to help anyone."

"Well you could help by carrying some of the shopping."

"That's not the help I do. Did you see the lady with rifle?" I asked

"yes"

"I don't have the benefit of an assault rifle I might need both hands. I'm your security and just in case I'm needed, I can't do anything quickly if my hands are full of shopping bags." Ellen wasn't happy with my explanation but rather than argue with her I let her walk away and watched the group from a short distance behind.

The lodge where we were staying would be picking us up at around nine tomorrow morning and the rest of the day was spent relaxing and chilling out around the pool. Most of the team were as fit as they were ever likely to be after whatever bug ailed them but a couple of them were a bit below par and were worried about the trek and if they would be able to make it successfully.

They decided to call a meeting to discuss the trek and how they were going to do it. This was unusual for this team their meetings were done and dusted before they even properly started no issues had been the order of the day since we got into Botswana. However, I was pleased that they had decided that if there might be problems that they would sort them before they happened.

We were sitting in the campsite at the picnic tables to discuss the trek we were about to do. This was the main trek of the trip and as such the one everyone should be looking forward to, but they had heard on the grapevine that no team had successfully completed the expedition this year as there was at least one person from every group rescued by the guys at the lodge. This had been enough to give them concerns again that if not all of them could do it should they all not do it?

As all of the team bar Toby had been ill optimism was not at its peak and truthfully it was almost at its lowest what should have had them all full of enthusiasm I now found them somewhat concerned and apprehensive. They had got over their illnesses, but it was almost now like they had all succumbed again to the bugs again that had previously left them debilitated and forlorn. They really needed a few extra days R and R but we didn't have that in our programme; not if we wanted to get everything done that they had set in their schedule.

Comfort food sweets, cakes, burgers whatever it takes to make people happy will do for me, so I suggested that we break out some of the chocolate they'd bought at Shoprite.

They told me everything that was bothering them again then they talked it out amongst themselves, which is what this whole trip is about. The idea is that they will come across problems that they need to resolve and by discussing the problems they will find a solution and then put into action any plan that they have worked out, I gave them a little help." Just something to remind you about. As I said a few days ago. You have flown all this way to get here you have become a team of ten. If you break the job down into small parts take each day at a time and work out what you have to do to get from the beginning of the day to the end, if you think as a team, work out how to help each other. Who needs a hand, how can I work to make this team better, and then you will complete this trek. This is what the whole meaning of the expedition is about, and you have this opportunity now to put this into practise and prove to yourselves and each other that you are the best team here. Just because other teams haven't made it together doesn't mean you can't.

Maybe they weren't teams maybe they were selfish or lazy or couldn't be bothered that's for others not for you. Some of you may not enjoy it as much as you thought you were going to do. You all might love every minute of it like I think you will. Whatever it is, you guys can do this, and I think that if you will believe in yourselves you will do it and you will do it well. All you have to do is take one part at a time and you will make it." Having said similar to them a couple of days earlier I figured they were then motivated enough but information about rescues whether it was accurate or not had taken the edge off their enthusiasm. I didn't care I was prepared keep repeating it and to bore them insane to get them through it.

We spent a while longer planning what, where and how and much later after minor discussions throughout the remainder of the day they all went to bed looking and feeling a lot more positive than when we started. Hell was it that long ago. I need to go to sleep.

We are packed and ready to go. Phil spoke to me asking for some advice re his girlfriend and his mate Charlie he was giving me a heads up as he was hoping we could have a chat later at the new camp and before we started the expedition. I promised him I'd find time to speak to him tonight. He thanked me and re-joined the rest of the boys. I'd made him a promise, but I didn't have a clue what I could offer him in the way of advice that wouldn't upset him.

Our transport spot on time; an open backed truck similar to the one they'd endured in Chobe National Park. But the day was warmer the sun was up, and the early morning chill of Botswana long forgotten. I rode up front with the lodge manager to check on the rumours about rescues and casualties.

 Lynn wished to ride in the back with the girls. They still hadn't fully integrated as a team and she decided to sit with them to see if there was anything she could instigate. The boys did as they always did, grabbed two bench seats and sat together. Our journey took us around an hour plenty of time for me to speak about the trek. I told him about them being ill etc. and filled him in on the last few days. You won't make it he said you will fail just pick somewhere easy to get you out from. You'll realise when you get down there how rescues can be difficult to sort.

We don't do failure I told him this team is a winning combination I don't think we need tell any of them about this year's rescues because they won't be involved in any. They might not be the strongest or the fittest individually, but they are a team. Lynn the teacher and I are just along for the ride.

He gave me a briefing on what to expect on the trek and how badly a number of other teams had fared. Some rescues were of teachers and students who really didn't want to make the effort . Injuries more imagined than real.

We've been on a four by four track for a while when after a sharp slow left-hand turn, he stops the truck "Your campsite is here. Pitch your tents on the other side of that small building. When the guides come tomorrow they will bring a driver with a flat back. Put anything you're not taking with you into bags and they will put it in a store for you until you get back. I will send someone up from the lodge who will mind you while you're here. His name is Maurice. If you want something ask him. He will sort it for you. I ask you not to visit the main lodge while you are here but liaise with Maurice. Our other guests pay for isolation and privacy. In case I don't see you tomorrow morning have a good trek and good luck.

Ready to rock as soon as they were off the truck and shortly after with tents up, we are getting instructions from the man who would take care of us whilst we were here. If he was not the gentlest man I have ever met in my life I don't know who is. He had the softest voice and we strained a little to hear what he was saying. We all listened intently, as if we'd been hypnotised. He was also our link with the lodge though only a short distance away from us but with its facilities and a bar and restaurant reserved for the people that stayed in the rooms.

At the edge of the small campsite a thatch topped rustic building housed a bush toilet and a shower that might have been made by a famous lager company. It ran on paraffin and a wick made from a sheet of toilet paper. Producing the best hot shower, I'd had outside, since the one in

Namibia a way back. It looked primitive, but it was absolutely brilliant. As long as you had a piece of paper for a wick and some paraffin you had hot water.

We camped that night in our tents and cooked on Trangias. Sorted our fuel and food and equipment and separated the kit we would not need on our trek. As the lodge would mind our tents we also dumped as much weight as possible including any spare clothes and anything that we could to save carrying it. After tonight we would sleep al fresco with just a mosquito net over us to keep the beasties off us.

Maurice spoke perfect English and we had an interesting conversation. He told me that when he was younger he was frightened of the white man and lived in constant fear. Unable to speak English or any other European language he had avoided all contact with white people. He had arrived at the lodge having been offered a job and here he had "learnt to speak English, communicate with the white people and most importantly for him, hold his head up high". His words not mine. His story I have found is not unusual and the blame is not necessarily all on one side.

Our evening meal was finished dishes done and only hot chocolate needed to finish the evening. We have minders tonight. Three men arrive at the camp. Maurice who has been with us on and off throughout the day introduces them and then makes his way back to the lodge to eat and sleep.

We knew that they would be arriving and when they did they built a big fire to sit around during the night and invited us to join them if we wished. We shared some hot chocolate with them before we turned in. Phil hadn't bothered to come and talk to me and I had no desire to pursue it myself and let it be.

Morning and the guards are still with us. The fire has gone down save for just enough to warm hands on and heat a kettle of water. We have coffee because we can and when it's finished they ask if it will be alright to leave. I see no problem why they shouldn't and after handshakes and thanks and please leave the fire I will put it out they depart expecting to see us again in about four days' time. Lynn joins me for coffee. "how's the adoption programme going?" she whispered. We were far enough here by the fire from the tents not to be heard as long as we kept it quiet

"I don't think any of them need adopting. They may have on day one but now they are sorted except possibly Ellen. The talent was there the cream sometimes needs time to rise to the top and I wonder if as you say, Ellen who you tell me shacked up with her boyfriend whether that's stifled her development. I think she might be the only one that needs some help. But it couldn't come from me she thinks I'm disgusting and that's your fault Mrs Jones".

I was smiling when I said it, but she started laughing. "I think up to now the expedition has done what it promised on the tin. Their development like everyone's isn't complete but it's grown substantially since we left."

"I've always said, even if they start they start an expedition at six feet six inches they will appear taller by the time they get home."

"I think you're right. About all of them including Ellen. But she will survive just think she'll be a late developer. We've another ten days yet and we've got the trek and the project and whatever else they have planned for the end. If it keeps on like this, it will have all been worth it. Even the blood the sweat and the tears."

"If there isn't blood sweat tears pain and death in Africa, you're doing something wrong."

"That's a development too far. Let's leave out the pain and death and we can enjoy the rest." Voices from the tents signalled the team waking and soon after queues were starting at the toilet and the washroom. Porridge was soon on the go and final packing up was starting. All the team are awake. I'm hoping that they have all slept well. Some are looking apprehensive if that's possible, maybe worried is too strong a word but not all of them are buzzy buzzy. It's quiet during porridge. "When I played rugby guys. I used to sleep in on the mornings we were playing because I used to feel sick before a game and I couldn't keep my food down inside me. Eventually I came up with four fish fingers on two slices of buttered bread and it stayed in there. That was my meal before every game. Butterflies were wearing boots in my stomach and getting my kit on was torture. Leaving the dressing room and going out on to the pitch I was as near ill as you could get without having anything wrong and being physically sick. The referee would blow his whistle one side or the other would kick the ball from the centre; the game would start, and butterflies left, sickness disappeared, experience took command, and for the next hundred minutes or thereabouts I would be having the time of my life. Fear makes the wolf more dangerous and fear is more often than not imagined not real. Lynn was smiling again and so were most of the team. "There aren't any wolves down there are there Rob?" Ellen from the back.

"No sweetheart there aren't"

"Well that's all right then shouldn't be any problems."
Because it was Ellen I'm not certain if the question was
legitimate or in support of the don't worry about it talk. In
the end it didn't matter we would be on the move soon the
bags that were staying here were packed, in a pile, and
ready to go. Two men have arrived in a Hilux pickup with
the site manager to take our spare kit into safe storage. We
loaded the back of the truck and the site manager
introduced the two men as our guides for the next four
days. Though I got the feeling he thought he would see
some of us before then.

We have two guides with us for this trek. One man is in his
forties with a younger apprentice probably early twenties
and they arrived at exactly the right time just as our talk is
finishing.

Our trek requires us to camp for three nights in the gorge
and as we don't have either a map or previous knowledge
it's going to be handy to have these guys along. We also
have to leave the gorge during day three and return down
into it having passed a part impassable at river level. And
as the journey itself is apparently difficult enough if we
need rescuing one of the guides will make his way back to
the lodge to organise the evacuation. I had explained again
to the other lodge staff that we didn't believe in defeat and
wouldn't require the rescue service. Like all good
organisations contingency plans were in place just in case.

The guides appearance has put minds firmly back in focus
again and a short time later we follow them to a path that
leads us down into the Botoka Gorge and the start of our
adventure.

The path is long and as we descend it gets noisier and noisier; until such time as we are at the bottom. There the roar of the Zambezi is spectacular and down at riverside standing near to it and looking back up and at the cliffs around I can see why it would be difficult to effect a rescue here. If this is typical of the next four days, I think we can look forward to a brilliant expedition. Across on the other side of the river is Zimbabwe. The river, which is also the border between the two countries, isn't exceptionally wide here, and consequently runs with some power and ferocity. High above at our campsite we were sheltered from the noise but now down here we are treated to its full volume and how difficult it is to be heard when we speak to each other; we need to SHOUT. There is wild water everywhere in this stretch and quite soon we witness the white-water rafters bouncing down in their inflatables, kayak paddlers too, some for the run, and some as safety and pickup guards for anyone tumbling out.

We spent most of the day clambering over boulders. Most too big to step over some too big to climb over safely. They worked as well as any team could. Lynn kept them amused by telling bad jokes and laughing all the time. She wasn't really built for climbing and scrambling but she was as fit as any of the students and had no more difficulty in doing the day than they did. The guides were happy with them too and I relayed their respect to the team over the evening meal.

We had been taking anti-malarial pills since before we left, and this was one time when we would be extra careful. Trees and humid conditions and no wind and though in theory not the right time of the year, is there ever a wrong time of the year? The potential for mosquitoes was quite high and the chances of getting bitten is always better under the right conditions. And these are as ideal as you can get. Apart from the ones that seem to spend their lifetime hanging around campsite toilets. We set a long rope up in the open that mosquito nets could be hung up on. We would sleep in a line There was no sign of mosquito when we all turned in and snuggled down in a sleeping bag the sound of the river bashing down the gorge stars in the sky clearly visible. I believe I have the best job in the world. And with that thought I went to sleep.

I slept right through and now it's dawn and most of the group are awake and some are moving about. The morning is cool again. There is light down the gorge, but the sun doesn't show its face for most of the day and porridge is high on the list of wants in the morning. I get water for the cooks.

The river runs fast and furious down the gorge; swept away is the probable outcome if you fall in. If it's a choice between me or a student I become expendable if someone is stupid enough to fall in the water, it better be me. The paperwork and enquiries for anyone else will go on forever and whatever happens I will be blamed anyway. I always get the water down here.

After breakfast I do the same with all the water bottles. The boys don't like the idea of not being able to get close to the edge and test themselves. "Personally, I'm in agreement with you guys" I tell them "but my hands are tied when it comes to this. Risk assessment tells me that one slip and you are away with the river running as it is." Lynn does her Mrs Jones again and kills off any argument from the boys and reluctantly they accept that they're not messing about in the river like they want to.

Day two and after a short while of the same boulder hopping we are in easier territory and making swift progress. We camp early and with little to do other eat and relax we organise some quizzes. We split the boys into three a side and then the girls into two per team. We are like dubious matchmakers trying to integrate this group and finally we get a result. Two teams in competition and successful integration. It's taken over two weeks but Hallelujah. Given that these and others were on their dangerous sports programme some three weeks ago they have been totally disinterested in associating with each other since. We will if things develop now and go the other way get into panic situation if anything further than what we were attempting to achieve starts to occur. One other good thing is that Phil appears to be enjoying himself and hasn't approached me again. We have a team and I couldn't at this point ask for more from them. After the quiz with daylight still here Toby Tony and Archie asked if they could go and sit with the guides for a bit as they'd been invited to see them do some fishing. I'm not certain if the guides were having to fish in order to eat or just as a way of supplementing they're food because the option to do so was here. I had been told that they would feed themselves, so I assumed that plans for their meals were properly in place. A little later Toby came back to tell me that the older guide was going to cut his thumb off as he had damaged it when an engine had fallen and crushed it and it wasn't getting any better and he figured if he got rid of it the problem would go to.

I took my first aid kit over to where they were camping to find Tony and Archie eating fish cooked on their campfire. I asked Papa the older guide if he would like me to look at his thumb. He put his hand out and wrapped in a damp bandage was a mess of blood and mangled bone and nail. What happened? I asked, and he told me how a water pump that was blocked that he cleared but it hadn't been switched off and when he cleared it the impeller attacked him. Spending time in a wet bandage probably hadn't done much for its looks but it was clean as it was going to get and as there was nothing loose to remove, I took a picture of it covered it in antibiotic cream non-stick dressing and a bandaged over the whole thumb and said I 'd look at again tomorrow. Surgery over and enough fish eaten by the boys and we all returned back to our tents, leaving Papa and his tyro to enjoy what remained of the day in peace. "Why did you photograph it?" came from Toby. "Tomorrow when I look at it I will be able to see if it's got any better or any worse" I told him.

Day three was going pretty much as day two and then we arrived at what had been christened Jacobs Ladder. This morning we need to leave the gorge in order to continue with our trek. The bank here disappears under water and consequently impassable, so we have to ascend a steep and long set of wide wooden ladders to the top of the gorge. I use the word ascend when I mean struggle to get our bodies up. The route is made up from wooden posts with steps lashed across them to allow the ascent. The rising posts are up to four feet apart and the cross poles about three feet apart. This is not an easy trip and we knew it was going to be arduous. But teamwork prevailed again and an hour after we started we arrived at the top of the gorge and took an early lunch. On the top the sun was out, and sweaty bodies dried nicely. Normally we would have needed to put more clothing on to stop the evaporation cooling us down but that was unnecessary with that extra heat. The heat hadn't progressed to Papa's thumb and after we reached the top I checked it over again. It was looking better already but then it wasn't mine to be worrying about, but he told me it was feeling better it hadn't got red or nasty looking so I popped a bit more cream on it and recovered it again.

The going is easier up on top and an hour or so walk further and we are on the way back down. What took us an hour to get out of, took ninety minutes plus to get down. In parts there weren't any ladders and with packs on our backs the chances of a serious accident, in the event of a fall, were high. One of the few times I go first and along with the guides, some careful planning, and that team that they had built for themselves we worked tirelessly to overcome the problem and mid-afternoon found us once again in the gorge. At the bottom we took a short rest, emptied our boots of the soil we had brought down and after a check over of scrapes and for any blisters we moved on the short distance for our final night on the river side. They were tired but now there wasn't much further to go, and they would be back on top and returning to the campsite.

After finishing the gorge walk our original plan had been at a village near to our exit point, where we should have taken on our project. Our kit would have been delivered to us there and when the project phase had been completed we would have one night back at the campsite where we would have our meal provided as part of the deal we had done with the lodge. We knew before we left the UK that things had changed for reasons unknown and we will return now to the campsite where we will have our celebratory meal at the lodge a few days early with project plan B unknown and still in the air. One job at a time.

Its morning we have eaten our porridge the guides are impressed with the team and I passed on this information. The confidence rope which has provided our hanger for the mosquito nets is stowed in my bag probably for the final time on this trip; and we have gathered as a small group, and there is an air of excitement about them. They are so pleased with themselves and I have to admit I am pleased with them and for them. But we still have today, and Lynn reins them in which saves me doing it. "We have the last few hours on the bottom and we still have to get out of here" she reminds them "let's do our congratulating when we're back at the camp." I took it from there.

"You've done well guys but let's not mess it up maybe three hours to the top according to the guides and then another hour at least back to the lodge. Application concentration ok? We're off and as usual I am at the back. Lynn has taking to floating between front and back. The guides know the drill and they are so experienced they don't need me to tell them what to do. She joins me for the final mile or so and we have a quiet talk and reflect on a job well done by them all.

Now we have to get out. There is a pathway out to be negotiated. We can see part of it winding its way through bushes sometimes disappearing and often looking dangerously steep. You follow the guides I tell her, and I will do the back as normal. If we get a slider hopefully I'll stop them before we have to go back to the bottom to get them out. You can call the group and organise the order with the guides. She looked at me like are you sure? "You're not stupid you know the team they'll probably organise themselves as well as they have been doing so you shouldn't have anything to do other than keep an eye on it all, but I really need to be at the back here just in case. Ok?"

"Right guys last push to the top take it slowly don't do anything too quickly we haven't had a problem let's not start now ok. I have every faith in you. Teamwork. And try not to crowd each other. I'll be at the back. And then following the guides we started the last time out of the gorge. I was sorry to say goodbye to it. Progress was slow but steady and uneventful. They'd learnt how to deal with steep soil and how to help each other. When in future life they would have to help another person up steep soil I will never know but there must be a lesson in there somewhere. The line is getting longer and I'm losing contact. I slowed them down so that they could get a bit nearer to each other for instant assistance. At the back in front of me is Shirley and she's struggling she is only slight and the heavy sac she's been carrying is getting too much. I tell her to leave it and I'll get it up to the top. I put it on top of mine and I'd swear it was heavier than mine to start with. Now the route has got easier because it's got harder and the vertical rise has changed into a zig zag to avoid it becoming impossible. The chances of a long slip have almost disappeared and as I was slowing down with the extra weight and rather than becoming the tragedy myself I balanced it against a tree followed up behind her and then went back for it. I shuttled it backwards and forwards half a dozen times and as the slope eased nearer the top I put it across my shoulders and pushed the last part until I was over the edge and on top where I joined the others who were all lying down so obviously knackered. The guides saw me come out carrying two bags and nodded to me. Ok? The younger man asked

"I am young sir." I said a bit breathless, but it came out without squeaking "I'll take a break with the others". I took off the bags and plonked myself on the ground. "Well done guys good job all round." Shirley took her bag from me, "Thanks Rob". "You're welcome I'm still a part of this team". I drank some water we shared some chocolate, guides included, and when we all had done the resting we needed we headed back to The Peregrines Nest campsite. We were hoping to make it for lunch, but tiredness got the better of us and rather than have an accident on some wobbly legs I suggested that a rest should be taken. We were travelling over gentle undulating ground with numerous patches of tree cover and finding a good one we stopped for lunch. The trees protected us from the sun that we had not seen too much of for the last couple of days and in the shelter there, after we had eaten the sandwiches and drunk a lot of water. most of us had a snooze. It was warmer for us than it had been down in the gorge and it wouldn't do any harm to siesta now though there was still a good distance to do back to the camp rested legs would do it easily in around thirty minutes.

We had put the tents back up. The manager came and shook my hand. "You were right" he said. "You are the only team that has got through this season." "Thank you" and "thank you to your guides they're good men."

"They think you're good too they have christened you Simba 'the old lion' you should be flattered I have never heard them say that about anyone before you must have earned their respect." I was taken aback "Also as an another first after the meal which will be outside under the pergolas and after the residents have left if they wish they are welcome to come into the bar and buy some soft drinks."

"I shall tell them of your offer thank you."

"See you at dinner time." He got back into his truck and headed back along the track to the lodge.

"Simba wow" Lynn was behind me and had picked up part of the conversation. "They're right." She added, and she walked away smiling, leaving me to indulge myself in a compliment from the guides that was worth just about everything to me. Some of them slept the remainder of the afternoon and whoever didn't just lazed around. Tiredness again creeping into their life but tonight they needed to make an effort and resting throughout the afternoon was the insurance policy being paid up to appreciate the evening meal. We cleaned ourselves as best we could and walked to the lodge. Maurice said he would watch over our camp until our minders arrive.

We were spoiled and indulged, served with everything, and overfilled with food. Whether not having to be rescued had anything to do with this I don't know but I was not about to go looking for a reason as I was too busy enjoying myself and later in the bar when the team were sitting around with glasses of juice or coke a coffee pot was placed in front of Lynn and myself with the instruction to drink what we wanted and it would be filled again should it need to be. The coffee was too good not to drink and I was hoping that my body would be tired enough after the four days to overcome the overdose of caffeine that it was getting.

Much later and a lot later than we were used to, we arrived back at our camp. Our minders were around the fire and after swift visits to the toilet most of the team headed straight for sleep. I gave the watchmen some coffee, sugar, milk powder and mugs excused myself and hauled my tired body into my tent and beat the caffeine until six the following morning.

I woke up desperate for a wee; I'd done well, I think I'd have slept through an earthquake and I was pleased to find that I was the only one awake so after the toilet I grabbed a shower and tried to ease all the aches and pains that I was in the process of developing. Simba was more old than lion this morning. The watchmen had finished the coffee I'd given them and as they didn't want any more, after I got out of the shower I let them go with my thanks and my handshake. I had been told not to tip anyone here and did as I was asked.

We have packed, taken pictures of our camp and the amazing toilet and shower, checked fire is out, rubbish is picked up and we make our way over to the lodge to pay our final account and get our lift back to Jollyboys.

From the office window is probably the best view I've seen out of any office in the world. 700 feet below we can see the white water breaking on the Zambesi and down part of the route that we finished walking less than 24 hours ago.

Our minibus from Livingstone has arrived and we pile in after one last round of handshakes. I'm sorry to be leaving it has been a fine adventure and the team is now excited by the project and the last week or so of this trip. They were still buzzing when we got back to Jollyboys Camping. Their achievement yesterday had created a euphoria that would hopefully carry them through the following week when they would be on their project and until they got home.

We have set up our tents in almost the same places they were in when we left a week back and unfortunately the food we left in the fridge was also still there very much the worse for it. We should have given it to the staff but forgot to let them know. I think they could have made some use of it. The security team that lived here during their shifts along with the other staff would be fed by the cook. She managed to spread out and share whatever they had to eat into a meal for all. This generally would be mealy maize on most of the plate with a small slab of vegetable that resembled spinach in colour and a piece of meat normally sausage around the size of a thumb to provide the day's protein. We spent five days here during our time in Livingstone and I think they had the same meal every time we were there. Our cheese had taken the same colour as the spinach I was talking about, so we sent what we thought was inedible which was most of what was left to the rubbish bin. We tried some that wasn't green, but it tasted green, so it followed the rest into the bin. An oversight that shouldn't have happened and I accepted responsibility for it. I should have remembered it was there.

This morning we are to meet the rep for the charity that's organising our project. He has been in touch with the staff at Jollyboys whilst we have been in the gorge to let us know that we will be making a start on the building a VIP toilet at a school about a thirty-minute drive from here.

It seemed an indulgence to be doing VIP toilets when so many other things could have been prioritised. A reasonable mistake for us, I suppose, as we know VIP as very important person whereas VIP here means ventilated improved pit. A VIP toilet is the same as a normal African long drop with the addition of a plastic pipe of 10 centimetres diameter which forms a vent. One end goes into the floor slab and then it finishes about a metre above the roof, not unlike a soil pipe on a typical house in the UK. The difference is that nothing goes down it save for light which then attracts any flies up the pipe to the top where they are trapped by a fly screen and die, keeping most of the flies out of the toilet.

It makes the passing of one's personal waste products a good deal more comfortable. It's not a perfect solution to the waste problem but carefully managed and sometime emptied it's better than no toilet at all.

Yesterday we booked our taxi for today with the man who brought us here from our campsite. He knew we didn't need a minibus as not all of us were going and this morning he is early and in a different car from yesterday. We are not expected until 9am and given that Zambia is still in Africa I will be surprised if anyone other than us arrives on time. I 'm in the front, with Richie our leader today in the back with Shirley and Charlotte. Seat belts only seem to be on other person's vehicles and, life being cheap as it appears to be, are an unnecessary expense. Our driver asks for a couple of dollars in advance as he needs to buy fuel and so after some driving around the streets we stop at a house. A man comes out opens the back of his parked car and pours some bottles of what I assume is petrol into our fuel tank. The deal done, and payment made we are on our way.

"What car you have?" we have hardly got going and our taxi man who did not say a word yesterday on the drive from campsite to campsite is starting a conversation. "Ford Mondeo," I told him.

"Bet you're a good driver" he continues. I shrug my shoulders non-committal. "You want to show me how good you are?" he asks "no".

"oh, why not?"

"Your job is to drive my job is something else."

"Come on show me how good you are" he's not quite pleading and we are slowing down. "I stop car and give you a go."

"Listen pal you're driving we are passengers you are the taxi and we are going to the school. Because that's what we're paying you to do." We've almost stopped, and he knows I've got annoyed. We keep going and around a couple more bends and there's a police roadblock. A line of vehicles in front of us are pulled up at the side of the road. A policeman waves us to halt a submachine gun across his arm for drivers that don't understand or ignore hand signals. He has buddies up front next to a red and white pole blocking this side of the road. He sees us in the car and waves us around after calling out to his pals up front and we carefully drive onto the wrong side of the road and bypass the barrier. The driver's hands are shaking as he changes gear and he knows that I know why he was going to let me drive this morning. The guys in the back have been quiet throughout this altercation and I turn around and give them a smile to assure them. I'm not certain if it was taken as assurance or me looking like a smug bugger having sorted out our man. Not long after and we arrive at the school. The taxi driver, if it is actually a taxi he is driving, wants to go. He also wants me to pay him. No way Jose you will take us back we booked you for here and back and a one-hour wait and here and back it will be. And to encourage you to hang around I won't give you any money until we're back at Jollyboys. Our driver has got the message; he's not happy but I don't care and now that he knows I don't care he has taken to sulking in his seat whilst he waits for us to return.

The school is quiet its Wednesday so there must be a holiday or end of term has arrived. I don't know the times here in Zambia as I've been to other schools in other countries at this time and they are open for business. No doubt the headmaster will tell us what's happening when we meet him. And I am assuming now that this is he the man walking across the grassy field towards us. I can see he is beaming even from a distance and is aware of our expected arrival. He comes directly to me shakes my hand in a conventional way then again in the African way. He repeats this a couple of times and each change he says one for you one for me one for you one for me. He has an unusual accent and as I listen to him repeating it all again with the students as I introduce them I see that he is wearing a hearing aid which almost certainly accounts for the effect in his speech.

We are welcome he apologises for being late which he isn't, but he is so grateful for our help in building this toilet he is treating us like royalty. I nipped that in the bud before we were overwhelmed with his thanks. Bullshit it most certainly wasn't this man was truly grateful for what we were about to help him with. As the school was not our original project, their position now at the head of a queue, for reasons still currently unknown, has been a welcome surprise.

The toilets will be behind a teacher's house on the other side of the field we are standing on. The field is around fifty metres by fifty . The school buildings are on one side with a couple of houses on the other. We can camp at the school side of the field as we then have easy access to toilets and wash basins and water for cooking and drinking.

The field doubles as a playing field for sport and as a recreational play area for the school children at break time. As we will use it as a camping site whilst we are here there will be a fire pit for us to sit around during the evening time after dark. The headmaster has all of this planned and all we have to let him know is when we will arrive so that he can organise a meeting with his staff and an introduction to the men who will assist with the building project. The school is closed now for the summer, so we won't be either disturbed or in anyone's way.

We agree on an early return tomorrow morning with a plan to go to the builder's merchants as soon after as possible, to order materials and then meet up with the teachers and the work force in the afternoon. We have a plan once again, not that it lasted for any length of time, but it was a plan sufficiently flexible to be altered as needed.

We all shake hands and the headmaster walks us to our car. We have been away less than an hour and our taxi driver looks like sulking is now a fine art form and I'm almost tempted to hang around talking to the headmaster and fill out the time just to annoy him. I don't if only because it's our time being wasted too. We are taking a different route back and spend a bit of time on dirt roads before we suddenly pop out onto our main road just down from the roadblock. The barrier is now on the other side of the road and our man is not hanging around now in case the policeman decides to call him back. He doesn't show any interest and his gun stays over his arm.

The driver's hands are no longer shaking, and I figure the danger for him is now past. We don't need to put any more fuel in, and we are shortly back outside our camp. Normally I would tip the driver when we get back to Jollyboys, but I figure as the car probably isn't a taxi and the driver is therefore certainly moonlighting with his or someone else's car he's out of luck and I think he is as pleased to see the back of me as I am to see him disappear down the road and away.

Richie made the payment and was a bit put out when I asked him not to tip. He realised why when I told him that the driver was working a fiddle of some sort and should we have been in any sort of an accident the likelihood is we would be on our own.

I suspect that would be the case under any circumstances here. Though we have a comprehensive insurance policy which provides us with any medical cover I would have a lot of explaining to do should anything have occurred.

Richie called a meeting to let everyone know how our morning went and what our programme was, and they put together a shopping list for food and necessities for a wander up to the shops after lunch. Lynn speaks quietly to me over lunch. I believe you had an argument with the taxi driver. There wasn't any argument I said he was told and he shut up. As he wasn't saying anything anymore there was no argument." "Richie says you get quite nasty."

"He's exaggerating, sweetness and light me."

"Pigs fly" she said. "They're a fragile bunch on occasions for all of their apparent worldliness" she continued "and I think you alarm them on occasions." "Not intentionally but I will take care of them." I don't think she believed me about sweetness and light, but the problem was past and after we finished sandwiches and coffee the whole team went into town.

They'd decided to have a half hour walking around in groups and meet back at the supermarket later. Lynn needed to change some money, so I hung around outside the bank keeping an eye on the team as they went about their window shopping. The guards didn't like me standing around like the lookout on a robbery and though their English wasn't particularly good I got the message and moved. They had their job to do and I wasn't about to make it any more difficult for them.

The traffic was busy outside the late afternoon traders were doing their banking business. They closed at 3.30 as we used to do in days of yore and numerous big 4x4's were dropping off the casually well dressed and the business suited people, before slowly moving away looking for a handy parking space.

Parking is just as difficult here as any street in any town centre. One or two double-parked until a police Toyota moved them off. Lynn came out into the sunshine and I could see her looking up and down the road for me. I called to her as I was walking over and having spotted me and joined me we made our way over to Shoprite to see who was there. They had worked their way through most of the aisles and were getting close to finishing. Phil came over to me clearly trying to whisper to me. "I didn't come back to you Rob he said "I'm going out with Shirley now, so I don't care about my ex whatever her name was and my ex best mate whatever his name was they can have each other. Saves me getting them a present each before I go home. He laughed, and I was pleased for him. At least I didn't have to suggest he dumps her and his mate and I was grateful I didn't have to do that, or I'd have got the blame again for something I wasn't in any way responsible for.

I let Lynn know that Phil and Shirley were now an item and may need slightly more watching. She looked a little horrified at the news. "I do the minding you do the watching" we both laughed, and I don't think either of us really knew why.

We have for this morning managed with the help of Jollyboys acquired a minibus to take us to the school. The driver and his mate are on time help with the loading and provide a quick and efficient service. They don't stop for some bottles of petrol on the way and fortunately yesterday's roadblock is somewhere else this morning.

Soon after nine we are at the school and again we are welcomed by the headmaster who has two others with him. One is his deputy a young tall and well-built man and the other a middle-aged lady smartly dressed in a floral dress.

She has made the other two look quite scruffy, and it is her house that the toilet will be built behind.

She tells me that she is looking forward to the work being completed. Currently she and her husband and all the teachers who live on site have chemical type toilets without the chemicals, what we used to call bucket and chuck it. Their only other option being a communal toilet attached to the school some fifty metres from their accommodation.

I remember when I was a kid. Going to the toilet down the yard if it was winter and we were lucky there would be a small lamp in there but most times it was out. When it was snowing we would be able to see where we were going in the dark with any reflected light, without we risked a fall both there and back. A picture of life once again is being put into another category the one of memory. I realised that living in a house with a potty, a tin bath and one five amp round pin socket to power the old valve radio, which had to be switched off if anything else needed plugging in, that I probably had a greater bond with these people in Zambia and many of the people in Africa generally than I did with the young people I brought here. I've spent a lot of time in bush toilets, squatting over holes in the ground and chasing off insect and animal life in African toilets that I now considered myself if not an expert but then at the very least I must come under the heading of "experienced".

Whilst we have completed the niceties of the morning meeting the rest of the team have brought all of the bags across and Shirley and Richie are organising the camping area.

Phillip is giving a hand or hovering around Shirley I'm not certain which but there is nothing but friendly working going on so that's Lynn's department at this time. The headmaster has accompanied the building team over to look at the work to be done. There is a hole around 1.5metres by 3 metres and 2 metres deep in the ground in the back garden. The sides have been built from rough brickwork that though new doesn't look well put together.

This is the obvious location of the toilet. What is required now is rendering of the side walls to seal the new brickwork in an attempt to make it waterproof hoping that any liquid will then go out low down at the bottom of the pit and not out of the side walls. When this is finished we will install some shuttering to create a floor slab on which the two toilets will be built. The slab will have four holes in; Two at the back for the vent pipes and, two, location to be confirmed, nearer the middle for the body's business end. The headmaster and his deputy with input from their building foreman have made a list of materials. I give it a quick look over and can't see anything wrong with what he's asked for though the steel seems a bit overkill when some mesh would be more than adequate. Maybe they don't have easy access to mesh here.

"You know about building?" he asks me. I tell him what I do when I'm back in the UK and he's now even happier as he thinks he has a project manager on site. I didn't realise the significance of this until the following day.

"If it's possible we need to get a taxi back towards Livingstone to order and pay for the materials." He will come with us as we need to go to different places for our goods. We make the arrangement for immediately after lunch and leave him to return to his house. He will order the taxi for 12.30, which will give us time to get to the builder's merchants when they open after their lunch. Our schedule as expected has altered but no one's hurt, keep going.

We have easy access to water and washing hands and dishes is not a problem. Some of the toilets have been blocked off and are not for our use whilst the four others have been scrubbed clean for our benefit. There is some long-standing staining impossible to remove that will remain until they are blown up but basically, they are as clean as could be got though.

Before we leave the UK, I have let everyone know that the problems in some places are not aids as it won't live outside of the body but some things like hepatitis, can hang around anywhere for anything up to months. The chances of catching them are remote but stomach upsets, diarrhoea, or vomiting are a doddle to acquire and therefore cleanliness is paramount. Without intentionally creating fear in the students I need to keep them focussed on hygiene. When you are cooking for a whole team and we all eat from the same pot. A dose of the runs can sprint through a team in no time. We still boil our water or treat it with iodine or chlorine to purify it. Iodine has been banned now for our use. Too much will cause problems for the thyroid gland. Not a concern for us here as there are no medical issues that will prevent team members using it and it's been a long enough since I last used it.

We had bought plenty of bread yesterday and as usual, cheese or jam or both provided lunchtime sandwiches washed down with coffee or tea if they wish. No milk here so we use powdered milk at least it doesn't go off in the heat and enough expeditions and you get used to whatever is available.

Shirley who is our leader today and Toby her deputy, who fortunately is on the accounts team as well, will accompany the headmaster and me to the builder's merchants. We three are squeezed into the back with the headmaster in front. Our driver doesn't speak English and needs directions as to where he's going. There aren't any seat belts, so headmaster is welcome to the front seat. There are the usual signs in the taxi saying things such as "in God we trust" I prefer brakes myself and taxi drivers that don't feel a need to text all the time. I spoke to the headmaster before we left, and he has taken the driver to task for using his phone whilst driving and this has disappeared and hopefully will remain so. We are in good time for the merchants opening after lunch as also are a number of others and we tuck in behind a couple of pickup trucks parked outside.

We have hired the driver for the afternoon, which works out if not necessarily cheaper, considerably more convenient for our purposes as we would now be standing around in the street, awaiting our turn at the counter. We are buying cement here as this company sells quality cement from South Africa other merchants are supplied from Zimbabwe and this is, according to my advisers, inferior. We have bought twelve bags of cement which we are assured will be delivered later this afternoon. Yes, they know where the school is as one of the "checkers" lives nearby and will deliver it personally. Tools are not required the school has enough to go around. Next our driver takes us to a different merchant where we buy steel reinforcing bar to go in the concrete. I quiz the headmaster as to the reason for the amount of bar when some mesh would be sufficient with maybe the addition of a couple of extras if they felt the need. His information had come from the building foreman who would supervise the job with me. We would meet him later along with the labourers and the charity agent who would also be there during the building programme. I was starting to get a feeling of too many chiefs and not enough Indians, but I lived in hope that I was worrying unnecessarily.

The steel would be on the delivery truck tomorrow morning and delivered by lunchtime. This was no problem as it was unlikely to be needed for a couple of days, as first we must render the block walls to keep in the waste and to avoid that seepage which might destabilise the surrounding ground.

The headmaster took me to one side. "I'm sorry to have to ask this. But would it be possible for you to buy me half a gallon of paraffin for my heater. It's cold in my house and I can't afford to buy any to keep my family warm." I wanted to buy him a gallon at least but all he had brought with him was a half-gallon container as this is the amount that he would normally get. I asked if it was possible to get another container here. But he knew that they couldn't supply one. He had a word with the taxi driver and we stopped in a garage on the return leg to school.

"I was presumptive," he said, "but I couldn't afford to let the chance go by that you might be able to help me".

Toby asked me what that was about but not wanting to risk embarrassing headmaster I told him "Maybe later". We had not spent a great deal of time shopping but a fair amount waiting to be served and our time away had been longer than we had hoped.

Lynn had been worried as the ETA back was an hour ago and sitting in the field next to our tents were twelve bags of cement dropped off as promised. They still do them in cwt bags here rather than the children's sizes we get back in the UK "We have a secure room to keep the cement in" headmaster told me "and in there we have a wheelbarrow and a sack trolley so moving them will be easy."

"Two people to a bag I tell them "and gently into the barrow. It looks older than me and I'll be surprised if it survives our week here".

Young men have a habit of trying to prove how strong they are and what I didn't need was strained backs and knackered knees before we'd even get started building. Hence the reason for children's size bags in the UK. Too late for me I have according to my osteopath three severe curvatures of the spine. After we had put the cement into the room the headmaster padlocked the door and handed a key to me.

"We both have one" he said, "this way you can get in here any time you want without having to find me."

"Does anyone else have a key?" I asked. He shook his head

"I hope not. Now if you will excuse me I must see my wife for my meal and I will see you tomorrow morning if that's ok." We shook hands and he walked quickly along the front of the school buildings to his small house, which was located just behind the main school. Cordoned off by an old seen better days picket fence, I assume that it went with the post, and given his lack of funds I suspected that that was the only saving grace to the job.

Toby came over to me when the head had left and asked me why we had gone to the garage. I told him the situation and he offered to pay me back from the group funds. I suggested instead that he might consider buying more paraffin before we left. He agreed saying that he couldn't see any objection coming from the group and promised to be discreet about what they were doing. Embarrassing the head was not the way we wanted to show our kindness. We had throughout the day had a number of deliveries of firewood to provide us with warmth and some extra light during the evening.

This was donated by local people who appeared with armfuls of timber, dropped their contribution and left. Most got as far as Hi or Hello and goodbye, but few spoke any English. And having dropped off their load they would only be wasting their time hanging around. Three men had appeared together carrying a small tree trunk. It had been stripped of its branches and twigs. They put it down in the area designated for fire pit and built the makings of a small fire around it and under it and then left. Not a word could we understand but we let them get on with it. Ellen asked what we should do with it? "Set it alight" I said. "All of the tree won't burn tonight but over the next couple of days we will manage to use it all. Tonight, it will burn in the middle and tomorrow we will have two pieces, which will be a lot easier to manage. But before we light it get two of the buckets that we bought today filled with water and keep them near. There won't be a problem unless of course we haven't got a contingency plan and there's enough water here not to be worrying about waste."

They are all looking forward to tomorrow and getting on with their project. Although this wasn't the main reason for the expedition it was a significant part and given the change of location they were hoping that this might be a long-term benefit and consequently possibly a better end product. Although we are in a large open area there is little wind and we are able to sit in a circle around the fire.

Trying to have a fire due to the wind in the gorge had been a precarious affair always risking a small piece being blown onto a mosquito net and compromising its usefulness in one go, but here I was pleased that we would have to be particularly stupid to create problems. I didn't need to cross my fingers this team was proving well capable of organising and taking care of business with only the smallest amount of input from me.

The tree had burnt in half and we pulled the ends away from the fire they smoked a bit for a while but by the time the rest of the fire had burnt down they too were out and it was safe to leave., though I did wet it down before I went to teeth cleaning and bed. It would be warm enough tomorrow to dry out again.

The team were ready and breakfasted by eight am and I had opened the door to the store-room and we had taken out a couple of bags of cement and shovels and trowels for this morning's work. There was a pile of sand that had arrived yesterday afternoon which I assumed was for the concreting, but I was unable to locate any plastering sand and I brought this up with headmaster after we had said our day's greetings. It wouldn't be Africa if this didn't happen. The sand which we use for concrete in the UK was our plastering sand as well as the concreting sand hence the truck load that had been delivered. It had been a donation from some of the parents which they had dug up from somewhere and had delivered to us. I decided anymore questions would be a waste of time and breath and headmaster and I waited for the team of labourers and the agent from the charity to arrive.

Shortly after nine, just after I had been introduced to the charity man, we saw the building team of three men walking across the field. They stopped momentarily, spoke to Lynn, who had remained at the camp with some of the girls to finish off the breakfast chores and then continued on to join us at the site. There was hostility in the air from the moment they appeared. Whatever had happened in the past I know not but when they saw the charity man an argument ensued. I didn't understand a word that was said but the tone and the body language gave enough information to let us know that all was not right with the world today.

The headmaster understood and filled me in later that day. It was all about who was going to be in charge of the job and these building workers weren't going to give up their time, free, to be bossed around by someone who didn't know what he was doing. According to them. The charity man stayed about half an hour. He had another appointment this morning and promising to return later or tomorrow he said his goodbyes and left. We didn't see him again.

We discussed the day's work and how it would proceed, and headmaster left us to get on with it. Here a cement mixer is a person with a shovel and eventually a bad back. I showed the team how to make a mix suitable for rendering without wrecking their bodies. Time had to be spent before mixing on removing the bigger pieces of gravel from the sand which gave everyone plenty to do except for the man who considered himself to be in charge who took to a plastic seat in the shade at the back of the house. With the other two volunteers I organised some planks to give us an in and out of the pit. A couple of blocks of wood nailed to one of the planks and you have a primitive but effective ladder. With the students mixing and the two guys on the trowels we were moving the job along quite quickly. The team organised a rota system so that the mixing didn't go too slowly, and so that everyone got a break. When one of the plastering team went for a break I dropped in and took his trowel and continued where he left off. The mix was horrible my friend big John, a man I used to work with, would have thrown it at his labourer if he'd served this up. But nevertheless it kept on going on the walls and although it wasn't as quick as we had hoped it did keep getting nearer to an end as the morning progressed towards lunchtime.

Lynn with help from the sensible girls, who didn't want to do building work, had organised sandwiches and water for us all with coffee or tea over at the camp if we wanted it.

"You are a saint" I said as she gave me jam sandwich and a mug of hot coffee. "Except for eating I don't like cooking or any time in the kitchen but I like dirty hands and blisters even less."

"Then you are only a part saint" I replied. She made to take my sandwich from me, but I got it away in time. Then we noticed that it had all gone quiet and the students were listening to the banter. Lynn returned to camp she's too old to blush I thought so the sun must have got to her though I hadn't noticed it until now.

The render to the blocks was completed in the early afternoon we cleaned the area and the foreman led his men with a promise to return tomorrow at eight. I felt sorry for him, as he seemed a bit stiff from sitting in that plastic chair all day. Perhaps he'll bring a cushion tomorrow. The team had done well, and they were pleased with my observations on the boss. It is said that sarcasm is the lowest form of wit, but I consider that, done properly, it's a fine art.

We got cleanish in the school toilets and spent the remainder of the day planning how we were going to finish what amounted to just over a week left of their time away.

Toby who was doing the juggling with the accounts reported that original plans as considered looked like they would go ahead and there was no reason why this couldn't and shouldn't be confirmed ideally as soon as possible. Lynn looked at me and I at her and we both shrugged shoulders almost simultaneously. Archie who was team leader today was not going to be telling us anything either. "Before we go any further I'm asking if this is something that should be run past me on health safety or security grounds?" They all had a look at each other. "I'm not asking to know what you have planned but I would hate to kibosh it when it's too late to do anything else."

"It's not a problem Rob"

"Fine that'll do me. I hope it works out."

"So, do we Rob you'll be with us anyway."

"By the way everyone, keep an eye on yourselves; if you are taking doxycycline as it can make your skin photosensitive and I've noticed a bit of redness about cheekbones is not unusual as well as between your fingers and toes if you wear flip flops." Lynn leaned over.

"You are sweet" she said.

The fire didn't get a lot of use as shortly after the meal they started to drift off to bed. I got a feeling that more than just our foreman was going to be stiff in the morning. It was dark but only just. Simone who was the group photographer was out with her camera painting with light she said. She was trying to get enough letters to make a word by making a panorama with her computer. She hadn't decided yet what she might want to say but she figured, rightly, that if she had the whole alphabet on her memory card then the words whatever they turned out to be would be easy. After a while she came and sat with me and Lynn at the fire.

"Rob do you need to know what we're planning?"

"No, I'm fine thanks. You guys have been a solid team and I trust you and if you say its sound that'll do for me."

"I don't want to tell you, but I want to be assured its ok and I'm in a quandary I'd hate it to go wrong as we've all been looking forward to this for the last year. And the only reason I'll tell you is so that that doesn't happen."

"If you all think it's ok than that'll be fine."

"Ok thanks goodnight Rob. Goodnight Mrs Jones." We said goodnight.

"She's a lovely girl I've taught her for a couple of years and assuming she gets her A levels which shouldn't be in doubt she's off to America to study graphic design. Her father lectures there and she and her mum will go out to join him. They have only been waiting for her A level results and this expedition."

"There all nice kids I said if all the teams were like this lot we'd be killed in the rush to go away".

"Not all good then?"

"I think it's the best job in the world but sometimes one tosser can spoil it for everyone threatening to send them home most times works I don't think even their parents would miss some. I took one team away once and I'll swear one boy's mother was disappointed when he arrived back in one piece."

"You're joking."

"Sadly, I'm not".

"On that note I shall wish you good night" she left me then. I was not unhappy sitting on my own by the fire and the heat from the embers for me on my own was enough to keep me warm. The wind had risen a bit and I'd put a hoody on after dinner for sitting around in. I'd had it on and off for three weeks or so and it was starting to hum to me. I rinse my clothes that will dry quickly through when I can, but I get an itch off some washing powders, so I try and avoid getting my clothes properly washed.

The wind has got up overnight not too blowy but sweater in the morning weather and the porridge goes down well. These have even learnt that a bit of salt in the cooking makes a lot of difference to the final taste. The headmaster tells me that there is some shuttering timber in the storeroom and we open up and although there isn't a lot we take it over to the workplace.

Our foreman and his team aren't here yet. Remember this is Africa I tell them. It doesn't take long to carry the timber over and shortly after and whilst we were doing so the steel that was promised for yesterday but didn't arrive was now on a truck driving across the field towards us. The driver knows nothing of what happened yesterday, when quizzed by the head and is keen to depart before he gets involved in an argument. The headmaster says I think the workers are on Africa time, which raised a chuckle.

"They know about Africa time?" He asks. I was at a festival a while back and even the master of ceremonies was telling the crowd to comeback when the clock said, "We are on proper time not Africa time."

It's something I always remember, but I doubt if he got his wish.

"Mexico is worse" offered Simone "Daddy worked there he had to leave he said manana doesn't mean manana it means if you're lucky the day after the day after or whenever."

I'm not really certain why we've got this amount of steel, but I suspect some is for other projects in the future. Our building force arrives. There are two extra men today and they are carrying what looks like a couple of old gates two men to each and our gallant foreman giving directions. They place the two gates over the hole and low and behold we now have shuttering in place for our floor slab. As far as they're concerned they don't mind leaving the wood in there as it would only get burnt anyway. These guys and their building practice are bothering me but there is nothing I can do about it. They have put two pipes in the pre-cut holes for the vents and cut two holes for the squat. They have lined around the outside of the timber doors with some planks that they have nailed together at the corners and beefed up the sides with some biggish rocks from a pile at the end of the garden. Yesterday's workers left after they had dropped the wood off. The two new men will be helping to mix the concrete for the floor slab. Headmaster has turned up with a hacksaw to cut the steel to length. "You won't get through it with a hacksaw headmaster it's been hardened. The two new men each have a go on cutting the steel to length until all the teeth have gone from the blade. They settle for bending the steel into shape to fit inside the shuttering. They also adopt the false idea that if you fill it up with steel it will be stronger. They then start a concrete mix and I realise that the pile of rocks that are at the side of the garden are part of our materials and given that some of these pieces are bigger than the gaps in the steel work I don't have any hope of this coming to a successful conclusion. I realised in retrospect that as long as the timber doors supporting the floor don't rot the toilet will remain in use. The team have watched in amazement at the goings on. They have not smiled since the workers arrived as they realise that all the planning and money spent is being wasted by incompetence. They in the end did most of the concrete mixing as the two other workers took a leaf from the foreman's book and slowly gave up work. They organised a rota with everyone giving a hand. I spent most of the morning on it with them and took a break for coffee back at the camp. I had instructed Lynn not to bring coffee up as I was reluctant to give lazy 'workers' drinks for doing nothing. We did what we could with what we had and late on before what was to be a late lunch we finished as best we could. The team tidied up and we left the volunteers sitting and chatting when we went to lunch.

"We have finished for the day" I told them and turned and followed the others back to camp. We scrubbed up and later got a visit from the headmaster. I felt sorry for him the politics was not helping his position although he was a local man well respected and well known he needed the support of the community to keep the school open and for that he was obliged to toe whatever party line he had to. At least half of the school fees remained unpaid in any year and these were to provide books pencils and salaries. Most years there is a major shortfall on all three.

Two of the girls quizzed him on the teaching as they had seen some maths papers pinned to a notice board. They had a lot of respect with the standard expected. They told me later that as A level students they found the paper when they read it to be hard. The fact that it was an end of term paper was seriously impressive and possibly almost as difficult as the A level papers they had just taken.

The afternoon discussions with the head and later we were joined by his deputy and the lady who lived at the house gave us an insight into the struggles teachers here had to get funding and deliver an education. They could suspend pupils whose parents didn't pay but they couldn't remember ever doing so. To a certain degree this is likely to have encouraged others to claim hardship unnecessarily and even though they were aware of this they still seemed unable to be tough enough to refuse the children an education. As I'd discussed with Lynn earlier on the expedition the norm in Africa is if there isn't blood sweat tears deprivation and death you're doing something wrong but here was an example of the other side of the coin, where to a certain extent the usual way would have offered a solution to the problem.

We chilled out the remainder of the day. The volunteers from the village tried to bum clothes, work shoes and money from the team and I had to sort of shoo them away. They got the message and soon after they had left headmaster came over asked what happened. I told him, and he said he would make certain it didn't happen again. It didn't.

We weren't due to leave until tomorrow morning expecting to work right through to the end of today, but time spent by the team chatting to the teachers about life here was as important to them as building a VIP toilet block. The expeditions are experiential and soaking up knowledge and other cultures will give them a better understanding of other lives than blisters from mixing concrete.

It's always a compromise what the benefits of an expedition might be for all of the interested parties. In an ideal world a project will leave something of use to the community after the visitors have left. Or if nothing is finished sometimes a project started and materials left to finish will have provided the wherewithal to be completed. Sometimes other teams will follow up in future instalments. Some projects have been in development for a number of years three and often four visits a year by a couple of linked schools properly co-ordinated can and often does bring enormous benefits to the community and still provide a good work experience for the students.

The last thing a community is to spend their time on a project with no obvious benefit to anybody but the visiting school. Their life is hard enough without wasting it on trivia and frivolous projects. A project well thought out and developed can on occasions create a link from one school to another, but this only has value if that link spells a bigger commitment and relationship between the schools and the community.

Everyone understood where I was coming from with this and this team's commitment in attempting an unplanned for job at this school has to be commended. We spent part of the afternoon discussing what I'd told them and when the head and the teachers said how pleased they were with the visit and it was also hoped that at some time before the remaining bags of cement went off that they too might be used for something useful.

The headmaster joined us for our evening meal he didn't really enjoy it but was gracious enough to commend the cooks. There wasn't anything wrong with it other than it wasn't a plate of mealy maize for its base which is what provides most of the carbs here.

We said our goodbyes. The headmaster looked embarrassed when I carefully gave him some fuel money, but I made him take it and he was sensible enough not to argue with me. Our minibus arrived, as arranged, at nine. We loaded up and returned to Jollyboys camping for our final couple of days. We have some shopping to do. We have a couple of things we must buy and most of the team are looking to buy some more souvenirs for home. Lynn and I will do our normal keep an eye on everything from any available vantage point we can find. Lynn has managed to get Simone to go with her whilst the others slip off to do their shopping.

As it's Sunday in Livingston and we need to change some money and Barclays is shut of course, as are all the other banks, we will use a bureau de change on the main street where there is a small queue waiting to do the same. All around the shop along the pavements are street traders of one type or another. Some guys just chatting others doing business, there is a general busy but relaxed atmosphere about the area. The students are inside whilst I wait outside, and I'm thinking maybe I should change some money myself. The rate at the bank was just over eight thousand kwacha to the pound the bureau is offering seven thousand five hundred to the pound which is not too bad and cheaper than going to the ATM and paying the service charge.

One of the dealers says, "you want to change some money?"

"Yes" I said "forty pounds"

"I'll give you same rate as the bureau. So that's quarter of a million for forty pounds,"

"Forget it. Its 300,000 not 250 000"

"ok 300,000." I get my forty pounds out of my wallet and show him my money He peels six fifty thousand kwacha notes off of a huge wad he's holding in his hand and tells his mate to check the count. As his mate passes me the notes I give our dealer the two twenty pound notes.

Instead of putting the folded notes straight into my pocket I flipped them open and fanned them out in my left hand.

His mate has palmed two of the notes and I only have 200.000 kwacha. That's twice he`s tried to rob me. My right hand has got a grip on his left now still with the money in it. I showed him the fanned out money. "You owe me 100,000 you`ve robbed me."

You`ve palmed it he shouts back at me. I`m starting to hurt him now 'cos' I've got a real good grip on his fingers which are still holding my money and I don`t care. This incident has got a lot of onlookers. I throw the 200,000 kwacha his mate has given me onto the pavement and his mate is down on his knees picking up the four notes. "Give me back my money" I shout back at him and still crushing his fingers I grab the two twenties'. He starts shouting to his mate "give him his money" he says "he`s hurting me". Six 50,000 kwacha notes appear, and the deals done. I let go of his hand.

"My friend" he says "you want to buy some diamonds? We could do you a good deal on diamonds"

"No thank you, goodbye" and I give him a polite wave and walk backwards away from him. The students had finished their transaction with the bureau and had witnessed me in yet another confrontation. They said nothing as if it was becoming the norm and we went off to buy the birthday cake we`d come for. I gave our currency dealer a smile as we left but he was in no mood to smile back. Nobody appeared to be surprised, interested or concerned about what had happened and had not got involved in any way.

This wasn't luck on my part as our dealer friend had got caught cheating. If the police had been about things may have been different, but I've found that you have to take care of yourself. You are on your own under these circumstances and there's a winner and if you are not the winner then you are a loser so with any means at your disposal you need to win; if it includes whacking someone then that's what you have to do or at least let them think that. If you don't you might find yourself as an unsolved crime on the BBC's 9 o'clock news.

Simone was kept occupied and out of the way while the others sneaked into the bakers to pick up the birthday cake, they'd ordered before we went on our project. Bagged, secreted away, and half the team headed back to Jollyboys to hide the cake. The rest of the shopping completed and everyone ready to go and we follow the route, now so familiar, back to camp.

The only one who is still camping though is me. The others have hired the bungalows to stay in for the final couple of nights. They were disappointed but not put out that I was happy to stay in my tent. Lynn was staying in a single next to the girls and the six boys had got the only six-bed room available. I joined Ellen and Lynn at the table near to the kitchen. Would you like a muffin Mr Platt? she asked. "Do you know I've waited nearly a month for you to ask that Mrs Jones"

"I bet you want a squirt of cream as well".

"That would be lovely" I replied. Ellen stood up horrified.

"You two are both disgusting" she shouted at us and tore off in the direction of the other girls. Presumably to recount the conversation. "Don't worry about Ellen she's not as innocent as she pretends to be. Now shall I go and get the muffins. Cook said they'd be ready soon and she'd had promised to keep me some if we weren't back in time."

"Then I'll pay for the coffees" I said.

"Deal done, I'll bring it all back on a tray. Funny that wasn't it?" she said "Worthwhile just to see Ellen's face." She was giggling, and I wondered how she managed to keep school life running smoothly when she had the mischievous nature as she did. I used to think yawning was the most contagious thing until I heard her laugh, you could not help but smile and join in when you heard her. She was built like a beach ball at least twice my size as fit as a butcher's dog and the sweetest person I had thus far taken to southern Africa. Her sense of humour was more anarchic than mine.

I did wonder though if it had been me making these dodgy comments double entendre and innuendo instead of her I figured I'd be arrested as soon as I landed at Heathrow. Thank goodness she was here and doing the jokes.

Simone was surprised to see the cake. We sang happy birthday, or they did. Ellen, who is leader today and is still finding it difficult to look either of us in the eye calls a meeting.

"As most of us know, we aren't having breakfast here tomorrow morning." Then she looked at us both.

"We are going to have breakfast on Livingstone Island." Cheers from the crowd. "The menu is Eggs Benedict and hot muffins" then she gave us another look "I don't know if there's any cream" she continued "but there will be tea and coffee." There's a lot of giggling going on. "But I'm certain they'll be just as enjoyable. "The minibus will be here at 7.30 on the dot they say. We have an hour on the island and it may be the only thing that does, but they run to time, we must be ready. And we must be washed and clean." The boys got a look that would turn lesser mortals to stone "Thank you". She sat down to cheers and laughter. "Will that be alright Rob?" Asked Simone "How can I refuse?" I said there followed more cheers and we break up. "A muffin competition never been to one of them" says Lynn and left me pondering what on earth she was on about as I could hear her giggling on her way to the kitchen with the tray of empty plates and coffee mugs. And I wondered too what breakfast on Livingstone Island had in store for me.

7.15 and the whole team is in the kitchen as smart as they could be given the rigours of the last few days on the project. But they have had a decent night's sleep and access to showers and they've not wasted the opportunity. The minibus arrives bang on time and we pile in and are away slick by anyone's standards.

We are dropped at the front of the Royal Livingstone Hotel. Reception directs us towards the back and to the river. We are above Victoria Falls on the bank of the Zambezi river in the gardens behind the hotel where set tables are ready and waiting for guests who want an al fresco breakfast. Today this is not for us, but we are directed towards the bank to await our transport.

One of a number of speedboats is returning from the island. Early breakfasters are being dropped off. We get lifejackets from the returning passengers and in small groups we are taken by speedboat on a circuitous trip around rocks and avoiding presumably strong currents to be met at the island when we then trade our lifejackets for oilskin ponchos to keep us dry. As we arrive people again are waiting to leave. It isn't rain it's water hanging in the air from Victoria Falls. There is a permanent rainbow during daylight here and although it's not cold the moisture hanging in the air here can make it feel so.

When we walked the Botoka gorge we were below Victoria falls now that we have moved topside and on Livingstone Island we are in the middle of the top of Victoria Falls. We are about to eat the best breakfast, in the best place to have it, in the world. Or in the world according to me. Which is near enough; as far as I'm concerned.

Long tables are set under huge awnings to protect food and diners from the water laden air. The food is exquisite. the tea and coffee hot and in abundance. The service and atmosphere something one might dream about. We are pampered and indulged.

Part way through and in small groups we leave our sanctuary, under the awning, and walk over to a position nearer the edge of the falls. One at a time directed by one of the hotel team, careful underfoot and we are standing on the edge of a wet rock holding onto a guide's hand as we peer over into the abyss that is the falls itself.

We can't see anything but white water below us but the size and beauty of the place as you look along the top really becomes so obvious from here. I have seen it all from the bridge below but this opportunity if you can put the money together is worth it. If you were to only go to Africa to see one thing I wouldn't know which one it might be, but this would certainly be high on my list of possibles.

Breakfast lasts an hour and too soon it's over. Though we have finished eating and drinking all we can we have a little time to wander about carefully. The sheer beauty and majesty of the setting is difficult to let go of. But let go we must and we reverse the clothes trading of ponchos for lifejackets to the hungry arrivals and return via speedboat back to the gardens from where we were picked up. We are dropped back at Jollyboys they are the happiest group I have ever had with me and they deserve everything that they have achieved. Tomorrow morning our transport will pick us up to take us to the airport at Livingstone from where we will fly to Joburg then Charles de Gaulle then finally to Heathrow. Although it's a circuitous route we are retracing our steps apart from the flight from Livingstone and waiting times between flights is not too long and although we need to pick up our bags at Joburg and check in once more, they will then go straight through to Heathrow, without us needing to handle them again.

I checked my sat phone as I had done every day since we arrived to find a text message asking me to phone ops room. I gave them a call. As I was going through Joburg tomorrow I was to pick up a party of four girls and a lady teacher who had been unable to leave the day before as two of the girls were sick and the carrier as per usual rules wouldn't take them on board.

Tickets had been rearranged and they were to fly the same route as us, times and flights exactly the same. I got the message and the details of the group and told ops room to confirm I would bring them back with our team.

I gave Lynn and the guys a heads up on what we had to do but it wouldn't affect our plans at all.

We have paid our final bill at Jollyboys. The transport they have arranged is on time and at a better price than we could ever have done. The airport lounge area is small. Seating is enough when we get there then it starts to fill, and fill and we are all flying to Joburg. I'm thinking you need a jumbo to get us all out of here when we're told that we are on the second flight out which will be a couple of minutes after the first. British airways are taking us to South Africa after South African airways are taking the other half of the waiting throng. I hope they don't race each other. We arrive at Joburg it's the normal heaving mass of humanity that occurs at international airports trying to get to the right gate at the right time and do everything else on the way. We've got our bags and my mobile is ringing I answer it to hear a woman's voice desperate and trying to find me. Where are you she's screaming at me like she's on fire. Picking up our bags then going around in a circle and then through the customs and then to our gate where are you. At the departure gate. Fine just wait there. I switched the phone to vibrate and we checked in checked out and headed with our tickets for our departure gate and this other part team of teacher and four girls.

To say she was stressed is an understatement. As far as she's concerned the girls could have malaria because they've got the runs. Have they shown any flu like symptoms?

No. But they've got the runs and runs are a symptom of malaria.

Not without headache shivers nausea high temperature there's a bucket load of pointers before the runs. They are not on their own likely to be pointing towards malaria.

yes, they are I've taken my first aid course with your company and I know what I'm talking about.

No you don't now sit down relax stop worrying and stop having a go at me because whatever it is it ain't my fault. Her mouth was open

"I'll report you."

Do so if you wish. But in the meantime, stop behaving like a six-year-old.

Lynn arrived just in time like a superhero and took the lady to one side and gave her a kindred spirit or whatever she gave her. But it calmed her down and she minded her throughout the journey home.

We have cleared immigration and we're by the carousel. According to the girls, she has apparently been like this since she left the UK, and the girls who are feeling perfectly fit and well are happy to be back. I remind them that should they get any flulike symptoms in the next twelve months that they should tell the doctor that they have been in an area where there is a possibility of Malaria. The teacher has stayed away from me since Joburg. Obviously, a lot brighter than I gave her credit for.

Lynn has waved goodbye to them and stands behind me.

"You're a hard bastard" she whispers in my ear.

"I'm sweetness and light me; told you that before."

"I think your right" she continued "you only showed me what we needed to see. You've taken good care of them and we will all thank you for that. I've phoned our minibus driver and he's handy".

You're all very welcome its best the exped I've ever been on. I will miss you all. We went through nothing to declare and I can see Nigel from our management team was standing just outside the barriers as we walked through. "Don't rush get yourselves packed and ready and I'll see you before you go."

"We'll be outside. In a school minibus"

"By the way I want to adopt all of them." I called after her. She turned, and She smiled which turned into one of her laughs. "I told you I could learn a lot about people with this."

 The teacher and four girls had spotted the sheet of paper Nigel was carrying with their school name and he shouted to me to come over. I needed to see my team off then we were caught up in a mass exodus. Lynn and the team were travelling back to near Plymouth by minibus. Any company kit was being picked up at the beginning of next term from the school and I was going home on the train from here. I was trying to ignore Nigel "in a minute" I was shouting but in that short time after we had come out into the waiting area I had lost contact with them. I headed for outside hoping to see them before they left but wherever they were now I didn't know. Buses and coaches disappearing into the distance could have been any one of them. Nigel caught up with me outside. "Why are you ignoring me?" he asked. "Because you're a fuckin nuisance" I told him. That shook him, and I didn't care.

"The teacher 's complaining about your attitude and I think she may be right by the sound of it. Had a bad exped have you?"

"I've just had the best month of my life with the nicest team I have ever taken away and that fuckin witch you dumped on me at Joburg and you have just spoilt the whole experience. I'm going home I'll send you my report. He was still standing there gobsmacked when I walked away. I don't know how long he stood there because I didn't look back to see.

I 'd lost them at the airport, and I was the nearest thing to lost without them. Sometimes I go away and I'm glad to see the back of the school. This team I liked every single one of them. I have taken a lot of groups away before and after these, but they are still the best team I ever went with. It wasn't a job it was a joy and a privilege and heavy hearted I caught the flyer from Heathrow. Got my train from Euston; and now there's a cloud of sadness creeping over me as I try to sleep on my way back home. I was going to miss those guys and that wacky teacher.

I have been home a couple of days and I'm running out of Doxycycline, my anti-malarial pills which I need to take for another month after I get home. I need a private prescription from my doctor. You can't get Doxycycline without one and you can't get them on national Health prescriptions, so you have to pay for them which I would do anyway. The difference is these are cheaper because you don't get them on prescription and my doctor does not charge me for writing one.

I'm standing at reception waiting for it when my doctor spots me. "Are you coming to see me?" He asks. "I've come for a prescription I said just need some anti malarials."

"You were supposed to come and see me when you got back."

"I've only been back a couple of days."

"Come in now" he wasn't having no for an answer, sit, roll up sleeve, needle, remove blood, roll down sleeve. "I'll send this for testing and phone you when I get the result which should be tomorrow morning. When are you away again?" "I'm back in UK until November."

"Right let's see what we get from this." He wrote me a prescription for my pills and said goodbye. I got the feeling whether I liked it or not he was going to fix my lack of bedroom related performance. Two days later I got a phone call from him. "I've made an appointment for you to see a member of the urology team at the hospital your appointment is at 2.30 on Friday I assume you can make it." I agreed I could "good that's sorted then" he said and hung up.

At the hospital I saw Mr Simpson and after my examination he told me that he wished to do a biopsy on my prostate as my levels weren't particularly high, it feels normal, but we can, so we ought to, so we will. He explained that he would take some tiny pieces from the prostate but before he did he would inject a small amount of anaesthetic before each one which would be enough to stop any pain. Results would follow soon after which I meant I would have it all sorted a week before school half term. I love it when a plan comes together.

This was a good time to get these bits done. Schools had gone back, and reports had been written next phase was going to be D of E training sessions most of which would take place during half term. Nigel from H and R got back in touch. The other school exped leader Peter Beatty would have been quite happy if a lion had dragged teacher off into bush and eaten her on day one. He confirmed she'd been a nightmare and he was more than happy to dump her at Joburg, but he would have preferred it if it had been Joburg on the way out not on the way back. Nigel apologised profusely for messing up my return and told me in addition that my team apparently couldn't have asked for anyone better. He said goodbye and promised to get in touch again soon.

H and R, it would appear had some second thoughts after the last mess up and had offered me a late season exped to Africa to take an Australian school up Mount Kenya. Hallelujah someone's taking care of me again.

Mr Simpson sent me a letter which told me my appointment was for the following week.

I have given myself the best cleaning job I can. I am wearing a smock with ties at the back I am on my side on a trolley surrounded by a team all in white. The guy who's talking to me says he's a nurse and not certain what his speciality is but he's holding my hands and my arms as Mr Simpson with his machine based on an original design of a medieval torture weapon goes to work. He seems to have forgotten about the anaesthetic he promised or he's in a hurry to get to another job. Maybe the hole in the ends blocked but if this is as it's supposed to be the statement it will be pain free I think it applies only to him. The specialist nurse has a good grip on my arms. I think his speciality is restraint and security he has more tattoos than I have and hands like a builder's labourer.

"Done" says Mr Simpson. He seems almost as pleased as I am. Thank god for that I'm thinking "You may experience some blood in your urine and in your semen. There's nothing to worry about. This will pass through then return to normal. You will get a follow up appointment in the post in the next few days." Then he was gone. You did well" said my nurse "hardly needed holding. Any problems come back. Some blood to be expected as Mr Simpson says otherwise nothing else if there is and it would be unusual if there was then don't hesitate to come back here.

The next day and I'm giving myself a test in the shower. Looks like a strawberry ripple. I wash the evidence away before it's discovered which was a pity the colours were nice. I should have photographed it.

I am back at the hospital it's the eighth of October I have a wheelbarrow in the back of my car to take my Viagra home. Then I have an appointment to see the tattooist about another part to my motivational talks. Mr Simpson arrives door held open by a nurse.

"You have prostate cancer it's not good. Numbers tell me that it should be removed sooner rather than later. I have spoken with the surgeon and he will do what's called a radical prostatectomy, which uses a robot to remove the prostate rather than cutting a hole into you and taking it out that way." He stopped momentarily to let the good news sink in or to get his breath whichever. "Do you read?" I just about got 'yes' out without sign of panic. "Good. Give Mr Platt an information folder. This is one of the cancer nurses she will liaise with you about the operation. The surgeon will take over from me now. He will be in touch as soon as there is a date for the operation. Any questions ask nurse. Goodbye." And he was gone. I feel like I want to be sick. He'd delivered the information like terms and conditions at the end of a radio advert. The lady in the blue uniform gives me a telephone number for the direct line to cancer nurse's office and a folder loaded with information about cancer, prostates and operations I have lots to read I need someone to tell me everything is going to be alright, but I'm not getting that from anyone, and I leave the clinic with a folder weighing heavy in my hand and fear weighing heavier in my insides. I'm sitting in my car digesting the situation I have to go home and tell my wife. It wasn't so long back that her sister died from cancer and now I've got some more news for her.

We had a discussion shed a few tears and decided to read what we had later.

I had an appointment made a couple of months back when I knew I'd be home with the man who had tattooed my arm he was about to do the other one and the philosophy of 'one life one chance live it love it' took on a personal meaning that had never been its original intention.

"How you doing, Rob what you been up to? The tattooist is pleased to see me

"Been in Botswana and Zambia"

"Good?"

"Brilliant" A short while later I am a bit sore and my wallet's quite a few pounds lighter and with my arm wrapped in cling film I headed home to continue with my new reading material.

We couldn't find some answers we were looking for in the folder so the following day I tried the direct line. Whether it was a direct line or not I'll never know. Every time I phoned it I got an answerphone but after leaving a number of messages and not getting a reply I gave up.

We came to the conclusion that whatever I'd done in the past about whatever the problem I had I'd taken responsibility myself; so, we said that's it then we will not be beaten we will nail this. I've survived everything thus far no sense in a change now. "Fuck it." I got a look that said I wish you wouldn't swear. But I had done. It was too late. Hopefully, it wasn't too late for everything else.

My first job is to phone the H and R teams at various companies and give them the news. Sometimes what you need is just a little support from somewhere else. "First off you got to get yourself fixed." I'm talking to Duncan and he's telling me what they're going to do. I don't have an appointment for surgery, but I am on standby if someone in the queue can't make it. They only do one operation a week with this robot. Kenya is out of the question for the end of this year and after that I have trips to Morocco then back to Namibia and then Uganda. We'll have to drop Kenya but He is going to keep all of the others open for me and when I have the op we can then work out how we play.

But first you get yourself fixed and anything you need give me a call. I can only say thank you he was giving me a lifeline and not about to write me off as some would do when I gave them the change in my work availability.

Irritatingly Kenya could have been done as Christmas came and went and then I got a date for March and that was confirmed. My operation would be on a Tuesday morning I would go into hospital on the Monday, Tuesday was spoken for, Wednesday was convalescence and Thursday I was to be on my way back home. That was their plan and I only have a wheel on part with little dialogue. Morocco. was looking unlikely at this time but even if it did go ahead it was only a meet and greet at the airport fly out do trip to Todra Gorge fly home send bill get paid there was no need to give a talk.

But first I had to give a couple of talks one on Namibia and the other on Uganda to the schools I was taking away.

I had an international school in France going to Namibia, which we would Skype with and then one in the north-east near Sunderland going to Uganda. I would travel there and give the talk on the Monday exactly a week before I was due in hospital.

I get another letter from the hospital. I have a pre-op the week before which I can make, as it's two days after my talk in Sunderland. The hospital is aware of how my work is sporadic and inevitably somewhere away and having given them dates they are fitting my appointments in perfectly.

Then I get another letter at the beginning of February they are going to do a colonoscopy next week as they want to check what else is going on before they operate. I have to drink what looks like an awful lot of liquid designed to empty my insides and not eat anything for 24 hours. Going without food wasn't a problem drinking all this liquid, which the longer I drank the worse it tasted.

By the time I've consumed most of it I seem just to be flushing the system through. What goes in one end seems to escape miraculously all be it a slightly different colour from the other end in hardly any time at all.

It's now Saturday morning and I'm lying again on a trolley with a nurse, female, without visible tattoos and two nice hands definitely not the building labourer type and two doctors who are going to work on the business end.

One sticks a cannula in my hand and pops some relaxing juice in whilst the other takes his walking stick with a box brownie on the end corners still attached and grubs around inside like a South African diamond miner with a large shovel. I make a lot of noise and the man with the sedative job waps me full of juice and I go quickly to sleep leaving my poor body to be violated in a further round of torture and medical mayhem.

A while later I come awake. The nurse is trying to get a reading off my fingers and doesn't seem to be able to. There's another doctor there monitoring me whilst the first 2 are in consultation on the other side of the room looking into their television screen. It's too early for the football so I figure they might be looking at the main feature. "I'm sorry to say you haven't emptied successfully. Did you definitely take all the laxative?"

"Yes".

"Well you need to come back again next Saturday we don't have much time before your other op so let's get it done then. We'll give you another course to take next Friday and you can come in early Saturday morning and we'll give you an enema as well. That should do the trick. That's it then see you next week."

The nurse wheeled me outside and with the help of a porter took me into a recovery room. They'd knocked me out and I couldn't go home until someone came to pick me up and was prepared to stay with me for 24 hours.

Another job for my wife. She was proving to be quite handy. The following Saturday I have had my insides flushed from both directions. There's more people here this time the man with the cannula seems to only have one job the other two are about to go down the business end again and today we have two nurses. Let's hope this time it works. "There's a lot of people said I'm full of crap. And you've got the pictures to prove it." He laughed and that was the last thing I heard. I woke up a while later in the recovery room. A nurse was taking my blood pressure and then stuck a thermometer in my ear. The doctor arrived. "Not perfectly clear" he said "but clear enough. We've removed polyps that we saw last week, and we'll send them for testing. When someone comes to pick you up you can go. He shook my hand" said 'goodbye' and went.

The nurse asked. "Can I phone someone to come and get you?"

"Kylie Minogue". I said Not an answer expected. "Well if you don't know her number you better try my wife. I think she's sitting in the waiting room anyway."

She didn't find me funny her loss I reckoned but I wasn't going to fret about it. I was hungry. I went home minus some polyps and ate for England when I got there.

I drove up to the school in Sunderland and after a long drive had a 30 minute meeting with the students after school, a bite to eat in the staffroom, courtesy of the two lady teachers who think they will be going. Then into the school hall for meeting the parents or them meeting me as the case might be. The hall was unusually full parents in attendance and 10 minutes talk and only surprisingly 20 minutes question and answer and it's all over. I was back home just after midnight and in bed shortly after.

The French school Skype call hit snags from the outset. I couldn't get a good picture and they seemed to lose the sound all the time. We called it off in the end and settled for a discussion if needed, in Charles de Gaulle airport, where I would meet them en route to Namibia.

My pre-op over and a week later I am standing with the ward sister who is looking for a bed for me. There isn't one but she's going to find one and if someone doesn't move, leave or die she's going to kill somebody for their bed, or my operation will be postponed. It's late morning so I go and sit in the waiting room. I am on nil by mouth so hanging around in the ward while they all eat lunch isn't a good idea.

They know I'm here and where I am so that's ok. There is little I can do other than sit around and read or fill in the crossword, which I will leave until later when I'm really hungry. I don't think sister killed anyone, but I now have a bed with a view. I'm next to a window which makes reading easy and means I only have to talk to people on

one side of my bed. I keep telling myself that it's an
experiment by mad doctors on a perfectly healthy man
intent on stopping me going up Mount Kenya. Just because
my father died from prostate cancer rather than just with it
as most men will. My doctor took it upon himself to try
and save me. I suppose I should be grateful but looking out
of the window it's a nice day out there I could be going for
a walk.

I tell the sister this story maybe humour only comes with
authority as she sees the joke and finds it, if not funny,
mildly amusing. I think she gave me a smile anyway. I
have visitors. A medical team on their rounds.

"As you know we are a teaching hospital do you have any
objections to student doctors being in attendance?" I tell
them no. The question has been asked by a young lady. I
didn't catch it, but she did give me her name. "I am Mr
Kumar's registrar" she says. Mr Kumar is the man who
will operate tomorrow. She took the sheets down while
giving a talk to the students and asking questions. She has
her hands in the loose paper underpants and is feeling
around at the top of my groin. How wonderful the national
health service is this is the sort of attention you would pay
good money for and I look closely at the doctor. She
doesn't look old enough for a paper round let alone being a
registrar and my concentration now is on avoiding
showing my appreciation of her examination. A student
now is doing the examination he's almost frightened to
touch me until he's given some encouragement and
direction by his teacher. "There are two lumps to the side"
she says, "if you can feel them."

"Yes, got them" he says. "We don't know what they are"
she tells him "but they could be linked. We don't think so,

but we'll keep an eye on them. And apart from them there is no obvious signs of anything amiss or any hint of cancer. Prostate is normal and not enlarged. PSA levels are at eleven which for an active man is not high either. The biopsy was what found the cancer." She'd covered me up while she was talking. "Any questions Mr Platt?"

I didn't think asking her if she was married was a good idea, so I told her no she left the nurse to open the curtains wished me a good day and went to another bed further down the ward. I was starting to like it here. I slept through the tea time rather than torture myself and sometime in the late afternoon, early evening, Mr Kumar visited me after he had finished his clinics gave me rundown on tomorrows programme.

I told him that there had been an attempt to put a catheter in a few years back for a check-up and they couldn't get it through. Don't worry he said we'll stretch you wished me a good night's sleep and left me to my crossword and painful thoughts about stretching.

I like cryptic crosswords interesting clue came up, 'where one might have a last sleep'. The answer was "deathbed" friends have told me they'd have got up and left the hospital then treating it as 'an omen and one not to be ignored. I saw little point in such over-reaction, but I did put the bloody thing down and try to go to sleep again. It was too late to do a runner anyway. My wife would have put the locks on the door.

I am lying on a trolley again. I think I've spent more time on trolleys recently than airplanes. I have had a really good shower, a nice clean nightgown, they have taken my false teeth stuck a cannula in each hand asked me what they were going to do to me this morning. That got me concerned if they didn't know what they were doing but its apparently so that I know. I didn't think that was important I figured it would be a good idea if they knew. But I know that they know that I know therefore they can go ahead. The clock says 8.45 over the door to the theatre I was counting down from 100 but I don't remember going through the doors. Now another clock on another wall says 3.05 and a man is holding my hand he's trying to get a reading off the end of my finger, my blood pressure is being taken again and he's talking to me I think. I can't see the clock now as I'm in a different place I recognise the voice it was talking to me before I'm still dopey but not as bad I was earlier how long ago I don't know but I'm alive and well. Ha. My brain is sluggish and so is my mouth, unusual. I have a sore throat swallowing is uncomfortable. "You're in recovery" says he who is minding me. There is no rush to do anything; stay still and all will be good later. I'm in no rush to go anywhere. I need to eat first. I've gone for thirty-six hours plus without food I'll be shrinking away. They stuck an oxygen mask on my face and I went to sleep and didn't properly wake up until Wednesday. I don't need to worry about going to the toilet as there's a bag on a small trolley at the side of my bed attached to me via what they call a catheter and I think it feels more like one of those green reinforced garden hoses. I think they stretched me like Mr Kumar said they would and to be truthful the only part that hurt during my stay was that bloody catheter. Its Thursday. Sister is here, and she wants my bed. Her surgical production line needs topping up and I'm a blockage. "Have you had a bowel movement?" she enquires. My thought is that there's not been enough time for the food to travel that far since my enforced abstention.

She says there is, and I can't go home until I've been. She is going to leave it with me. She hasn't asked to see it, so I suppose I could lie but I don't fancy going down that path in case I do something wrong or more accurately get caught. My ability to move around has been greatly improved by the addition of a sort of garter, which now has my urine bag strapped to my leg. Activities such as cartwheels or handstands are not a good idea but I'm hoping that walking around albeit with some difficulty is probably good to get my body into the right mood to go for my required bowel movement. The other advantage this has is that it gives sister back the bed and she can open up her route again. Now all I have to do is move myself open up my route and then I can phone home and order my lift.

Sister gives me some paperwork and advice when I'm leaving later. "Is everything understood" she asks. "Thank you all's fine" I tell her.

"Happy with the process with the bag?'

"The good thing about that is for the first time in my life I can shake the drips off by banging it on the side of the pan whilst still standing up. Never done that before." I get a quick goodbye and she's gone. I can't blame her really.

Sleeping is fun. The bag as it was in the hospital is on a frame at the side of my bed. Lying on my back in bed and going for a wee is a technique I have got familiar with. My concern is that when they take the catheter out it's a habit I'll immediately have to get out of. I would like my catheter removing of all the expected discomfort and pain possible to experience after an operation to only be bothered by a catheter seems an inconvenience too far. The only blood visible when I left was where my surgeon said he'd stretch me and looking at where the dried blood was, now long washed away, I think stretched was the operative word.

I have returned to hospital to have the tube removed I am again on a trolley. "Cough" I'm told and its whipped out painlessly and gone. Euphoria is short lived. I must pass water through my system what goes in must come out. If it doesn't the return of the catheter is imminent. Like my catheter implant or not as the case might be, the staff too are overstretched and three times I have to go after I have had my drinks measured and the nurse who's monitoring the procedure is gowned up and working on someone else. Eventually we co-ordinate our ins outs and professional availability. "You can go home" big sigh of relief. Return to euphoria "Any problems phone here immediately." The National Health Service is spoiling me, and I can only feel huge gratitude for what I've had. My wife is here to pick me up. I again realise I had made a good choice there. Getting one with driving licence and car. If one is to give out thanks it would be criminal of me not to thank my wife who has put up with me longer than a life prison sentence. I shall do her a favour and phone work and see if I can go back to Africa. Morocco is too soon. But the international school in France is an easy comeback and then Uganda.

I was going to write a book about travelling around Africa my journey in different countries that would maybe provide some amusement and entertainment to the readers. In addition, I have ended up with an attachment about a personal journey that to some extent naturally slotted into the narrative. My mantra of "pain is temporary giving up is forever" can easily apply to more than just physical effort. Whether its struggling to pay the mortgage on your dream house to be debt free and comfortable at some time in the future; carrying an overloaded kit bag up to the summit of a mountain or dealing with an illness in order to come back again. Without the pain the achievement might not be so obvious, without the stretch out of the comfort zone not so fulfilling or satisfying. Stretch, pain, achievement are different things to different people there is no right answer or level of discomfort or sacrifice. 'Pain is temporary giving up is forever' is more than my mantra, it's also my metaphor for life. I realised, that for myself I had written more than a walk around parts of Africa but also, I told a short story of a part of my journey through life and as it isn't over yet I'm going back to Namibia I'm going to get paid again and I'm wondering what all the fuss was about.

Printed in Great Britain
by Amazon

81699064R10206